That Damned Fence

The Literature of the Japanese American Prison Camps

HEATHER HATHAWAY

OXFORD
UNIVERSITY PRESS

OXFORD
UNIVERSITY PRESS

Oxford University Press is a department of the University of Oxford. It furthers the University's objective of excellence in research, scholarship, and education by publishing worldwide. Oxford is a registered trade mark of Oxford University Press in the UK and certain other countries.

Published in the United States of America by Oxford University Press
198 Madison Avenue, New York, NY 10016, United States of America.

© Oxford University Press 2022

All rights reserved. No part of this publication may be reproduced, stored in a retrieval system, or transmitted, in any form or by any means, without the prior permission in writing of Oxford University Press, or as expressly permitted by law, by license, or under terms agreed with the appropriate reproduction rights organization. Inquiries concerning reproduction outside the scope of the above should be sent to the Rights Department, Oxford University Press, at the address above.

You must not circulate this work in any other form
and you must impose this same condition on any acquirer.

Library of Congress Cataloging-in-Publication Data
Names: Hathaway, Heather, author.
Title: That damned fence : the literature of the Japanese American prison camps / Heather Hathaway.
Description: New York : Oxford University Press, 2022. |
Includes bibliographical references and index. |
Contents: Pt. 1. Topaz, a literary hotbed—After the bombs: the experience of Toyo Suyemoto—Writing as resistance in Topaz: TREK and All Aboard—Toshio Mori: a literary life derailed—Miné Okubo: an aesthetic life launched—Pt. 2. Writing elsewhere—The Pulse of Amache/Granada—Dispatches from tumultuous Tule Lake—Internment novels: Toshio Mori's the Brothers Murata and Hiroshi Nakamura's treadmill—Jerome's magnet—Humiliation and hope in Rohwer's the Pen.
Identifiers: LCCN 2021049877 | ISBN 9780190098315 (hardback) |
ISBN 9780190098322 (pdf) | ISBN 9780190098339 (epub) | ISBN 9780197628317
Subjects: LCSH: American literature—Japanese American authors—History and criticism. |
American literature—20th century—History and criticism. |
American literature—20th century—Periodicals—History and criticism. |
Japanese Americans—Forced removal and internment, 1942–1945. |
Group identity in literature. | Japanese Americans—Intellectual life—20th century.
Classification: LCC PS153.J34 H38 2022 | DDC 810.9/3529956073—dc23/eng/20211117
LC record available at https://lccn.loc.gov/2021049877

DOI: 10.1093/oso/9780190098315.001.0001

1 3 5 7 9 8 6 4 2

Printed by Sheridan Books, Inc., United States of America

This book is dedicated, first and foremost, to Japanese Americans who were incarcerated and to their descendants. It is also dedicated to my parents. To my father, who loathed being constrained, and to my mother, who experienced a different type of confinement, about which she was both silent and unjustly shamed.

Contents

That Damned Fence

They've sunk the posts deep into the ground
They've strung out wires all the way around.
With machine gun nests just over there,
And sentries and soldiers everywhere.

We're trapped like rats in a wired cage,
To fret and fume with impotent rage;
Yonder whispers the lure of the night,
But that DAMNED FENCE assails our sight.

We seek the softness of the midnight air,
But that DAMNED FENCE in the floodlight glare
Awakens unrest in our nocturnal quest,
And mockingly laughs with vicious jest.

With nowhere to go and nothing to do,
We feel terrible, lonesome, and blue:
That DAMNED FENCE is driving us crazy,
Destroying our youth and making us lazy.

Imprisoned in here for a long, long time,
We know we're punished—though we've committed no crime,
Our thoughts are gloomy and enthusiasm damp,
To be locked up in a concentration camp.

Loyalty we know, and patriotism we feel,
To sacrifice our utmost was our ideal,
To fight for our country, and die, perhaps;
But we're here because we happen to be Japs.

We all love life, and our country best,
Our misfortune to be here in the west,
To keep us penned behind that DAMNED FENCE,
Is someone's notion of NATIONAL DEFENSE!

Anonymous Japanese American incarceree[1]

Acknowledgments

Humanities research requires funding and I am grateful to be part of an institution that strives to provide it. I thank Marquette University's Committee on Research, the Office of Research and Innovation, and the Department of English for its support of this project. I am also grateful to colleagues in the Association of Asian American Studies, the American Studies Association, the Society for the Study of Multi-Ethnic Literatures (MELUS), and the Western Women's History Association who have provided both inspiration and valuable feedback as this project evolved. Of particular value was the small but powerful 2013 "Captivity Writing Unbound" conference, hosted by the University of Southern Alabama, which I attended in the early stages of this project. My understanding of comparative captivities was enriched by the excellent papers delivered by colleagues here.

The community of survivors, scholars and activists who research and educate people about the incarceration are among the most dedicated I have met. Hisaye Yamamoto provided the initial impetus for this work when she visited Cambridge, Massachusetts many years ago. Greg Robinson generously shared his wisdom and encouraged the project from its beginnings. The anonymous Oxford Press reviewers offered valuable suggestions and direction at a pivotal point the development of book. Eric Muller and Jasmine Alinder assisted me in obtaining permission to use the stunning cover image of young Billy Manbo, who was incarcerated at Heart Mountain as a child. To Mr. Manbo himself I express deep gratitude for use of the photo, which was taken by his father, Bill Manbo, Sr., during the incarceration. Finally, Frank Abe and Lily Yuriko Nakai Havey provided helpful comments and corrections during the final stages. I thank all of you, most sincerely.

The influence of a small set of intellectual partners is present in all my work and to them I owe special thanks. Werner Sollors' expansive, analytical mind and passion for knowledge, as well as his wicked sense of humor, has and will always have a role in shaping my research. James A. Miller modeled for me the most ethical of academic lives grounded in the pursuit of equity and justice. James C. Hall is my longtime collaborator who I wish lived closer to me so that we could spend more time conjuring up projects together. To friends and colleagues, Amelia Zurcher and Nigel Rothfels, I owe deep appreciation for reading drafts, listening to my ruminations, and providing insightful and often surprising perspectives on the material.

The real heroes of any archival project are those who find, catalog, and maintain historical documents. Jane Beckwith, who fought for years to establish the Topaz Museum in Delta, Utah, is one. The archivists at the Japanese American National Museum are others. Tom Ikeda, founder of the Densho Project, and the entire Densho team deserve the highest gratitude. Densho's mission is to preserve the history of the Japanese American incarceration through oral history interviews, photos, newspapers, and other primary sources that document the experience. Without Tom Ikeda's initiative, the historical record of the incarceration would be dispersed among libraries across multiple states or lost altogether. He and his crew provide an invaluable service to scholars, survivors, and students who seek to bring the history of this injustice into the light. The Asian American Curriculum Project, generated by the Asian American Studies Center at the University of California at Los Angeles, is also to be commended for its remarkable work in preserving Asian American writing in the United States. I am deeply indebted to all of these organizations.

My Oxford editor, Nancy Toff, expressed interest in the project at the outset and patiently saw it through to the end, always with good humor even when I was lacking it. Zara Cannon-Mohammed, also of Oxford University Press, managed the final stages of production with skill and grace.

Finally, I am grateful for the Hathaway and Rothfels families, who have cheered me on along the way: my brothers, George, Bill, and the joyfully newly-discovered Michael; my sister-in-law, Sharon; my nieces, Hannah, Sophie, Sarah, and Meghan; and my nephew, Will. Mike deserves a special award for being the only family member to have read the project, cover to cover, through his duties as volunteer proofreader. May the MLA colon forever live on, Mikey! Jay Johnson deserves an award, as well, for his support and patience as I focused on my work over the years.

My two greatest companions in researching and writing this book, however, have been Kathy and David Rothfels. Kathy, my mother-in-law, who lived in Salt Lake City and accompanied me to Delta, Utah numerous times, never missed an opportunity to inform me about a book, documentary, newspaper article, or radio program that she saw or heard about the incarceration.

David, my son, has been my constant champion along the way. From the time he sat as a little boy taking notes in the corner of the old Great Basin Museum in Delta and up unto this day, he has always known exactly what to say to inspire me, to lift my spirits, and most importantly, remind me of the purpose of this project.

Introduction

Toyo Suyemoto, an up-and-coming young poet living in Berkeley, California, remembered exactly what she was doing on the morning of December 7, 1941. In her memoir, *I Call to Remembrance*, she recounts:

> I turned on the radio to catch the early broadcast before I picked up the baby out of his crib for his first morning feeding. The news that the harried announcer was presenting at that hour was unbelievable and horrible. He was describing the attack of Japanese planes on Pearl Harbor, the naval station on the island of Oahu in Hawaii. How could it be? It was beyond my comprehension. In my mind, I was shouting, "Why? Why?"
>
> When the broadcast ended, and the announcer had finished with the local news, I sat still, stunned, with Kay held in my arms and my thoughts in a turmoil. We were Japanese too. What would happen to us? I learned soon enough.[1]

Just as other generations know precisely where they were when they heard of the Kennedy assassination in 1963 or the attack on the World Trade Towers in 2001, those whose lives were changed by World War II know the same about the bombing of Pearl Harbor—especially Japanese Americans living on the West Coast.

Suyemoto was reasonably fearful about her family's future: on February 19, 1942, just ten weeks after the bombing of Pearl Harbor, President Franklin Roosevelt issued Executive Order 9066, which set the stage for the mass incarceration of Japanese Americans. Suyemoto soon learned that she and her son, along with more than 110,000 other West Coast Nisei, American-born citizens of Japanese descent, and Issei, Japanese immigrants to the United States, would first be forcibly expelled from their homes and confined to makeshift assembly centers, some in fairgrounds and others in race tracks, for a number of months. They would then be incarcerated in isolated and primitive relocation centers for a number of years.

That Damned Fence. Heather Hathaway, Oxford University Press. © Oxford University Press 2022.
DOI: 10.1093/oso/9780190098315.003.0001

This book explores those events using as its lens the writing produced by Japanese Americans during the period of their detention. In five of the ten relocation centers established by the War Relocation Authority, the government agency established to manage the imprisonment, occasional literary magazines were published alongside weekly newspapers. The newspapers were primarily used by the camp administrators to communicate necessary information and events to the detained, but the literary magazines contained creative works written by incarcerated Japanese Americans themselves. In the Topaz camp, officially named the Central Utah Relocation Center and where Suyemoto was detained, *TREK* magazine captured the distinctive culture and community that developed there. The *Pulse* did the same for the Granada/Amache camp in Colorado, as did the *Dispatch Magazine* for Tule Lake in northern California, the *Magnet* for Jerome, and *The Pen* for Rohwer, both located in southeast Arkansas.[2]

These literary magazines contained fiction, poetry, journalism, and drawings that provide insight into the daily realities and emotional experiences of the incarcerated. They demonstrate how factors such as the physical locations and geographic features of each camp, the points of origin and professional and educational backgrounds of the detained, the gender and generational demographics of the population, and the attitudes of the camp administration combined to create not a monolithic experience of "the camps," but rather five unique communal modes of survival. Reading these literary magazines comparatively illuminates how and why one camp differed from another. Reading them collectively confirms the tenacity, humor, sorrow, anger, despair, resistance and resilience with which Japanese Americans faced their wartime incarceration.

When studying historical injustices such as this, the terms used to describe them are especially important because the words chosen can implicitly emphasize or diminish the magnitude of what took place. Toni Morrison, in her monumental novel *Beloved*, which recounts the disastrous and ongoing impact of African American slavery in the United States, alludes to this dilemma when she observes that "definitions belong to the definers, not the defined." She means that those in power hold the rhetorical reins when it comes to defining things and, in that role, they possess a tacit authority to shape perceptions of reality. To refer to someone who is held against their will and forced to work for another without pay as a "slave" rather than as an "enslaved person," for example, defines the individual as a thing or an object—a slave—rather than acknowledging their full humanity as a person who has been subjugated by an oppressive social, political, and economic institution.

The imprisonment of Japanese Americans during World War II provides another example of how language can shape understanding. President Roosevelt himself, as early as 1936 and as late as 1944, described holding facilities for Japanese Americans as concentration camps, but after the war they became more commonly referred to as internment camps.[3] "Internment," however, describes the legal confinement of nationals from a country with which the United States is at war. Three-quarters of Japanese Americans detained during the ward were US citizens, thus making terms that relate to imprisonment more accurate. People who are imprisoned typically have committed a crime, though, as determined by a judge or jury, and are locked away as punishment. But the vast majority of Japanese Americans who were sent to War Relocation Authority "camps" had broken no laws.

The forced expulsion of Japanese Americans from their homes and the dispossession of their property was described at the time as an evacuation, but really it was a wholesale eviction, not a protective measure for those involved, as the government argued. Upon their release from the camps, only a small percentage of Japanese Americans returned to the homes, businesses, and property they had owned before the war.[4] Areas in which thousands of people were confined and surrounded by barbed wire and armed guards were officially labeled "assembly and relocation centers," but they were really low- to mid-level security prisons. Most held only Japanese Americans (some held people of Japanese ancestry from Central and South America, as well), thereby marking the prisoners by their indelible skin color and phenotypical features rather than a convict uniform that could be removed at will. So, even if inmates could temporarily leave the camps on work releases, for example, they were recognized as prisoners nonetheless. Although survivors, scholars, activists, and legislators do not wholly agree about which terms most accurately describe the tragedy, most share a clear understanding that the words used to refer to this dark period in American history do matter.[5]

In 1980, for instance, Congress formed the Commission on Wartime Relocation and Internment of Civilians to "review the facts and circumstances surrounding Executive Order 9066, issued February 19, 1942, and the impact [it had] on American citizens and permanent resident aliens . . . and to recommend appropriate remedies." In the 1982 foreword to the commission's final report, special counsel Angus Macbeth addressed the language issue head on:

> The Commission has not attempted to change the words and phrases commonly used to describe these events at the time they happened. This leaves one open to the charge of shielding unpleasant truths behind euphemisms. For instance, "evacuee" is frequently used in the text; Webster's Third International Dictionary defines an evacuee as one "who is removed from his house or community in time of war or pressing danger as a protective measure." In light of the Commission's conclusion that removal was not militarily necessary, "excludee" might be a better term than "evacuee." The Commission has largely left the words and phrases as they were, however, in an effort to mirror accurately the history of the time and to avoid the confusion and controversy a new terminology might provoke. We leave it to the reader to decide for himself how far the language of the period confirms an observation of [British writer] George Orwell: "In our time, political speech and writing are largely the defense of the indefensible. . . . Thus political language has to consist largely of euphemism, question-begging and sheer cloudy vagueness."[6]

Whether in Orwell's historical moment of the 1940s, special counsel Macbeth's of 1982, or our own, acknowledging that the language we use to describe things significantly shapes how they are perceived, responded to, and acted on is a matter of both ethics and justice.[7] Moving beyond euphemistic and vague political speech to define more accurately historical truths, including exactly what happened to Japanese Americans after the bombing of Pearl Harbor in 1941, can be achieved by looking at firsthand accounts written in the moment by those who lived it. This is the goal of this study.

Literature about the incarceration is now plentiful, but this want not always the case. Shortly after the war, a number of Japanese American creative writers sought to pull back the curtain on what took place. Artist and author Miné Okubo's graphic memoir *Citizen 13660* was published in 1946, the same year that the last prison camp closed.[8] Okubo combined line drawings of daily life in the Tanforan Assembly Center and the Topaz Relocation Center with her own commentary to document her experiences. Published within an immediate postwar cultural and political context, Okubo's critique of the government was necessarily limited in *Citizen 13660*, but it remains a valuable initial record of daily life in captivity.[9]

Other works were written during the incarceration but not discovered until years later, and these complement Okubo's memoir. Hiroshi Nakamura, held in the Salinas Assembly Center and the Poston (Parker, Arizona) and

Tule Lake (Newell, California) camps, wrote an especially revealing "documentary novel" titled *Treadmill* while he was imprisoned. It was not discovered in the National Archives until 1974, however, and was not published until 1996.[10] Similarly, Toshio Mori penned a short novel, *The Brothers Murata*, while held in Topaz, but again, this was not published until 2000. In 1953, Tule Lake inmate Hiroshi Kashiwagi, then a graduate student at the University of California at Berkeley, wrote a one-act play that was set in the camp and titled *Laughter and False Teeth*. In this he wove subtle commentary about the decline of morals and morale experienced by inmates as a result of their captivity. The play was produced in 1954 by the University of California at Berkeley drama department and also by a community theater, but it, too, was shelved until its rediscovery by activists in the 1970s.[11]

The best-known work of fiction that explores the immediate effects of the incarceration during the 1950s is John Okada's *No-No Boy*, published in 1957. *No-No Boy* is less about experiences in the camp itself than it is about the postwar ramifications experienced by its protagonist, Ichiro Yamada. Okada's main character refused to serve in the US military during his incarceration and upon his release, he was again imprisoned for two years for draft resistance. The decision about whether to enlist created dissension in all of the camps, provoked as it was by the infamous "loyalty questionnaire," a test administered by the federal government to determine a person's patriotism. Okada writes about how the social and political tensions that emerged in the prison camps continued to play out in one family and community after the war. *No-No Boy* received some attention when it was initially published, but, like much of the literature about the incarceration, it has grown in recognition and reputation since.[12]

Creative works by Japanese Americans about internment waned somewhat between the 1950s and the beginning of the redress movement which began in the 1970s, and more recently a number of Sansei (children of the Nisei) writers are reimagining the experience in fiction. Academic scholarship on the event has been produced consistently since the war, however.[13] Two of the earliest studies, *The Spoilage* (1946) and *The Salvage* (1952), were products of interdisciplinary social science research conducted under the aegis of the Japanese Evacuation and Relocation Study (JERS) at the University of California at Berkeley during the war itself. Led by Dorothy Swain Thomas, a prominent sociologist, the methods used in these studies were far from perfect. One main problem involved the employment of internees themselves as "community analysts" in the camps. Their role was to collect the ethnographic data on Swain's behalf, which made them the subjects of their own research.[14] This obviously compromised their objectivity. Nonetheless, much of the raw data collected by JERS has been valuable to subsequent scholars.

Following the publication of Swain's two foundational if flawed studies, scholarship on the incarceration has been plentiful. One large vector of scholarship focuses on the political causes and consequences of the event, with considerable attention given to the internal dynamics of the Roosevelt administration and its foreign policies.[15] A second vector examines the legal aspects of the incarceration in terms of the denial of the rights of citizenship and civil liberties, the treatment of dissidents, and forms of resistance. These tend to be anchored in the two most notable legal cases involving these concerns. *Hirabayashi v. United States* (1943) held that curfews imposed on racialized or other minoritized groups were constitutional if the United States were at war with the ancestral nation of that group. In *Korematsu v. United States* (1944), the Supreme Court ruled that the incarceration was based on "military necessity" and not race prejudice.[16] A subset of the scholarship that focuses on the rights of citizenship, and particularly the right to free speech, addresses censorship in the camps.[17] A third vector concentrating on politics and law chronicles the movement toward redress and reparations.[18]

A great deal of work has been done on the cultural history of incarceration, as well. One subset of scholarship attends to art and craft work produced by the detained, which ranged from the making of furniture, toys, and tools to shell jewelry, painting, and ikebana, the Japanese art of floral arranging.[19] Much of this creative output was determined by the natural resources available near individual camps. Tule Lake was set on an ancient lake bed, for example, which enabled residents to make jewelry and other decorative objects out of shells. Desert mesquite surrounding Poston and mangrove forests near Rohwer and Jerome gave rise to both functional and aesthetic woodworking. An important environmental history of the camps explores how the natural spaces in which they were located could alternately empower or defeat incarcerees.[20]

Photography in the camps has also received considerable attention. Internees were prohibited from having cameras, though some were eventually smuggled in or built by inmates. The majority of existing photos, however, were commissioned by the War Relocation Authority itself. Given this, photographic studies examine how the contexts in which the photos were taken affect what they capture on film—that is to say, how does the identity of

Peggie Yorita, an incarcerated Japanese American, makes jewelry using tiny seashells found in the drained lakebed of Tule Lake. Making jewelry became a diversion from boredom among the incarcerated, and the intricately arranged and painted shells, formed into brooches depicting flowers, birds and other natural objects, are now treasured artifacts from the tragedy.
Densho, ddr-densho-2-58, courtesy of the Bain Family Collection

In the shadow of a guard tower, Japanese Americans search for seashells in the drained lakebed of Tule Lake. Acquiring shells to make into jewelry became a competitive enterprise among the incarcerated.
Densho, ddr-densho-2-47, courtesy of the Bain Family Collection

A Poston inmate, Mr. Hitori, paints a carved bird made from desert mesquite to make into a decorative brooch. Mesquite, the most common desert tree, was readily available in the area surrounding Poston, and the wood was collected and used by inmates to create both aesthetic and functional objects ranging from jewelry to furniture.
Photo by Hikaru Iwasaki, courtesy of the National Archives and Records Administration

the photographer, his or her employer, and the purpose for which the photos were to be used inform our understanding of what is portrayed?[21] Both Dorothea Lange and Ansel Adams, who also visually chronicled the Dust Bowl and Great Depression, figure prominently in several studies on the complexities of camp photography. Color photographs are rare, but a series of Kodachrome shots taken by the internee Bill Manbo, depicting life in the Heart Mountain camp in Wyoming, were recently discovered and published in 2012.[22]

Education has been studied as well, focusing on how it took place in the camps and on the college release program, which enabled college-age students to be released from confinement to continue their education at universities in the Midwest and eastern United States. Healthcare has been explored from a variety of perspectives ranging from oral histories of incarcerated physicians who led hospitals in the camps to quality assessments of the care provided by the War Relocation Authority. Finally, the formation and histories of individual camps round out the scholarship of internment culture.[23]

The literature studied here—the writing produced in the camps during the incarceration itself—fills a notable gap in Japanese American literary history in that it provides a crucial link between Japanese American writing as it existed before and after the war. Many writers who contributed to the camp magazines were active in Japanese American literary circles in San Francisco and Oakland prior to their incarcerations. Because people were assigned to camps based on their residential addresses, a number of these writers were assigned to Topaz. Professional artists and journalists were sent to the nine other camps as well, and many continued their writing endeavors while imprisoned. Amateur writers also contributed to the literary magazines and, like the painting and drawing done inside the camps, their words indicate the ways in which creative work served the valuable function of coping with depression, boredom, isolation, and anxiety.[24]

As a whole, the literature published in the camp magazines demonstrates how the racism at the root of the incarceration traumatized those involved. At the same time, however, this writing also reveals how Japanese Americans resisted the incarceration and the prejudice on which it was based. From inside the prison camps, in fact, these writers posed solutions to the "race problem" in the United States in which they, themselves, would play pivotal roles. Developing a better understanding of the Japanese American incarceration through the writing of those who directly experienced it informs us about how and why it has left an indelible imprint on Japanese American writing ever since.

PART I

TOPAZ, A LITERARY HOTBED

1

After the Bombs

The Experience of Toyo Suyemoto

Beginning in the late 1920s, community newspapers and journals including *The New World-Sun*, *Kashu Mainichi*, and *Current Life* began to publish young Nisei writers, who were perceived as potentially linking the cultures of Japan and the United States through their literature. The single edition of *Gyo-Sho: A Magazine of Nisei Literature*, published in 1936 by the English Club of Cornell College in Mount Vernon, Iowa, stated this explicitly: "the Nisei [are] an interstitial cultural group [that] will bridge the chasm between the cultures of the East and the West."[1] The writer Hisaye Yamamoto also recalls this expectation: "[T]he awareness of one's Japanese connections was omnipresent then as now, and some Nisei who gave the matter thought tended to look at themselves as a bridge between East and West."[2] Toyo Suyemoto, an emerging poet in the San Francisco area, might be considered the perfect embodiment of this cross-cultural ideal.

Suyemoto was as Japanese American as a person could be: her parents, Japanese emigrants Tsutomu Howard and Mitsu Hyakusoku Suyemoto, deliberately raised their eleven children with feet planted firmly in both cultures. Her father immigrated to the United States in 1905 to obtain an education and studied engineering at the universities of Nevada and California-Berkeley. Ten years later his wife, a teacher, joined him in the United States. Suyemoto, the oldest of their ten children, was born in Oroville, California, and her siblings were born there or in Sacramento, California.

While the couple maintained Japanese cultural practices at home, they also encouraged their children to live fully in the land of their birth: they chose a Baptist church over a Buddhist temple, for example, and an English, rather than a Japanese, language school. "When very young," states Suyemoto in her memoir, *I Call to Remembrance: Toyo Suyemoto's Years of Internment*,

That Damned Fence. Heather Hathaway, Oxford University Press. © Oxford University Press 2022.
DOI: 10.1093/oso/9780190098315.003.0002

> I did not think it strange that our family celebrated both Christmas, with tingling anticipation before its advent, and the more ritualistic Japanese New Year's Day; both a fire-crackery Fourth of July and *Hina-matsuri*, the Dolls' Festival for Girls, on March 3rd; Easter and Thanksgiving along with *Tango-no-sekku*, the Boys' Festival, on May 5th. Belonging to a racial minority on the West Coast was not as earth-shaking in my childhood as it was to be in a much later time."[3]

Indeed, Suyemoto remembers playing regularly with "children of other nationalities—Chinese, Black, Mexican, Italian and White." But she also discovered that "the differences of ethnicity were never completely melted down. . . . The very fact of our being born American was generally qualified by the biological adjective of 'Japanese'; we were the Japanese Americans."[4]

The mix of the Suyemoto children's names reflects the family's two worlds: Suyemoto's mother chose Japanese names for all the girls—Toyo, Hisa, Mae, and Masa—while her father selected more traditionally "American" names for the boys—William, Howard, Joe, Roy, Lee, Benjamin, and Franklin.[5] "Growing up in a family like ours meant learning to make ourselves understood bilingually. Our parents expected us children to speak correct Japanese and English."[6] Upon the bombing of Pearl Harbor, however, "Japanese"—the term she once thought of merely as an adjective modifying her American identity—suddenly supplanted all the rights associated with her US citizenship.

Suyemoto's life before the war was fairly typical of those of middle-class Nisei living on the West Coast. After high school, she attended the University of California (UC), Berkeley, and graduated with majors in English and Latin in 1937. She had also launched a literary career focusing on poetry, in particular, and her formal preferences reflected her bicultural background. Some of her prewar work demonstrated an affinity with American female poetic predecessors and resembled, perhaps most obviously, the work of Edna St. Vincent Millay or Emily Dickinson.[7] Consider, for example, her poems "Welcome" and "Afterwards" from *America Bungaku* (American Literature), a collection of Nisei writing published in Tokyo in 1938.

Welcome
Should she come, oh, timidly
To you, Death, all uncomforted,

Take her by her hand and gently
And lift her heavy head.

Call the lonely heart, taut with
Its brittle fear, to take note of
Your concern for her and, Death,
Your deep, enclosing love.

Afterwards
Sunlight aslant a garden wall
Can make me muse upon
The hour when you will not be here
After the day is done.

But I will not call out, though you
Be gone; no broken cry
Will part my lips, no hasty step
Of mine will bear me by.

The old forsaken path . . . Perhaps,
The passing wind will know
(And I, oh, I, shall not forget)
That you were glad to go.[8]

While "Welcome" strongly evokes Dickinson's poetry about death, "Afterwards" treats romantic love with the gravity of Millay. When speaking to a school group in 2000, in fact, Suyemoto referred to herself as a "Nisei Emily Dickinson."[9]

Suyemoto also valued, however, the challenges posed by writing Japanese forms such as haiku, tanka, and senryu, all of which are characterized by strict syllable and line constraints. Haiku, in their original Japanese form, are unrhymed poems consisting of three lines and seventeen sounds (or syllables, when written in English) that portray a single image in an instant of time. Structurally, the lines consist of five syllables in the first, seven syllables in the second, and five in the third. Senryu are similar to haiku in form, but they humorously or satirically focus on aspects of human nature.

Suyemoto's own sense of humor can be seen in two senryu she wrote about her family members in 1940:

I drop the paper
I am reading, and see you
Gravely reading me!

I explored his mind,—
A pleasant hallway that reached,
At last, a closed room.[10]

Suyemoto's appreciation of Japanese poetic forms stemmed from her mother who was an amateur poet herself and highly knowledgeable about Japanese literature. Suyemoto states:

> I am always mindful of [my mother's] admonition to treat the haiku or tanka form with respect for their rigorous discipline. I do conform to the syllabic count of 5, 7, 5, for the haiku, and that of 5, 7, 5, 7, 7 for the tanka. According to her, I must set the premise of the poetic thought in the first line (the first five syllables) and add solidity, or descriptive strength, in the following lines, so that the meaning is extended, or defined, by the reader or listener.[11]

To pursue her art, Suyemoto began graduate studies in English at UC-Berkeley in 1939.

In 1940, however, Suyemoto paused her education to marry Iwao Kawakami, a San Francisco journalist and creative writer. Kawakami had been active in Nisei writing circles since as early as 1929 when, as an editor of the community newspaper *The New World-Sun*, he created an English-language section directed specifically toward Nisei. He referred to his peers as "The Thinking Japanese Young People" and encouraged them to produce creative works reflecting the distinctiveness of Japanese American experiences.[12] He attempted to do so in his short story "First the Seed," which captured the daily lives of three young Japanese American ranch hands working on a collective farm. This story appeared along with Suyemoto's work in *America Bungaku*. Both at home and abroad, the couple was achieving recognition among a vanguard of Nisei writers who were poised to chart the course of Japanese American literature in the United States.

The war changed everything. Just two months after the birth of the Kawakami's son, Kay, in October 1941, Pearl Harbor was bombed.[13]

Almost immediately, Suyemoto could no longer shop at the local grocery and instead had to walk for blocks to an open farmers' market, where some vendors still would not sell to her. "I began dreading to walk that distance because I felt accused by the eyes of every passerby," she recalled. The neighbors upstairs, who also had a young child, now refused to speak to her. She learned that the FBI "was interrogating Japanese families, making numerous sudden arrests, and taking the Issei away on the slightest suspicion." She feared this would happen to her family as well, and she expressed her anxieties in her writing:

> The japonica, or flowering quince, had started to bloom in December, and the scarlet flowers graced the bushes before the leaves appeared. In my mind, even as a child, I had equated the blossoming of the japonica with the promise of spring. But now, with the declaration of war, I was not sure what the coming spring portended. So two weeks after Pearl Harbor, I wrote in haiku.
>
> Beyond mind's torment,
> Reach out and grasp a sprig of
> The flowering quince.

Suyemoto admonished herself to maintain her mother's faith in the inevitable return of spring, as the flowering quince promised, but "the immediate situation of uncertainty and fear," she recalls, "bound [her] in chilling doubts."[14]

The uncertainty and doubts triggered by war only grew with time and they ultimately destabilized Suyemoto's personal life. As tensions mounted about "the Japanese problem" nationally, so, too, did those in the Kawakami home. After war was declared, Suyemoto wanted to return to Berkeley to live with her family, but her husband preferred to stay in San Francisco to run his newspaper. The two could not find a compromise so on Christmas Eve 1941, Suyemoto and Kawakami separated. They never reunited, even though both were sent to Tanforan and Topaz, and eventually they divorced. Suyemoto's marriage was her first casualty of war.

Suyemoto's contribution to the January 1942 edition of *Current Life*, "Waiting Daylight," alludes to her despair during this period.

Waiting Daylight
With the
Unfolding of the day
I find is come to me a sense
Of restless
Expectation.

Oh, will
The dawn be late
In coming to my heart
Now that I cannot
Wait?

I am
Engulfed in night . . .
And the hour before the dawn
Drags slowly, waiting
Daylight.

In February 1942, she wrote the following modified haiku in her notebooks and rediscovered them when composing her memoir:

Will it be simple
To uproot the clinging heart
And toss it aside?

Let us turn away—
Darkness falls even as we
Contemplate the day.

I cannot say it
In measured phrases, but I sense
Winds troubling the grass.

The soft scent of peach
Follows after the rain—
My heart is shaken.

> Look at these petals
> I gathered from the peach tree,
> Few moments of spring.
>
> I grasp selfishly
> At these delicate moments
> Against later loss.[15]

The loss was imminent. On February 19, 1942, President Roosevelt issued Executive Order 9066, requiring the expulsion of all Japanese Americans from the West Coast.

The first phase of this involved a voluntary relocation out of the military zones to states in the intermountain West, but Suyemoto's family stayed in Berkeley for educational and employment purposes. "We ourselves could not have moved voluntarily because most of us were intent on finishing out the school year, and Bill was teaching bacteriology at the university."[16] In the end, only about 5,000 West Coast Japanese Americans were able to relocate voluntarily, the majority of whom settled in Colorado and Utah.[17]

Throughout the spring, the rights of Japanese Americans who remained on the West Coast were steadily whittled away by the government. Curfews were imposed between 8:00 p.m. and 6:00 a.m., and the Wartime Civil Control Administration (WCCA) was established to manage the assembly centers, developments which led Suyemoto and her family to confront their impending forced removal.

> One weekend, Father and I packed all of our books and had them stored with a Caucasian acquaintance. Much remained to dispose of, but once the bookshelves were bare and we began discarding our belongings, we realized with sudden intensity the finality of the moving, the fact that we might never be permitted to return.[18]

Like other Japanese Americans living on the West Coast, throughout April, the Suyemotos gave away or sold, at fire sale prices, most of their possessions. They also destroyed anything that might have been misinterpreted by governmental officials as signifying ties to Japan.

Suyemoto describes as especially painful the loss of intimate artifacts such as letters, photos, and papers documenting the family's history:

> Mother had kept letters from her relatives in Japan whom she had not seen since she left home in 1915 and never returned to visit. That night Bill made a bonfire in the backyard and burned these letters, to which were added kindling, scraps of clothing, the debris of school papers, the clutter of family living. The Brownie box camera that we had forgotten to turn into the police was smashed with Father's axe, and it was tossed into the fire. All night long the bonfire burned, consuming once significant possessions."[19]

The government prohibited Japanese Americans from possessing cameras, believing that they could be instruments of espionage. With the dispossession completed, the family functioned in a state of suspended animation, waiting to learn what would happen next.

The answer was delivered by Suyemoto's brother, who called unexpectedly from the university to tell the family that they would be removed from Berkeley early the next morning and taken to an assembly center designated by the Wartime Civil Control Administration (WCCA). Suyemoto was shocked: "I recalled the earlier hours of the morning, the beds made, the clothes picked up, even the familiarity of the patterned wallpaper. My eyes viewed the pattern, diamond-shapes and lines that flowed together. Now, at once, the pattern was not to be."[20] The WCCA issued the family the number that would replace their surname for the remainder of the war, 13423, and the next day they were taken to the Tanforan Assembly Center.

Suyemoto likened her experience to that of a refugee—but she was a refugee within her own country:

> I was but one of many other exiles in war-torn countries who were evicted from their homes with whatever belongings they could manage to carry. All of them, including my own family, had been caught in the flood tide and swept away. . . . I realized that a pattern of living was being altered, and that an unprecedented process of transplanting was taking place by government order. . . . Where we would eventually settle, no one knew.[21]

While the "transplanting" did indeed invoke the experiences of exiles in war-torn countries, Suyemoto's description recalls even more accurately the expulsion of Native Americans from their ancestral lands, by government order, nearly a century earlier.

The Suyemotos found the conditions at Tanforan, formerly known as the Tanforan Racetrack, to be dismal:

> A large, imposing grandstand loomed before us when the buses finally halted. At the racetrack gates there were armed soldiers to remind the Japanese evacuees that this was their entrance into protective custody. . . . We were herded into the racetrack grounds, families huddled in bewildered groups and then led to the side of the grandstand. My son in my arms looked about at the strange surroundings with a child's steady stare. The young people were quiet now, finding no tongue for their uncomfortable feelings as they looked around at the high, barbed-wire barricade, the sentry-boxes situated at intervals along the fence. Their faces spoke their reaction.[22]

The intake process began. First, all detainees were subjected to physical inspections. As a woman, Suyemoto found this especially humiliating: "I felt hands pass over my body, and I recoiled inwardly, but kept my face averted from that of the inspector. I watched Mother submit to the inspection with calm dignity."[23] Next came a "medical examination," a cursory glance in the throat and at vaccination scars, followed by the assignment of housing. Suyemoto experienced a moment of sheer panic when a clerk insisted she be housed with her estranged husband because their last names were the same: "Assuming my husband's identification number would have meant living with him and his father in his barracks, apart from my own family." [24] She protested strongly, however, and was allowed to stay with the Suyemotos.

Finally, the Suyemotos were taken to their new "home." It was a shock to all:

> We passed other buildings which were stables, and finally the guide stopped to point out one, and said, "There it is!" It was another stable. . . . Our living quarters had once housed race horses, and now human beings. . . . The original stalls had been extended with wooden partitions so that there were two rooms, with the swinging half-doors serving as dividers. The ceiling sloped from the back room to the front, and below the rafters an open space stretched the entire length of the stable. The rear room showed distinct evidences of the former tenants, with deep, rough hoof-marks imprinted on the walls, bits of hay right-angled stiffly in the cracks, nails jutting out at random, all whitewashed in slap-dash manner and somehow incongruous to our sight. Cheap mahogany-red linoleum covered the unscrubbed boards in the back room, and on damp days, so frequent in the Bay region, a rank, pervasive odor hung in the air. My son, who developed allergies during the internment period, retained even in his teen-age years a positive

four-plus reaction to horse dander even though he had never come in contact with a horse.[25]

Tanforan's stables were obviously not fit for human habitation, and the environment, combined with the stress of being evicted and incarcerated, took a toll on the psychological and physical well-being of inmates. Sleep was hard to come by, given hay-stuffed mattresses and constant noise. Privacy was nonexistent. A whole host of animal and plant allergens aggravated respiratory ailments.

The poor quality of the food in the assembly centers contributed to the health-threatening conditions and climate. In addition to being nutritionally unbalanced—the early meals consisted of kidney or navy beans, boiled potatoes, and white bread—the food was prepared in facilities lacking adequate

Horse stalls were repurposed to confine Japanese Americans in the Tanforan Assembly Center, formerly the Tanforan Racetrack, a thoroughbred racing facility. The War Relocation Authority quickly whitewashed the stalls, which were made of roughly hewn wood, and still smelled of horses and manure while inmates were forced to live in them.
Densho, ddr-densho-151-20, courtesy of the National Archives and Records Administration

sanitation practices. Suyemoto recalls watching "young men on kitchen duty sweeping off uneaten food from the plates with their hands into slop cans, stacking the dishes in a square wire basket and sloshing them through soapy water and then into rinse water, and placing them on shelves to dry. No wonder," she observed, "there were scraps of food still clinging to the hastily washed dishes.[26] Food-borne diseases struck regularly. Spoiled Vienna sausages, for example, caused widespread dysentery at Puyallup and apparently threw the assembly center into temporary pandemonium because the illness struck at night. As inmates rushed to distant latrines, flashlights in hand, the guards in the towers feared a rebellion and responded with a crackdown.[27]

Communal living made the spread of infectious diseases especially dangerous. Tuberculosis was an ongoing risk, while the conditions for isolating patients were minimal.

Japanese Americans line up in the hot sun, waiting for lunch outside the mess hall at the Tanforan Assembly Center, against the backdrop of barracks and the horse track. The experience of waiting in line daily for meals, showers, and other activities is a distinctive memory of the incarcerated.
Densho, ddr-densho-151-60, courtesy of the National Archives and Records Administration

The hastily built healthcare facilities at the assembly centers were not equipped to handle the basic medical needs of the incarcerated, let alone serious maladies. While the conditions were dismal for everyone, they posed a particular danger for Suyemoto and her infant son. Kay had entered Tanforan with a mild cold, but the horse dander, dust, and cold drafts turned it into something quite serious.

> Kay had been a healthy, contented baby, but the mild cold he had caught before we left Berkeley lingered on at Tanforan. His chest began to sound raspy, and when I bathed him, Mother would urge me to hurry, her eyes observant and concerned. I worried too, as he weakened. The chill at night, rushing up through the gaps in the floor, and the damp smell of the horse stall did not help his difficult breathing. His infection became far more serious than the early stages of his cold.... Fever burned in his weakened body so warmly that I could feel it through his clothing and mine as I held him in my arms. His face began to lose its roundness. His soft, smooth cheeks turned dry, and patches of skin on his face scaled off. He had lately begun to eat solid foods along with being breast-fed, but now he could not retain anything in his stomach, not even milk. He did try to eat, when coaxed, but as soon as he took something, all that he had ingested would be spewed out in a volatile vomiting. He became listless and limp, his cheeks hollow, his eyes sunken into their sockets . . . the once happy baby began to resemble a wizened mockery of a starving old man.[28]

Typically, a Caucasian physician and nurse were assigned to each center to "oversee" the healthcare system, but in the early days, the Tanforan infirmary was staffed only with what Suyemoto described as a "graduate nurse." With an as-yet-to-be-stocked pharmacy and no real expertise, she could provide little assistance to the worried mother.

Those who eventually did provide healthcare in the camps were detainees themselves, Issei and Nisei physicians, nurses, or other medical professionals. They were assisted by high schoolers who were trained in camp to serve as nurse's aides or technicians. They worked under extremely challenging circumstances including excessive heat and cold, with limited equipment in non-sterile environments.[29] Fortunately for Suyemoto, a young physician named Eugenie Fujita had also been assigned to Tanforan and when the doctor reported to the center, Suyemoto requested that she examine Kay. Dr. Fujita was concerned about Kay's dehydration but had no means of treating him. Under the circumstances, all she could recommend was that he be given liquids as often as he was able to ingest them and that Suyemoto try to regulate his fever by sponging him off with water.

Kay's situation was not unusual: the incidence of children dying from dehydration in the camps was high. Inadequate insulation, extreme heat, and cold winter drafts proved to be a fatal combination for many infants.[30] The War Relocation Authority documents 98 stillborn deaths and 133 neonatal deaths (infants under six weeks of age) during the incarceration, with the highest number of stillbirths occurring in the two hottest centers, Gila River and Poston. But this was also a problem at Rohwer. In April 1944, the acting Chief Medical Officer reported to the Procurement Office that:

> [A]ir conditioning in the Nursery may save infant lives. Last summer in the extremely hot weather this situtation [*sic*] became very acute. Several expedients were resorted to save infant lives. Dispite [*sic*] these desperate efforts the temperature in the nursery for hours at a time was above 104°. Such a continuous temperature is a definite hazzard [*sic*] to infant life. The hospital management will continue to do everything possible to help the babies live this summer but it cannot assume responsibility for infant mortality from this preventable cause.[31]

The elderly and young children fared little better. One father remembers rushing his son, who had contracted German measles, "to the hospital, but there weren't too many doctors there. That night the lights weren't on in the hospital and no water. My son was real sick. So my wife stayed with him all night and kept trying to cool him down.... Because of that he can hardly hear in one ear."[32] Unfortunately, Kay fared no better than this little boy. Despite Suyemoto's efforts to keep her son cool, Kay did not improve and he had to be hospitalized.

The layout of Tanforan, as with most of the assembly and relocation centers, made getting to the hospital difficult. Camp hospitals were located near the entrance to facilities, along with the other administrative buildings, rather than centrally, in a way that would best serve the needs of patients who had to make their way there by foot. This meant long walks in excessive heat, wind, or cold for the sick who needed care. At Tanforan, this was also the case for Suyemoto:

> The walk to the hospital seemed unending as the wind blew up the dust from the racetrack. I decided to cut across the inside field, but I kept stumbling on the uneven, grass-matted ground. I pulled the blanket over

> Kay's face to protect him against the wind and dust as he lay passive in my arms. . . .

When they finally arrived, the nurse exclaimed, "Just look at his lips! He is cyanotic and needs oxygen!" She instructed Suyemoto to return to the family's quarters and bring back diapers, undershirts, and nightclothes, because the hospital had no such supplies.

Suyemoto recalls this second trek through her lens as a poet, as well as a traumatized parent:

> Going back across the racetrack, without Kay, is a blurred memory. I somehow recall noting the slant of sunlight on the grass, the heads of weeds nodding in the wind, the evacuees promenading around the oval [racetrack]—and none of them aware of my inner turmoil, the silent outcry against the conditions of this camp into which we were herded. Back at the horse stall, I soberly gathered together the baby garments.[33]

Once again, Suyemoto slogged back to the hospital, willing her son to get well.

In cases of serious illness, patients were occasionally sent to local hospitals for medical attention. Suyemoto, upon returning with Kay's clothes, learned that the another of the camp's physicians was so concerned about Kay that he had requested from the administration a transfer of the baby to a better-equipped community hospital in the local vicinity. While Suyemoto found this news cause for hope, she was upset to learn that she could not accompany her baby. She was, as a Japanese American, allegedly too dangerous to be trusted outside the confines of the race track. When the ambulance arrived, Suyemoto was taken aback that the vehicle carrying her helpless and harmless infant "had to be escorted to the outside hospital by an army jeep carrying armed soldiers."[34] Following Kay's departure, Suyemoto stated that the long walk back to the barracks as the sun set was "even more bleak" than her previous journeys. The young, single, nursing mother was behind bars while her child was alone in an intensive care unit miles away.

During their separation, Suyemoto had no way of knowing how Kay was doing. Eventually, a friend suggested she write to the head nurse on the pediatric floor of the hospital and send self-addressed stamped postcards to be returned to her with updates. The nurse obliged and after the first week, Suyemoto learned that Kay was in an oxygen tent and receiving intensive care. At this point, Suyemoto herself also faced physical challenges: "By this time, I was having a problem with engorged breasts so I expressed the milk into a basin and pitched it out on the grass. The neighbor women commented on the waste." She struggled psychologically, as well: "at night, as I lay awake, I could visualize a pediatric ward with numerous cribs, sick children, doctors and nurses on their rounds, and one strange, oriental baby in that room."[35] After two weeks of little information, Suyemoto was told that Kay would soon be discharged.

Upon Kay's return to the assembly center, he required exceptional care. The physicians told Suyemoto to request a kerosene heater and ensured that the camp hospital would approve it. This benefited more than Kay, Suyemoto recalls:

> I soon learned that other mothers in our barracks who depended on bottle formula for their babies needed the heater even more than we did. Some of them had electric plates for heating baby bottles, but so often a fuse would be blown at an inconvenient time that they would come to our room to ask that the heater be lighted. Then there would be half a dozen small pots on the heater with baby feedings warming in them.[36]

In time, Kay improved and grew into an active and happy toddler with no real understanding of what was taking place.

The same was not true for Suyemoto, of course. She suffered physically in the form of ulcers and psychologically, probably in the form of depression. She recalls the dissonance between her son's juvenile oblivion and her adult recognition of the reality of their incarceration. Throughout her confinement, Suyemoto used poetry as a means of coping with the traumas of the situation. At Tanforan, during the acute period of Kay's illness, she wrote very little, but what she did produce clearly reflects her despair:

> Day in, day out, thoughts
> Are woven into time's fabric
> I finger with grief.
>
> Here, the harassed mind
> Pauses to cry out, at last:
> I can bear no more.[37]

But bearing no more was not an option. In late September 1942, the family was sent to the Topaz Relocation Center, located in a desert in central Utah.

This second removal was even more difficult than the first, for Suyemoto:

> The thought of leaving California without prospect of return wrenched my mind. The Japanese idea of *furusato* (one's native place), the sense of belonging to a place where I had been born, schooled, and grown up, was not mere nostalgia, but an indefinable attachment to place. As much as I hated the sight of the tall, enclosing fence topped by barbed wire and sentry-posts . . . of Tanforan, . . . we were still in our home state. The grass flourished abundantly in the center field of the race track; the eucalyptus trees swayed gracefully in the wind outside the forbidding fence; the trees within the camp were still green in the full growth of their leaves.[38]

Suyemoto's feeling of being indefinably attached to a specific place seems almost a human universal. Whether referred to as *furusato*, *oikos* (a sort of "homeland of the heart,") or topophilia (a literal love of or strong emotional attachment to a particular geographical location or space), feeling grounded in a particular location or ethos enables us also to feel safe interacting with the larger world beyond.[39] Being torn from this place, or having this place obliterated, can be psychologically traumatic.

In the case of the 2011 earthquake and tsunami in Japan, for example, people lost not only their homes, land, property, neighborhoods, schools, and places of religious worship; they also lost the feeling of security and belonging that emotionally attached them to the physical location and history of their communal identities.[40] The experience of Japanese Americans during World War II was not that different. Suyemoto describes a comparable sense of placelessness and disorientation upon her arrival in Topaz: "I had had no distinct concept of how the Central Utah Relocation Project would appear, but I had not expected such a desolate place, hemmed in by barbed wire and the elements." She contrasts this with Tanforan, noting that "despite the degradation of being penned in horse-stalls, Tanforan was still California. There we had viewed the grass and trees, as well as the gardens that the evacuees themselves had planted. Here was not a single blade of grass or even a stunted bush." She continues, commenting on the psychological feelings engendered by the physical environs:

> As far as eyes could see, the camp stretched out on the flat, dry, grassless plain, with rows and rows of low, black tar-papered barracks, burrowed into

> the ground. The entire panorama was depressing. The surrounding barbed wire fence with sentry-posts located at regular intervals around the site was reminiscent of Tanforan. But there the resemblance ended. Boundaries of this camp were identified with red warning signs posted one hundred yards apart . . . forbidding egress.[41]

Suyemoto was not alone in her sense of alienation and disappointment. In her memoir, she captures the reactions of her peers to the place where they would be held for an unknown period of time:

> As our bus entered Topaz, the unvoiced, shocked dismay on the faces of the passengers was eloquent. Even the lowly dandelion, the bane of neat lawns, would have been a welcome sight here. Momentarily there flashed in my mind my Father's garden in Berkeley and its profuse array of colors. Here was unspeakable dreariness and gray, stifling dust everywhere."[42]

Clearly the visual climate of Topaz, a world effectively cast in blacks and whites and grays, challenged the emotional health of many incarcerees. The physically remote and isolated relocation centers led Suyemoto, among others, to view the landscape itself as oppressing as the sentry towers, barbed wire, and tar paper barracks hastily strewn upon it.[43]

Several of the poems Suyemoto recorded in her journal during October and November 1942 reflect her physical and emotional struggle. "Dust Storm" exposes the oppressive dust and its physically entombing nature:

Dust Storm
The dust blows up from desert soil
And taunts air with its maddening dance,
A swirl of gray along the roads
To mock the cautious glance.

How can a sudden twist of wind
Veil all the camp in choking cloud
Until eyes cannot tell the sky
From earth, wrapped in this shroud!

"In Topaz" weaves together Suyemoto's emotional and physical reactions to this new and alien environment:

An aerial view of barracks at the Topaz prison camp in Delta, Utah. 504 barracks, each holding approximately 25 inmates, were set within the one square mile area of the camp.

Densho, ddr-densho-37-833, courtesy of the National Archive and Records Administration

In Topaz

Can this hard earth break wide
The stiff stillness of snow
And yield me promise that
This is not always so?

Surely, the warmth of sun
Can pierce the earth, ice-bound,
Until grass comes to life,
Outwitting barren ground!

After months of confinement at Tanforan, the traumatic experiences surrounding Kay's illness, and under "the full realization that we were here [in Topaz] to stay for the duration of the war," Suyemoto reached an emotional breaking point. "This was the permanent camp, and here we would remain until the government which had condemned us decided to release us." Topaz felt to her like a prison because it was one.

Topaz comprised one square mile of barracks located in the aptly named Sevier (pronounced like "severe") desert of Utah. The closest town, Delta, was fifteen miles away and its predominantly white population of roughly 1,300 in 1942 was dwarfed by the more than 8,000 inmates in Topaz. The barbed wire holding the prisoners in the camp was immaterial: there literally was nowhere to go. To escape in the summer would result in death by desert heat and dehydration. To escape in the winter would result in death by hypothermia. All the "relocation centers" were intentionally situated in comparably isolated areas so as to "protect" the incarcerated from hostile nativists (white Americans who mistrusted Japanese Americans), according to the government, but the WRA was as interested in ensuring that the incarcerated were in no position to "collude" with Japan.

Over time, these carceral states came to be known by other more sanguine terms, but Suyemoto records in her memoir that "in a press conference the same month we were inducted into Topaz, President Roosevelt himself called [the relocation centers] concentration camps, referring to them using the nomenclature that would, later in the war, characterize the horrors of the Holocaust in Europe."[44] The differences between the Japanese American and European camps became clear upon learning of the genocide of Jews, however, and the term "concentration camp" was no longer ascribed to those in the United States. Regardless, both of these wartime atrocities inflicted traumas on their victims that would resonate for generations.

In the midst of Suyemoto's inner desolation about her family's fate, Kay's improving health provided some cause for celebration. By the time the family was transferred to Topaz, he had learned to walk and was developing like a typical toddler, even if in profoundly atypical surroundings. "For a child," Suyemoto recalled, "this dismal environment did not seem to matter as long as he was circled by those who loved him."[45] But Suyemoto, herself, did not adjust as easily.

> [I]n the evenings, as I looked about our room and saw the unfinished walls, the cots lined up in a row, Mother and Father quietly reading, Kay asleep,

the mending on my lap, my mind protested: How long are we to be here in this forsaken place? What will I tell my son when he grows up? I could not openly speak of the pain I felt or ask the questions that assailed me, and poetry was my outlet:

Time threads the needle.
I sew blindly, because tears
Obscure my slow hands.

Grief chokes in my throat.
I cannot speak; tomorrow
Stretches far away.

Doubt haunts me: I ask,
Will there be another spring
To justify breath?[46]

Suyemoto's turn to writing as a means of coping with her confinement proved crucial to the maintenance of her mental health. It did the same for many detainees.

Whether through diaries, notes, letters, or creative works, captive Japanese Americans and their descendants have used writing as a means of processing, recovering from, and resisting the long-term traumas of being imprisoned.[47] Psychologically, putting painful experiences into words gives us the ability to tell our own stories and thereby have some control over, rather than being victimized by, them.[48] Physiologically, the emotional catharsis that writing offers can protect against depression and enhance the body's ability to fend off ailments and disease, an especially valuable asset given the heightened communicability of illnesses in the camp.[49] Most importantly, however, through writing, Suyemoto reconnected with other Issei and Nisei writers from the Bay area who had also been sent to Topaz. Together, they created the premier literary journals produced in the camps, *TREK* and its successor, *All Aboard*. This artistic camaraderie eased her feelings of "pervasive loneliness" as she weathered her days of incarceration.

Suyemoto and her family were released from Topaz in the fall of 1945, the war having ended, effectively, with the bombing of Hiroshima on August 6, 1945. "So came the end to a peculiar, catastrophic experience, our American experience," Suyemoto recorded.[50] The West Coast was not welcoming

Japanese Americans—"disturbing news of shootings, arson, assaults and threats against the returning Japanese swept through the camp and aroused mixed emotions of fear, helpless anger, and uncertainty"—so Suyemoto, her parents, and Kay began a new life in Ohio, where her brother Joe had been sent to study at the University of Cincinnati by the National Japanese American Student Relocation Council.[51] Suyemoto, who had been the librarian at Topaz, earned a degree in library science and made a career of that work first at the University of Cincinnati and later at the Cincinnati Art Museum. But Topaz was never far from her mind. In November 1951 she penned the poem "Stalked":

Stalked
I had long shaken dust
From feet that once had walked
The unpaved roads of camp,
But quietly dust stalked

And would not let me be,
Sifting upon the wind
Of memory into
The crevices of mind.[52]

At the time, she did not know just how much the dust of Topaz and Tanforan would haunt her: in August 1958, Kay, still suffering from the severe asthma and allergies he developed during the incarceration, died unexpectedly while hospitalized for a respiratory illness. During the reparations and redress movement of the 1970s, Suyemoto began telling the story of her experience to public audiences, in an effort to ensure that the incarceration and the losses it inflicted on Japanese Americans would neither be forgotten nor, she hoped, repeated.

2

Writing as Resistance

Topaz's *TREK* and *All Aboard*

The 1930s signaled the emergence of Nisei writing in the San Francisco/Oakland area, not unlike the African American renaissances concurrently exploding in Harlem and, to a lesser degree Chicago. The Japanese American naissance, however, got far less attention from the white American public. James (Jimmie) Omura, a prominent Nisei newsman, describes the goals of the West Coast cohort:

> Larry Tajiri and I had ambitions to write The Great Nisei Novel. The others discussed it, but they all agreed that somebody else should write it. . . . I suppose in his Great Nisei Novel, he would emphasize Nisei who had achieved a niche in their field, advanced in their profession and obtained some worth of status. . . . We all felt the Nisei weren't getting their proper recognition.[1]

Isshin Yamasaki echoed Omura's concerns. Yamasaki edited the 1938 bilingual Japanese and English collection *America Bungaku* (American Literature) in which writing by Toyo Suyemoto and her husband, Iwao Kawakami, appeared. In the introduction to *American Bungaku*, Yamasaki lamented that though the Nisei were US citizens, "they are not accepted as Americans." But Yamasaki saw that this may be a strength. Because of the Nisei's experience of living amid two cultures, Yamasaki believed that "their contribution to literature will be a [*sic*] uniquely different one because of their parental background and American environment. . . . A true Nisei literature is the hope of not a few who silently watch the Nisei venture in this field."[2]

To promote American-born Japanese authors, Omura founded *Current Life*, initially subtitled *The Magazine for the American Born Japanese*, and later, *The Only National Nisei Magazine*.[3] *Current Life* ran for fifteen

That Damned Fence. Heather Hathaway, Oxford University Press. © Oxford University Press 2022.
DOI: 10.1093/oso/9780190098315.003.0003

issues between October 1940 and February 1942. In the inaugural edition, Omura emphasized two key points. First, he explained that white American aggressors failed to understand that "a gulf of difference" divided Issei, Nisei, and "Japanese in Japan" from one another culturally and politically. Second, he announced that racist efforts to deny Nisei their "inalienable rights" as US citizens must be resisted through writing. "*Current Life*," Omura proclaimed, "will endeavor to be a true mirror of Nisei life. It will reflect the opinions and sentiments of these people. It will be a defender of the American-born Japanese against the unscrupulous politicians and rabble-rousers."[4] In this respect, Nisei writers of the late 1930s and early 1940s echoed the artists of the Harlem Renaissance who also believed that literature could serve as an important tool through which to effect political change. *Current Life* would become the primary organ through which to fight this battle.

Toyo Suyemoto's poem "Yellow," published in the February 1941 edition of *Current Life*, embodies this goal.

Yellow
The other children pointed fingers at me
And cried, "Yellow, yellow, inside and out!"
Because my skin was a shade different from theirs.
They ringed me in a circle of distrust
And mocked me with repeated taunts
I held my hands fisted against my ears
And shouted, "No . . . no . . . no!"
And still the words crashed heavily
And thundered in the brain:
Yellow . . . yellow . . . inside and out.
See, my skin has not changed color,
But it may be that I am stained inside.[5]

"Yellow" is rare among Suyemoto's poems in terms of its overt reference to racism. Although it remains grounded in her personal experience, which is a common feature of her writing, its direct engagement with the social realities of discrimination and hatred distinguish it from the rest of her works.

"Yellow" is similar to the personal yet political poems from the Harlem Renaissance. Consider the African American poet Countee Cullen's 1925 poem "Incident," for a parallel.[6]

Incident
(For Eric Walrond)
Once riding in old Baltimore,
Heart-filled, head-filled with glee,
I saw a Baltimorean
Keep looking straight at me.

Now I was eight and very small,
And he was no whit bigger,
And so I smiled, but he poked out
His tongue, and called me, "Nigger."

I saw the whole of Baltimore
From May until December;
Of all the things that happened there
That's all that I remember.[7]

World War II brought an abrupt halt to the aspirations of both Nisei and African American writers' efforts to use "words as weapons" to counter prejudice, to quote the Harlem Renaissance author Richard Wright.[8] For African American writers in Harlem, the patronage of wealthy whites, on which many artists relied on to sustain their work, waned during the Great Depression and then dried up altogether upon the start of the war. The incarceration, for Nisei writers, similarly stymied the progress of their literary movement.

Despite the radical disruption that imprisonment caused in the lives of Japanese Americans, however, Issei and Nisei writers refused to be silenced. On the contrary, this enterprising group of artists found ways to express political resistance, build camaraderie, and find emotional release in the newspapers and literary journals that were produced in the camps. Under the sponsorship of the War Relocation Authority (WRA), these publications were intended to divert attention and curb boredom among the detained.[9] Daily or weekly newspapers, which were issued in all of the camps, contained informational bulletins, editorials, sports results, wedding announcements, and other features intended to resemble community newspapers in typical American towns. Their primary function, however, was to serve as the official means of communication between camp administrators and inmates. The newspapers were selectively staffed by WRA-approved detainees and were subject to varying forms of supervision or censorship, depending on the material in question, by the government reports officers appointed to the task.[10]

The most common "supervisory" tactic involved an extensive prepublication review by multiple officers within the camp administrative hierarchy, as the "Jankee," a "Japanese American Yankee," cartoon from the October 27, 1942, edition of the *Topaz Times* illustrates. Although the WRA frequently asserted that the detained enjoyed freedom of the press—as the various mastheads of Manzanar's paper, *The Free Press,* shouted loudly and clearly—in reality, the official position of the WRA was that "all legitimate complaints and criticisms by evacuees should certainly be aired, but the Reports Officer . . . should be authorized . . . to examine them carefully before they are permitted to appear in print."[11] The WRA perceived such authority to be necessary to prove to readers inside and outside the camps that those held were being treated justly and fairly while imprisoned. A confidential memorandum from the WRA stated that "any statement that may be misinterpreted to indicate that the evacuees are receiving harsh treatment, that they are subject to unnecessarily stern restrictions, or forced to live under unfavorable conditions should also be strictly censored."[12]

Of particular interest to censors were articles that were translated into Japanese, primarily for Issei who were not fluent in English. These were carefully scrutinized at the national level in Washington, DC, not just in the camps themselves. Norris W. James, the reports officer at Poston, explained to the House Special Committee on Un-American Activities in June 1943 that:

> the presumption is that . . . the Department of Justice in Washington or these other Intelligence services . . . [reviewed the translations] . . . and if anything popped up they would be able to handle it. These [Japanese] translators [and editors] know that somebody is riding herd on them in Washington in the Intelligence service—they know that and I believe that is why they haven't stepped out of line.[13]

The government allowed Japanese translations of the papers in an effort to dispel mistrust by the Issei and engender among this generation affinities with the United States that would be stronger than those they held with their native homeland of Japan. It was a convoluted and ineffective endeavor, however. Because nearly no war officials were fluent in Japanese, they created a system in which a detainee translated the English material into Japanese and

"Jankee" was the camp mascot, created by inmate Bennie Nobori, of the Topaz camp. This Jankee cartoon, published in *Topaz Times* on October 27, 1942, mocks WRA censorship of camp news. Humor was often used as a means of critiquing the conditions of camp life.

Densho, ddr-densho-142-11, courtesy of the family of Itaru and Shizuko Ina

On the masthead of the Manzanar *Free Press*, the bold block letters seem intended to emphasize an absence of censorship, but the production of camp newspapers was carefully supervised by the WRA.
Densho, ddr-densho-125-21, courtesy of the Library of Congress

then a second detainee translated the Japanese version, without access to the English original, back into English. The camp administrator then compared the two English versions to ensure that no secret messages were being relayed in Japanese.[14]

Newspaper staffs were also subject to formal and informal "meetings" with the reports officers, which further inhibited full freedom of expression. These meetings were allegedly arranged to discuss how to improve the papers and allow them to best meet the needs of their readers, but they were also used as a means of coercive, if subtle, censorship. The camp management overtly overruled decisions of Japanese American editors if any controversies might arise based on published materials.[15] Most camp newspapers did not report on conflicts taking place in the camps.[16] Some of the most challenging problems at the Rohwer facility, for example, were never addressed in its daily newspaper, the *Outpost*. There was no mention whatsoever of the tension between Hawaiian seamen sent to the camp and Japanese American workers that eventually resulted in violence, a riot, and an FBI investigation. The shooting of a young inmate by a local white resident who assumed the youth was escaping was not reported, nor was an assault on an incarcerated truck driver by a local resident when the driver was simply trying to make a delivery.[17] At Jerome, the administration suppressed an article on mess hall workers' demands for higher wages, while at Minidoka, the administration pulled an editorial that negatively compared the creation of an all-Nisei combat unit in the US Army to segregated African American military units.

The literary magazines, by contrast, faced less oversight. According to Suyemoto, although Topaz's *TREK* "was monitored by the Reports Division, there was no suppression of what could be printed in" it.[18] The validity of her claim is hard to document, but because literary magazines were perceived as entertaining diversions for the detained akin to art classes, jewelry-making workshops, and traditional floral design contests, they very well may have received less scrutiny. Writers, in turn, were able to take more risks within their pages. In Topaz, two former newspapermen, Taro Katayama and Jimmy Yamada, took full advantage of this opportunity to use their writing as a tool of resistance.

Katayama began his journalism career in 1932 when, at eighteen years old, he served as an editor of the first Japanese American literary magazine in the United States, *Reimei*, published in Salt Lake City. In the spring 1933 edition he contributed a short story, "Haru," which, though written well before anyone could have imagined the incarceration, is as bleak as the stark desert landscape of Topaz. In it, Katayama wrenchingly portrayed the life of a young Nisei who, as the daughter of a poor farmer, is forced into an arranged marriage with another farmer's son. The barrenness of her life is made clear in the opening lines of the story:

> The realities of her world were those that were forced upon her by the unalterable fact of her being what she was. Haru was the daughter of a poor Japanese farmer in western United States, and therein lay the beginning and the seeming end of her whole existence.[19]

Although the story is an admirable work of social realism, a literary genre popular in the 1930s that critiqued social and political structures that oppressed the working class and the poor, "Haru" appears to be the only fictional work Katayama ever published. Upon arriving in Tanforan, he shifted his focus to journalism and was instrumental in the creation and maintenance of the *Tanforan Totalizer*, the assembly center's newspaper.

The *Totalizer* was subject to multiple layers of censorship. According to one Tanforan journalist:

> Here is how our copy goes now. I get data (say from the Finance Department) and write it up. Then it goes to McQueen (official Army censor) for his ok. Then it goes to Davis (center manager) for his ok. Then it goes to the head of the department for his ok. Then the dummy is set and it gets an ok, again from Davis. Then the stencil is cut and sent up to Davis again for his ok. Then it gets sent to the supply room and it sits on the desk of the chief until he gets around to giving it final approval and checks to see if it has Davis' signature on it.[20]

As editor, Katayama found this oppressive oversight maddening. According to Charles Kikuchi, a fellow member of the *Totalizer* staff, "'TK [Taro Katayama] says that he doesn't give a damn about the paper because it is so limited and could not have any value as social documentation.'"[21] Katayama found more freedom when writing for *TREK*, however, and he exercised it in a brilliant rhetorical piece titled "State of the City," which opened the first volume of the literary magazine. In this, Katayama simultaneously recorded the daily details of the incarceration for the Reports Division's purposes *and* passed by censors his commentary on the injustices of it.

Katayama's title, "State of the City," immediately evoked the State of the Union addresses government leaders deliver annually. Katayama's title subtly but clearly drew attention to the incongruity between the reality of his status *not* as an elected or government official but rather as an American citizen imprisoned by such agents. He based his title on the way Topaz was referred to in mainstream newspapers at the time: "the city of Topaz." At its peak population of 8,130 "residents" on March 17, 1943, Utah newspapers heralded "the city of Topaz" as the state's fifth largest, and that language remains on the historical marker that now memorializes the camp's existence. It certainly dwarfed the actual incorporated municipality nearest to it, Delta, whose population was approximately 1,300 throughout the 1940s. Some white Delta residents recalled the two as merging into one mini-metropolis, but in reality, fifteen miles of farmland and desert established a clear and intentional boundary between the two. "Residents" of the "city of Topaz" were confined to one square mile surrounded by barbed wire and guard towers.

Toward the end of the war, however, in the waning months of the camp's existence, Topaz inmates were allowed to bus into Delta to pick up basic goods that were not available in the camp, an experience Toyo Suyemoto recalls as a rare moment of freedom:

> [By January 1945] block-shopping had been instituted in the camp, and one could apply a week in advance for a permit to go to Delta for shopping. A bus provided the transportation, and the sentry at the gate checked our passes before we left and when we returned. The stipulation for such a trip to Delta was that shopping be done for everyone else in the block, so when permission was granted and names posted, the shopper would receive lists and money for desired items that ranged from groceries to a toy for a baby or a spool of thread. The first time I went block-shopping, I was exhilarated by the bus ride because I had not been outside since we settled in

> Topaz [in October 1942]. Instead of chatting with fellow passengers, I kept looking out at the small homesteads, the farm animals, and the open stretch of countryside free of the barracks. I relished this brief spell of liberty.[22]

Inmates were allowed out of camps for other purposes, as well. Incarcerated Japanese American farm laborers were pivotal, in fact, in securing the sugar beet, potato, and cotton harvests in several western states during the war. The Topaz boys' basketball team was bussed into Delta to compete against the local high school, and the incarcerated were allowed to hike, with permission and typically under supervision by a camp employee, in the desert areas surrounding Topaz. With the assistance of the Delta newspaperman and geologist Frank Beckwith Sr., one group discovered a meteorite in the desert that Beckwith helped them send to the Smithsonian.[23]

On the surface, then, "the city of Topaz" might have appeared to be less prison-like than other camps, but Katayama's "State of the City" address clearly implied otherwise. For example, in describing the camp itself, Katayama referred to it as "one of ten similar forced-growth communities into which an America at war has funneled something over 100,000 human beings."[24] His use of "forced" and "funneled" implicitly condemned the removal of Japanese Americans from society and the funneling of them into captivity. Later in the essay, Katayama referred to Topaz as set in "'wilderness,'" using quotation marks to indicate the term used by the WRA to explain "the type of territory toward which the WRA was driven by circumstance in its selection of sites."[25] His mockery of the term "wilderness" and the phrase "driven by circumstance" called attention to the alleged rationale offered by the WRA to justify the remote settings of all the camps: namely, the delusion that West Coast Japanese Americans would communicate with the Japanese army by some type of code to enable acts of sabotage.

A few paragraphs later Katayama commented on one of the most troubling aspects of the "wilderness" surrounding Topaz: the choking alkali dust that so aggravated Suyemoto's son's respiratory illness.

> Asked what the infant city was like, those first residents might have, with some justice, summed it up with one word—dust. For dust was the principal, the most ubiquitous, ingredient of community existence at the beginning. It pervaded and accompanied every activity from sleeping and eating and breathing on through all the multitude of other pursuits. . . . It obscured

> almost every other consideration of communal life just as, when a wind rose, it almost obscured the physical fact of the city itself.[26]

Suyemoto corroborated Katayama's description but added to it the debilitating psychological effect these storms had upon the community: "We were soon exposed to the unremitting dust storms, more violent and smothering than anything we had experienced in Tanforan—and demoralizing." Suyemoto's description is worth quoting at length because it illustrates just how oppressive the ubiquitous gray powder was in Topaz:

> When the fierce winds blew and stirred up the fine silt, visibility became nil. The nearest barracks, just a few feet away, disappeared from sight. Puffs of dust drove in under the door, around the windows and over the sills, and the rough grit sifted over the scrap-lumber table, stools, beds and the cast-iron space heater. A layer of gray covered everything. When we went outside during a storm, we would return with whitened hair and eyebrows. Chiffon scarves tied over our faces or wet handkerchiefs over our noses gave little protection against the grains of sand beating on our skin. In the mess hall, the cups of tea, poured as the diners filed in and stood in line, would be powdered with dust, and the food we ate had an added texture that ground sharply on the tongue and teeth.[27]

These storms were frequent and could last for three days or more. Later in life, the sensation of sand in her mouth would bring Suyemoto, in her mind, right back to Topaz.

Katayama condemned the physical conditions of Topaz due to its location and hasty, inadequate construction and management by the WRA. He then emphasized that the only reason the incarcerated could survive in this desolate "city" was due to their own labor and adaptive skills. He used a classical rhetorical strategy of alternately praising his Japanese American peers and blaming government administrators to make his point.[28] He commended the inmates for adjusting to their forced "community" of "arbitrarily" assembled individuals and families, for example, while implicitly indicting the WRA for failures in planning, organizing and governing it. He celebrated detainees' initiative in developing a dry goods store, a barber shop, a theater, and radio repair shop, while deploring the "inadequacy of supply to demand" of basic necessities. He noted, as an example, how "wartime priorities" had denied the children milk because of increased demand for it outside the camps. [29] This example pointedly illustrates that, in a period of wartime rationing during which Japanese American farm laborers played a key role in "sowing the seeds of victory" (the slogan of the Victory Garden campaign) of the war effort, the needs of white citizens outside of camp trumped those of non-white children detained within.[30] Although the WRA wished to present Topaz as a new and industrious city, Katayama exposed how the organization failed to uphold its own civic duties.

Katayama also highlighted the ways that the incarceration negatively affected the war effort. Imprisoning Japanese Americans contributed to the labor shortage in the nation at large. While some inmates did work in local agricultural production, far more professionals, farmers, fishermen, and other workers were stuck inside camps, unable to participate in the maintenance of the US economy. Katayama directly challenged WRA propaganda that presented employment in the camps as providing inmates with the opportunity to "perpetuat[e] existing skills or [to] develop new ones" in preparation for postwar relocation.[31] All sectors of the Japanese American economy on the West Coast grew to a halt upon the incarceration, so those who had served the needs of their local communities were now wasting years of education and experience by performing primarily menial labor in the camps. In the end, Katayama's allegedly purely informational description of the "state of the city of Topaz" was, in reality, a political address that read, between the lines, like a jeremiad bitterly lamenting the incarceration.

Framed by the text of Katayama's "State of the City" was a poem by Suyemoto that underscores the tone of his essay.

Gain

I sought to seed the barren earth
   And make wild beauty take
Firm root, but how could I have known
   The waiting long would shake

Me inwardly, until I dared
   Not say what would be gain
From such untimely planting, or
   What flower worth the pain?[32]

Others have rightly interpreted this poem as indicating Suyemoto's reflections on the barrenness of the landscape of Topaz, both literally and figuratively.[33] In light of what had transpired in her personal history by December 1942, however, it also seems plausible that "Gain" might have alluded to the challenges she faced raising a young child in the desolation of a prison camp. Though her husband, Iwao Kawakami, was also held at Topaz, during the nearly four years of their confinement he never visited his estranged wife and their son.[34] The "wild beauty" with which she "sought to seed the barren earth" might very well refer to Kay, the child whose "untimely planting" is at once a "gain" but also potentially filled with "pain," given what appears to be an unexpected pregnancy, their imprisonment, Kay's serious respiratory condition, and the unknown future they all faced as Japanese Americans in the United States. Sadly, if read this way, Suyemoto's poem was prescient: Kay died at sixteen as a result of an asthmatic condition that stemmed from his infantile exposure to racetrack and desert allergens in Tanforan and Topaz.[35]

Many of the concerns to which Katayama alluded in his first essay received greater and more explicit attention in his second, titled "Beyond the Gate," which appeared in the spring 1943 issue of the magazine. Katayama's growing forthrightness should not, perhaps, be surprising given the tensions that had arisen surrounding the WRA's efforts, beginning in September 1942 and in full force by February 1943, to push people out of the camps and into cities in the interior of the United States as part of the resettlement initiative. Realizing the short-sightedness of the original imprisonment plan in terms of its economic, social, and political consequences, less than a year after Topaz opened, the government's goals shifted to closing it down.

Economically, the WRA finally recognized that the inclusion of Japanese Americans in the workforce would help ease the wartime labor shortage. Socially, the heads of the WRA believed that the dispersal of Japanese Americans to multiple cities across the nation would break up the population density of Japanese Americans on the West Coast that created such irrational fear in the white public. Politically, the WRA deemed resettlement a necessity to prevent a population of incarcerated individuals, particularly the elderly Issei who were too old or sick to obtain work in unfamiliar cities, from becoming permanently dependent on governmental assistance.[36] So, having first been evicted from their original homes and then incarcerated in guarded camps, Japanese Americans next became pawns in a new phase of the war effort: "resettlement" in disparate locales and communities. The consequences of this plan damaged more than individuals: through this process, many "Little Tokyos" or *nihonmachi* in West Coast cities were permanently destroyed, thereby obliterating the sanctuary cities that had historically provided refuge for Japanese Americans.

Katayama's article about life "Beyond the Gate" portended the concerns that arose among Japanese Americans who were forced to "resettle." Using a much more confrontational tone from that of the "State of the City" address, he opened the essay by retelling a story that circulated widely among journalists and activists during the war. In it, an incarcerated boy tells his parents, "I don't like it here" and asks, "when are we going back to America?" Katayama used the anecdote to emphasize the "abnormality" of life for US citizens living in prison camps during a war "dedicated to the preservation of democratic principles." He chastised the hypocrisy of politicians who spoke of fighting for freedom abroad while not enacting it at home. Finally, he pointed out the irony of the government's reversal of its initial decision to deny Nisei from enlisting in the US Army. Soldier shortages and strategic military needs caused the government to "re-open" the army to "citizens of Japanese ancestry as an official token of their reinstatement as loyal Americans." Suddenly, incarcerated Nisei were now suited to fight on the nation's behalf.[37]

Katayama also articulated in "Beyond the Gate" the community's concerns about whether resettled inmates would be able to find jobs at reasonable wages. Most of those incarcerated lost their businesses, property, and professional reputations when they were evicted. The degree to which Japanese Americans could succeed economically, he argued, would be the key determinant of whether "relocation is to be considered as something more than the mere dispersal of a concentrated minority group."[38] He emphasized the chasm that would undoubtedly be created between detainees' prewar and postwar lives. Incarcerated Japanese Americans in Topaz were a predominantly urban population, the majority having come from the San Francisco Bay area. Many were college-educated and professionally or technically skilled. Katayama rightly predicted that racism would likely limit this group to jobs as domestics, service workers, and farmhands upon their release.[39]

Finally, Katayama anticipated that the incarcerated would never recover the financial losses they incurred as a result of their imprisonment. After disagreement among WRA leaders about how to manage the economic disenfranchisement of detainees, in 1948 President Truman signed into law the Japanese American Evacuation Claims Act, which was intended to compensate prisoners for material losses resulting from their incarceration. This failed. First, the government never acknowledged violating the civil rights of Japanese Americans citizens and forced those filing claims to agree to demand no compensation for their incarceration beyond a single claim, limited to financial and property losses. Second, Congress limited compensation to materials and property held at the time of eviction, excluding lost profits from aborted professional services, anything pertaining to personal suffering, and any costs related to removal and confinement. Indeed, in what is perhaps the clearest indication of government subterfuge, the government required receipts and other proof of losses, going so far as to contest even the definition of a "loss" in this context.[40]

While Katayama subtly wove critiques of incarceration through his essays "State of the City" and "Beyond the Gate," he was more biting and satirical in his editorials titled "Digressions," which appeared in all three editions of *TREK*. In each, he underscored the quintessential "Americanness" of detainees and emphasized the different realities of those living inside and outside camp fences. But, in a fitting play on the meaning of "digression"—a diversion intended to attract attention away from the main issue—Katayama coded his criticisms under a veil of humor.

In his December 1942 piece, for example, he compared Christmas 1941 with Christmas 1942 to show that consumerism, Christianity, and patriotism intersected for detainees in the camps, regardless of their actual religious affiliation, just as they did for other Americans. In so doing, he demonstrated how radically the experience of Japanese Americans had changed in just one year:

> We have been in a mild quandary the last few days. With the war's second Christmas near at hand, we find ourself [*sic*] a little disquieted at its sudden appearance on the pathway of our consciousness. Frankly, we don't quite know how to greet the approaching holiday. It is as if an unexpected guest were at the front gate, and both ourself [*sic*] and the house wholly unprepared to receive him. Just what sort of mien, physical and spiritual, ought we to put on? None of the formulas of salutation which sufficed us in the past seem quite apropos.
>
> For one thing, we are devoid for the first time in our life from the familiar external concomitants of the season—the shopping and the crowds, the street corner Santa Clauses, the neon blandishments of holiday commercial art, the red, green and tinsel, . . . and the general feeling of anticipation and festivity boozily welling up in society's collective breast. Knock out these

> props, and you have practically destroyed the foundation on which most of our Christmastime responses . . . have been built.[41]

Recalling the state of relative personal sovereignty among Japanese American during the 1941 Christmas season, though it was admittedly underscored by deep trepidation, he noted:

> The personal and collective calamity of December 7 had left us in a state of mind and spirit which combined anger, awareness of a seemingly irremediable hurt and premonitions of still other woes to come. As for greeting the annual holiday, to mouth its traditional merriness would be, we felt, a painful mockery both of our plight and our actual feelings.

Still, reflecting the surge in patriotism common to most Americans after United States' entrance into World War II, he reminisced about homemade Christmas cards in 1941 that featured "a row of bristling bayonets and grim, helmeted soldier faces placed in melodramatic juxtaposition to a quite conventionally serene Star of Bethlehem." Through such clashing images, Katayama stated, a combination of "tradition and our own lacerated feelings were thus both served—and, we felt, with just the proper heroic effect."[42]

From his current perspective confined within barbed wire and policed by armed guards, however, Katayama noted sardonically that "last year's gesture to the Christmas spirit strikes us now as being a little too theatrical to serve this season's need. . . . We still don't think 'merry' is precisely applicable to a wartime Yule, . . . we don't feel, either, that a combination of bayonets and starlight and a pointed interpolation to the Atlantic Charter is needed to express the idea."[43] So, he concluded:

> All we know is that we haven't sent, and don't intend to send, any cards this year. . . . Our shopping, if one can call it that, has been extremely meager, casual and vicarious—courtesy of the Sears Roebuck and Company. We haven't any tree to trim, and we aren't hanging up any stocking. Nor are we conscious of any special seasonal augmentation of our normal flow of good will toward our fellow men, for whom we have always entertained pretty tolerant and hospitable feelings anyway. And so apparently, we aren't going to meet Christmas, 1942, in any particular manner. We'll just open the door and let it in.[44]

This sober resignation to a holiday in the midst of war was at once shared by all Americans, many of whom had loved ones serving in the military, and at the same time, completely different for those who were confined to prison camps.

In his second "Digressions" editorial, contained in the February 1943 edition of *TREK*, Katayama turned his attention, seemingly light-heartedly, to the dangers of seductive advertising during a period of war rationing. Between the lines, however, can be found yet another commentary on the injustice of being imprisoned. On the surface, the article focused on what Katayama termed the "Tantalus school of advertising": namely, the practice of advertising goods, complete with tempting photos, which, the buyer learned only after attempting to purchase, would be available only when the war was over and rationing was lifted. Again this is a circumstance common to all Americans during wartime, but it was particularly painful experience for those whose future was both unknown and indefinitely "on hold."

In this same editorial, Katayama twice likened the position of Japanese Americans to that of lab rats and warned that tantalizing the confined with postwar freedoms could "engender some kind of frustration complex or schizophrenic manifestations," much like the techniques "used in laboratories to bring about nervous breakdowns in rats and other trusting animals."[45] Later he stated that the authorities should teach inmates to "'Learn How to Approach a Certain Type of Magazine and Newspaper Advertising in War-Time'" so as to prevent "a lot of potential future customers from becoming vacant-eyed equivalents of those laboratory rodents, twitching between desire and doubt and mumbling incoherently about tomorrow and tomorrow and tomorrow."[46] Finally, Katayama's editorial reflects serious concerns held by the WRA and Japanese Americans themselves about how a sustained period of idle limbo would affect detainees in terms of postwar motivations to begin life anew.

Katayama's third "Digressions" appeared in June 1943, after he had enlisted in the army. In it, he described the complicated experiences of Nisei soldiers who were released from the camps to fight in the war. Playing on the government's reduction of incarcerated human beings to objects by replacing surnames with numbers, he jousted:

> If we should ever attempt a volume of reminiscences about our life since evacuation, we think we might call it "Our Days Were Numbered." Ever since that already incredibly remote day, a little over a year ago, when the

> WCCA (Wartime Civil Control Administration. Remember?) slapped on our first brace of Arabic tags—family and ID numbers—our existence has been a numeralogist's [*sic*] opium dream. Bed number, stall number, barrack number, train group number, block number, apartment number, resident identification number—in that procession of digital combinations lies the whole story of our career as an evacuee, from civil control station to WRA.[47]

Confronting the reality that, as one going to combat, his days literally may "be numbered," Katayama devoted the essay to his experiences as a soldier. He acknowledged that in the shift from prisoner to private, he felt like an "uncomfortable impersonat[or]" in a military uniform that didn't quite fit. He then provided, however, several anecdotes that illustrated the goodwill of the men he encountered in the military to show how soldiers lived out democratic ideals, even though their government leaders did not.[48] In this "digression," Katayama revealed his own personal struggle to reconcile his self-perception as an American citizen with the realities of first, his forced incarceration and second, the expectation that he was now asked to risk his life in war to prove his patriotism.

Another *TREK* contributor, Jim Yamada, criticized the incarceration through satire, often under the pseudonym of Globularius Schraubi.[49] Though Yamada seems to have written little after the war, he was well known at the time among other incarcerated authors. The short story writer Hisaye Yamamoto, who was confined in Poston, included Yamada among Topaz's literary elite in her description of *TREK* as "that most serendipitous of all camp publications" thanks to the "chance assembly of several of the top Nisei artists and writers: Miné Okubo, Jimmy Yamada, Taro Katayama, Toyo Suyemoto, others." The playwright and fiction writer Wakako Yamauchi also refers to Yamada as one of the "real artists" who were incarcerated "in Topaz."[50] Yamada's "Falderol" pieces ("falderol" is defined as trivial nonsense), as their title suggests, were clever commentaries that demonstrated his keen sense of humor, but they also tackled significant issues facing incarcerees.

In a February 1943 piece, for example, which Yamada published in *TREK* after his transfer to the notoriously hot Poston facility, he challenged the widespread rumor that inmates were receiving better food and treatment by the government than were those outside the camps. White supremacist and Mississippi congressman, John Rankin, formally expressed this falsehood in Congress when he accused the WRA of "coddling the Japs."[51] Yamada responded:

> It wasn't until we arrived in Poston and heard first-hand accounts of last summer's heat that we learned the true significance of the charge that the evacuees are being coddled. Previously, in our naïve way, we had interpreted "coddled" as "to pamper," and were having some difficulty reconciling that definition with existing conditions in the relocation centers.
>
> Now that dawn has finally broken, we want to retract all the mean things we said about the people who were pressing that accusation. Particularly, we want to apologize for that time when we wished that they were in our apartment, breathing through a damp handkerchief, while the wind was having hysterics outside and the dust sifted into the room between the panels of sheetrock on the ceiling.

Yamada concluded:

> For obviously what they meant by "coddle" was the alternative definition: "to cook slowly and gently, as eggs or fruit, in water just below the boiling point." Though this doesn't precisely describe the situation, it comes close enough so that we know clearly what they're driving at. And we appreciate their solicitude.[52]

Through clever word play, Yamada at once amused his fellow detainees and challenged external misperceptions about the conditions in the camps. He was backed up by none other than First Lady Eleanor Roosevelt.

The "coddling controversy" so offended Roosevelt, in fact, that she protested in an article she wrote for *Collier's Magazine*. Roosevelt was against the internment and tried to persuade her husband, President Franklin Delano Roosevelt, not to issue Executive Order 9066. When that failed, she did her best to ensure that the incarcerated were treated humanely. In the *Collier's* article, she contested congressman Rankin's accusation by explaining that food rationing was practiced equally across the nation and that "even the War Relocation Authority cannot buy more than is allowed for the number of people they have to feed." Based on her April 1943 visit to the Gila River camp in Arizona, she testified to the size and needs of the prisons: "if you have a city of 14,000 people living in a camp such as the one I went to in Arizona, even in these days you have to have more on hand than the average small community."[53] Unfortunately, rational arguments, even if expressed by the highly popular First Lady, did little to quell criticism grounded in the same anti-Japanese racism that engendered the incarceration in the first place.

Yamada attempted to cushion his fellow incarcerated Japanese Americans from the psychological wound of such irrational hatred through humor. Under the pseudonym "Globularius Schraubi," a nonsensical moniker that can best be translated, by combining Latin and German, as something akin to "pretentious blob or glob," Yamada sharpened his critique of the incarceration. Schraubi signaled his tone to readers in his explanation of his use of the initials "M.A." following his name:

> the initials attached to GLOBULARIUS SCHRAUBI's name do not mean master of arts; they do not even mean master of asses. In fact, they signify nothing; he puts them there because he likes them. Schraubi, incidentally, has written a large number of poems in blank verse. Naturally, these, being blank, have never been found worth printing.[54]

This "author profile" encapsulated the nature of Schraubi's humor: it is replete with parody, satire, and wit.

In his December 1942 entry, "Yule Greetings, Friends," for example, Schraubi contributed a burlesque of H. L. Mencken's linguistic analysis of *The American Language* (1919). In this study, Mencken documented and celebrated the idioms, dialects, and slang used in "American" English, in response to British critics who claimed that it was a perversion of their superior mother tongue. Schraubi praised Mencken's work as a "magnificent" study of the "slanguage and haranguage of this garrulous nation" and then proceeded to spoof it with an analysis of "Evacuese," or the "language of the camps," in which he, like Katayama, drew attention to the way in which Japanese Americans were treated like animals.

Schraubi referred to the camps as "Little Nip pons or Nip-Pounds—not that they are shelters for nipping canines," for example, and identifies the incarcerated as "alingual," seemingly alluding to the ways in which they were silenced by the WRA.

> What concerns us at the moment is the alingual status of Japa-Mericans in the Areas into which they were recently imported and where they are now concentrated. The term "alingual," as used here, should not be construed, of

> course, to mean that they are dumb or that they do not speak, even though they may be speechless under the circumstances. In fact, there is a good deal of tongue locomotion going on in all the Areas. Just how they wag their tongues, and in what tongues, is a subject of profound speculation in philology and socio-psychiatry.[55]

In referring to the "Areas" as "concentrated," Schraubi may have been alluding to the change in government nomenclature from "concentration camps," which was what the government called them during the early months of the war, to "relocation centers." This euphemism was adopted to ease criticism about the camps, though none of the conditions—being surrounded by barbed wire, floodlights, and armed guards—changed along with the title.

Schraubi's reference to speculations in philology and sociopsychiatry recalled the aims of the Japanese American Evacuation and Resettlement Study (JERS) led by the sociologist Dorothy Swain Thomas from the University of California, Berkeley. Thomas recruited Nisei social science students as well as some white observers to document the daily activities, behaviors, and attitudes of detainees. This proved to be a controversial enterprise because of the inexperience of many of the recorders, the poorly defined methods and objectives of the study, and the general feeling to which Schraubi alluded—that incarcerated Japanese Americans were being inappropriately "analyzed" as sociological or psychological lab subjects.

Schraubi extended his critique of the incarceration in a satirical commentary on the forced removal of Japanese Americans from their homes and livelihoods to the Tanforan and Santa Anita racetracks, where the detained were housed in horse stalls. Breaking down "Evacuese," he claimed:

> *Neigh* is a word which should be gone into rather thoroughly. It is equivalent in value to the French "nes ce pas" or the English "eh, what?" though it is used in a less precise manner. The word originated at Tanforan, Santa Anita, and other race tracks in which the Evacuese language was born. (Which goes to show that the language is not only sacred but also colorful, aromatic, and full of sporting spirit.) As every good horseman knows, good horses neigh when they are pleased. *Neigh*, therefore, is a word of rejoicing; and why not rejoice in view of the stable nativity of the language?[56]

By juxtaposing the sacred site of the Christian nativity with the profane conditions of the horse stables in which incarcerees were detained, Schraubi elaborated on his critique of the ways in which Japanese Americans were objectified from humans into beasts.

Finally, Schraubi commented on tensions within the camp among the inmates themselves, again using animal imagery. The term "inu," which means "dog" in Japanese, referred to spies in the community who informed the FBI about anyone they felt was not wholly committed to the United States. Many Japanese Americans believed that "inu" had identified Issei community leaders for arrest and detention in Department of Justice jails and prisons immediately following the bombing of Pearl Harbor. Leaders of the Japanese American Citizens League (JACL), a patriotic organization known for its pro-American attitudes, were especially suspect.[57]

Schraubi alluded to these problems when he made the "inu" the subjects of derision: "Dead men tell no tales. Dogs tell tales with their tails. Good dogs, however, wag them not at all when at a crucial moment, and as a result the merit of a dog is judged by the time, place, and manner of their tale-wagging."[58] Expressing a view held by many of the detained, Schraubi mocked those "inu" or dogs in the camp who preached cooperation with camp administrators when doing so made them complicit in their own oppression. Schraubi's reference to "dead men's" inability to "tell tales" likely implied the ways in which "inu," or informants, were threatened and even beaten by fellow detainees.[59] "Good dogs," by contrast, according to Schraubi, wagged their tails/tales "not at all when at a crucial moment," thus earning them "merit" or the respect of those around them. Indeed, the multiple puns on dog may also have been an attempt to cast doubt in the minds of camp administrators whether the tail or the tale—the stories told to them by alleged "inu"—were wagging the WRA dog, or vice versa.

Schraubi's language play continued as he mocked the common Japanese "shikata ga nai," or "it can't be helped," which has been widely interpreted as signaling either a sort of superhuman stoicism or a stereotype of passivity among Japanese Americans in the face of their incarceration. "Shikata ga nai" was punned, in Schraubi's translation of the "Evacuese," as, "Matter key na sigh neigh!" which, he claimed, was an "abbreviated way of saying something quite complicated. The nearest we can come to a literal translation would be: 'No matter if you sigh or neigh, so long as we have the key to the jarnt you can't have what you want.'"[60]

Through satire, James Yamada joined his fellow journalist, Taro Katayama, in making excellent use of the pages of *TREK* to resist and critique their incarceration. Other artists, such as Toyo Suyemoto, Miné Okubo, and Toshio

Mori, also found *TREK* to be a valuable venue through which to continue their creative pursuits while incarcerated. On one level, the community of writers and artists confined in Utah found ways to continue to practice their craft while imprisoned and, in so doing, were able to serve as a link in the chain of Japanese American literature as it existed before and after the war.

On another level, however, the promise of a career in the arts or journalism that seemed possible for many writers prior to the incarceration proved hard to achieve after it. The intentional dispersal of the Japanese American community to cities all over the Midwest and East Coast broke up the literary and artistic circles that had provided inspirational aesthetic foundations in San Francisco and Oakland before the war. The economic hardship suffered by the families of these artists and writers, as a direct result of the incarceration, forced many to take on postwar employment unrelated to their artistic ambitions. Sadly, we will never know what great work might have been produced if these artistic cohorts had been free to thrive.

3
Toshio Mori
A Literary Life Derailed

Toshio Mori, a Nisei living in Oakland, California, was motivated to write, in part, to counter the stereotypes of Japanese Americans he saw in 1930s popular culture:

> I was really trying my best to reach the white American readers . . . because I found that most of the writings by white Americans were concentrated on Japanese subjects through humor. . . . most of them were based on detective, suspense or mystery stories with the main character, a Japanese detective. But as far as I was concerned, they didn't typify the Japanese community at all, and I started thinking that perhaps I could reveal some of the true Japanese lives.[1]

Unlike some of the other up-and-coming writers in the San Francisco Bay area at the time, however, Mori had to relegate writing to a pastime. He could not devote his life to it because he had to work in his family's flower business. Still, he disciplined himself to write daily between 10 p.m. and 2 a.m. and, after six years of trying and countless letters of rejection, he achieved his goal of seeing his stories in print, "as a professional" in his words, in a magazine directed toward white American readers. In 1938, at age twenty-eight, Mori published his first two short stories, "Tomorrow and Today" and "The Brothers," in *Coast* magazine, a journal focusing on matters of interest to people living on the West Coast.[2] By 1941, Mori's writing had appeared in several of the Bay area's literary periodicals, and he had also composed his short story cycle about daily life in a small Japanese American community, *Yokohama, California*.

In *Yokohama, California*, Mori had come close to creating "The Great Nisei Novel" sought by Larry Tajiri and James (Jimmie) Omura.[3] A collection of stories rather than a full-fledged novel, *Yokohama, California* was the first extended work to portray Japanese Americans in rich complexity. Mori

That Damned Fence. Heather Hathaway, Oxford University Press. © Oxford University Press 2022.
DOI: 10.1093/oso/9780190098315.003.0004

explained that in it he "tried to present some of the life patterns of a Japanese Issei and Nisei . . . community to reveal to the people in general some of the small details for living that would appeal to the reader of any nationality."[4] As such, *Yokohama, California* stands alongside other modern classics of ethnic American writing such as Henry Roth's *Call It Sleep* (1934), which portrayed Jewish Americans in New York city's Lower East Side; William Saroyan's short stories and plays, which portrayed Armenian Americans in Fresno, California; and Jerre Mangione's *Mount Allegro* (1943), which focused on Sicilian Americans in Rochester, New York.

As a short story cycle, *Yokohama, California* also closely resembled Sherwood Anderson's 1919 classic, *Winesburg, Ohio*, which Mori admired greatly. Mori later recalled that Anderson's stories "used to puzzle" him so he read "everything of Sherwood Anderson's to understand him. . . . One day I started to feel akin to his characters and at the same time I started to find that I, through the combination of characters I knew in the Japanese community, became more fluent in characterizing the typical Japanese people within my community."[5] He accomplished his goal: *Yokohama, California* is an underappreciated literary gem.

Encouraged by the immigrant author and friend William Saroyan, Mori had contracted the book with a small publishing house in Idaho, Caxton Printers, for publication in 1942. Saroyan was impressed with Mori's stories in *Coast* and reached out to him. According to their fellow writer, Hisaye Yamamoto, the two men shared a special bond:

> The fact remains that it wasn't any of us [Mori's fellow Nisei writers] who helped Toshio Mori when he was starting out. That was William Saroyan who . . . got in touch with him, went for walks with him, sat over café meals with him. . . . That was Saroyan encouraging him to get more of his work into print.[6]

Saroyan and Mori both published throughout the thirties, and by 1940 Saroyan had met success: that year he won the Pulitzer Prize in Drama for his play *The Time of Your Life*, which explored the social interactions among a culturally diverse group of people in a San Francisco bar. Saroyan held Mori's work in high esteem. In the "Informal Introduction to the Short Stories of the New American Writer from California, Toshio Mori," which Saroyan wrote for the intended 1942 publication and which was included in the 1949 edition, when the book was finally published, he described Mori as "probably one of the most important new writers in the country."[7]

Mori's publishing path did not parallel Saroyan's, however. The Sansei poet Lawson Fusao Inada (incarcerated in Fresno, Amache, and Jerome), describes *Yokohama, California*'s publishing history in his introduction to the first reprinting of story collection in 1985:

> The publishing history of *Yokohama, California* is a story in itself; it spans the times. It is both landmark and watershed, representative of key periods in Japanese-American, American history: before the war, the camps, after the war, and now, whatever this period might be called, when there is talk of redress and reparations. . . . It's all right here in the book: 1942, 1949, 1985. . . . The book was written in the late 1930s and early 1940s although some of the stories might take place in the 1920s or earlier. The book was accepted for publication in 1941, slated to be issued in 1942, finally appeared in 1949, and went out of print.[8]

Inada attributed the lack of general interest in the work to Mori's ancestry, not his writing abilities.

> While before the war, people might have been moderately interested in a book by a Japanese American, an Oriental, a Nisei, even a Jap (the term was nothing new), by 1949, all this was something else indeed. It was as if, in the interim, Toshio, the "new writer," had become many different things—all variations of Jap.[9]

In effect, the war and the incarceration rendered *Yokohama, California* not a promising literary debut but rather, as Inada describes it, a book "not to be read so much as inspected. It had been tarnished, not burnished, by time. . . . By its very nature, it was destined for obscurity," according to Inada.[10]

While historical events may have stripped *Yokohama* of its rightful literary acclaim in the short run, however, it was not "destined for obscurity" in the long run and remains the first Great Nisei "novel." Inada himself recognized it as such:

> This is the book—the first real Japanese-American book. This is the book—the one people ignored and rejected. This is the book—the one that "was

> postponed." This is the book—by "the first real Japanese-American writer." This is the book—a monument, a classic of literature.

Inada understood that *Yokohama's* importance extended beyond literary circles. He continued:

> This is more than a book. This is legacy, tradition. This is the enduring strength, the embodiment of a people. This is the spirit, the soul. This is the community, the identity. This is the pride, the joy, the love. This is *Yokohama, California*. This *is* Japanese America.[11]

Hisaye Yamamoto, who was detained in Poston, acknowledged the same. She stated that as of 1979, "one fact remains incontrovertible: [Toshio Mori] is the first and only Japanese American to have had a book of short stories published in this country."[12]

Since then, in 1988,Yamamoto herself published a brilliant collection, *Seventeen Syllables and Other Stories*, which has been widely read and celebrated. Nonetheless, she was correct in her assessment that in Mori's writing alone can be found "the panorama of Japanese America in the early 1930s, in the later 30s as the storm clouds gathered, and in the concentration camps of 1942–45, stretched on a canvas from here to there, a veritable Floating World. No one else has kept this account of our lives, in fiction and in personal essay, in such detail, with such compassion.[13] *Yokohama, California* is at once the foundational work of Nisei creative writing in the United States and an invaluable historical record of Japanese American life before the war.

Mori captured this "Floating World" in nineteen stories, all of which warrant serious critical attention individually because of their beauty, depth, and mystery. But threaded throughout the collection is a theme that, when traced, reveals differences in Mori's writing before, during, and after the war: this theme involves the inherently American nature of the inhabitants of "Lil' Yokohama." Nearly all the stories illustrate the firm embeddedness of the fictional town Yokohama, California, in the larger American social fabric. In each, Mori shows the extraordinary ordinariness of this small town by illustrating that Japanese Americans are, indeed, "just like everyone else."[14]

In "The Woman Who Makes Swell Doughnuts," for example, Mori tells the familiar tale of a friendly neighborhood woman who welcomes everyone into her home:

> All her friends, old and young, call her Mama. Everybody calls her Mama. That is not new, it is logical. I suppose there is in every block of every city in America a woman who can be called Mama by her friends and the strangers meeting her.

First, Mori universalizes her as a maternal figure for whom ethnic or national signifiers are meaningless. At the same time, however, he also firmly locates her as Japanese American. "Mama's" house, in Mori's story, is strewn with "magazines and books in Japanese and English." She is "the best cook" the speaker has ever known, not only of doughnuts, but of both "Oriental dishes [and] American dishes."[15]

The most important aspect of being with the woman, according to the narrator, is that with her, he does "not have to be on guard."

> Sometimes we sit many minutes in silence. Silence does not bother her. She says silence is the most beautiful symphony, she says the air breathed in silence is sweeter and sadder. That is about all we talk of. Sometimes I sit and gaze out the window and watch the Southern Pacific trains rumble by and the vehicles whizz with speed. And sometimes she catches me doing this and she nods her head and I know she understands that I think the silence in the room is great, and also the roar and the dust of the outside is great, and when she is nodding I understand that she is saying that this, her little room, her little circle, is a depot, a pause for the weary traveler, but outside, outside of her little world there is dissonance, hugeness of another kind, and the travel to do. So she has her little house, she bakes the grandest doughnuts, and inside of her she houses a little depot.[16]

Steven Mori, Toshio's son, described his father as valuing the quality of "satori, the intuitive inner light that is most sought after in Zen Buddhism."[17] Achieving satori is the point of this story. Toshio Mori first refers to the "little depot" as part of the woman's house: "I understand that she is saying that this, her little room, her little circle, is a depot, a pause for the weary traveler, but outside, outside of her little world there is dissonance, hugeness of another kind, and the travel to do." But in the final line of the passage, Mori shifts gears and states that the depot is within the woman herself: "inside of her she houses a little depot." This is satori and it is her gift to him: she models the quality of a self-knowledge that yields contentment. Mori pairs classic American slang and imagery, "swell doughnuts," with his description of the woman's heightened sense of being to show just how firmly Japanese American she is.

Another of Mori's stories, "The All-American Girl," similarly situates Issei and Nisei at the center of the American experience. In it, Mori describes two boys' infatuation with the beautiful young woman who walks past their house occasionally:

> We call her the All-American Girl, my brother and I. . . . We used to sit on the front porch of our house in the city and every once so often she used to walk past. "Here comes the beauty," Hajime said when she came down the street. "An All-American if there ever was one."[18]

When she disappears and the two discover she has married a "promising doctor in Los Angeles," they learn her name for the first time. " 'Her name was Ayako Saito. That is our All-American Girl,' Hajime said." Though the boys continued their porch-sitting for many months, they never saw the All-American Girl again. But they were "quite sure no girl we saw ever struck the note that the All-American Girl accomplished with her smile, departure and mystery."[19]

Like "The Woman Who Makes Swell Doughnuts," this story carries multiple meanings. On one level, the boys are content with seeing an ideal without the need to possess it—the ideal being the young woman's qualities. They embrace the Buddhist concept of detachment. They grow in adoration for the young woman, but from afar, whereas trying to engage with her might lead to becoming attached in a way that can create misery. So the boys rely on a Buddhist sense of equanimity in the midst of their admiration of the All-American Girl. On another level, Mori proves yet again the enmeshment of Japanese Americans with US culture as he portrays the "All-American Girl" as clearly of Japanese ancestry.[20]

Mori further emphasizes the American nature of Yokohama, California in a story titled "Lil' Yokohama," which portrays the small town as like any other in the 1930s United States. He begins by firmly situating "Lil' Yokohama" alongside many other typical cities:

> In Lil' Yokohama, as the youngsters call our community, we have 24 hours every day . . . morning, noon, and night roll on regularly, just as in Boston, Cincinnati, Birmingham, Kansas City, Minneapolis, and Emeryville.

> When the sun is out, the housewives sit on the porch or walk around the yard, puttering with this and that, and the old men who are in the house when it is cloudy or raining come out on the porch or sit in the shade and read the newspaper. . . . The people of Lil' Yokohama are here.[21]

In the next scene, he describes the community watching a game of the great American pastime: baseball. (Mori himself was an outstanding shortstop and at one point had aspirations of joining the major leagues.)

> Today young and old are at the Alameda ball grounds to see the big game: Alameda Taiiku vs San Jose Asahis. The great Northern California game is under way. Will Slugger Hironaka hit that southpaw from San Jose? Will the same southpaw make the Alameda sluggers stand on their heads? It's the great question.[22]

By mixing baseball with Japanese American team names, Mori emphasizes the jointly Japanese and American nature of this community:

> Papa Hatanaka, the father of baseball among the California Japanese, is sitting in the stands behind the backstop . . . great lover of baseball. Mrs. Horita is here, the mother of Ted Horita, the star left fielder of Alameda. Mr. and Mrs. Matsuda of Lil' Yokohama; the Tatsunos . . . the Nodas, Uedas, Abes, Kikuchis, Yamanatos, Sasakis . . .[23]

Then he closes the image: "The big game ends, and the San Jose Asahis win. The score doesn't matter. Cheers and shouts and laughter still ring in the stands. Finally it all ends—the noise, the game, the life in the park; and the popcorn man starts his car and goes up Clement."[24]

Mori's goal in this tale is to present a week in the life of this typical American community. He chronicles the same activities that take place everywhere else in the United States—deaths, births, illnesses and partings, marriages, loves, and losses. He ends the story emphasizing just how unexceptional Lil' Yokohama is:

> And today which is every day the sun is out again. The housewives sit on the porch and the old men sit in the shade and read the papers. Across the yard a radio goes full blast with Benny Goodman's band. The children come

> back from Lincoln Grammar School. In a little while the older ones will be returning from Tech High and Mc Clymonds High. Young boys and young girls will go down the street together. The old folks from the porches and the windows will watch them go by and shake their heads and smile. The day is here and is Lil' Yokohama's day.[25]

This is not a narrative of assimilation; it's just the reverse. Mori does not seek to show how Japanese Americans "blend in" to the "melting pot" of America: rather, he seeks to demonstrate how they are intrinsically foundational to it.

In "The Brothers" (the story published in *Coast* in 1938), Mori goes one step further to definitively distinguish the beliefs and values held by Japanese Americans from those evinced by the totalitarian regime of the Japanese nation-state. The story emphasizes from the very first line that "this is really about George and Tsuneo, two tiny Japanese boys who are brothers" but it is not. Instead it is an analogical commentary on Japan's invasion of Manchuria in September 1931. The writer Hisaye Yamamoto recalls that,

> particularly in that time of tension in the thirties when Japan began to occupy Manchuria under the eyes of a disapproving world, and Japanese in the United States began to feel some of the backlash on top of the already existing prejudice, . . . it seemed necessary to begin taking a stand of some kind. Several of Toshio's stories of that period touch on this theme.[26]

"The Brothers" takes a stand on world politics through the story of two young boys.

"The Brothers" is structured around the point of view of a patient who made weekly visits to his dentist and who, through conversations with the dentist, became preoccupied with the relationship between the dentist's two sons.

> Tsuneo is three and George is five and they are typical of their age regardless of their nationality. Likely as not they could have been the sons of a German or British or French or Russian or Chinese or American or Eskimo. Their age is of time when their activities are completely of their own sphere and when the adult influence has little to do with their actions unless the child is willing accede to the adult.[27]

As the story progresses to describe the slow encroachment and appropriation of the older brother's property by the younger, the seemingly superficial plot takes on additional connotations. The speaker states that "once the adventure of these two tiny boys was mentioned by the father, little else was of interest. It began so innocently and naturally, the drama of these two tiny lives, and it was not so easily picked up but came slowly to me toward the end or the climax of recent episodes."[28] Just as the awareness of an encroaching totalitarianism slowly becomes apparent to those it oppresses, so, too, does the patient grow in gradual awareness of the dangers inherent in the brothers' behavior.

The patient spends most of his time with the dentist focusing on the conflict between the boys. Early on, the dentist explains that "there are four drawers in the desk, three on one side and one just above the knees. He said he made George relinquish the lower drawer to Tsuneo so the younger one, too, would have a part of the desk. Territory, he called it." Mori then makes clear that the battle of the boys serves as the conceit for world politics:

> At that time the Manchurian affair hogged the headlines and everywhere he went there was the talk of war and war clouds. So when we discussed the problem of George and Tsuneo and their struggle, it was a timely one. The father had been aware of its relation long before this; that was why he spoke of his two tiny sons and shook his head and smiled. "What barbarians," he would say.[29]

The dentist's reference to his own children as barbarous is multivalent: it suggests his own belief that he, a Japanese American living in United States, views the imperialistic acts of Japan as brutal and also that, just as he can distance himself from the behavior of his two sons, so, too, can Issei in the United States distance themselves from the political activities engaged in by their "mother country," Japan.

The patient, however, cannot let go of his concerns: "every Tuesday," the speaker comments, "I was there with interest and alarm." When he discovers that the younger has occupied another drawer, he asks the dentist, "Why doesn't George do something about it?" The dentist replies:

> "That is where the phenomenon of nature takes hold of each one. Tsuneo, the three-year-old, is the strongest because he has less fear of losing his

> possession. He is strong and powerful by simply having little and he covets all and stakes for a gain," the dentist said.
>
> "And George?" I said.
>
> "He is five and lot stronger," the dentist said. "But he has many more things to mind. He must police all his belongings and that takes much of his strength out of him. At five he knows enough to give in a little and lose few than to lose much more by antagonizing."[30]

Following this foray into political theory by the dentist, the narrator then offers his own:

> There is no end nor beginning in possession of things. According to their father, George and Tsuneo had in their possession all the things they were to require and receive later. When the struggle for the drawers commenced, simultaneously everything in their range and knowledge began to move and the ruthless comparison of who had more began.[31]

The battle between the boys intensified and culminated in "the inevitable fight," after which "Tsuneo, the little one, was still defiant a little but George was all for settling peacefully."[32] Or so the father thought.

During breakfast the next morning, the father realized that battles of this nature are perennial. Initially, they all sat quietly eating together, and the father had begun to forget that the fight had even taken place. But then he came to a realization:

> But as the boys sat in front of him the father did not like the quietness found in time and place and as he watched his tiny sons quietly gobbling up the corn flakes, he knew that behind silence, behind little heads, their little eyes are for coveted things and their hands are to paw and smash, and the brewing trouble which is the worry and the sadness of the earth is once again stirring.[33]

This international analogy, "The Brothers," also somewhat anticipates a novel that Mori later wrote while incarcerated, *The Brothers Murata*. In both, the inescapable "worry and the sadness of the earth" that is caused by differences in values, ideas, politics, and possessions divides the closest of siblings. If this can happen to brothers, Mori seems to question, what can it do on a global scale? He found out with the outbreak of World War II.

Yokohama, California, as it was originally conceived, offered a nuanced portrayal of prewar Japanese American life that emphasized the equal weight of those two adjectives for Nisei: Japanese *and* American. The war, however, changed that balance. Because of their Japanese ancestry, Mori and his family were incarcerated first at Tanforan Race Track and then at Topaz. During this time Mori continued to write and he published five pieces in the literary magazines produced in Topaz: *TREK* (which ran three editions) and *All Aboard* (which consisted of just one edition). Four were short stories: "Tomorrow Is Coming, Children," "One Happy Family," "The Travelers," and "The Trees." One was an editorial titled "Topaz Station." All reveal a shift in Mori's feelings about, in his words, "the experiences that an immigrant and his family have, trying to find their home in America."[34] Most could only have been written after December 7, 1941, and the American cultural catastrophe that ensued, just as those in the original version of *Yokohama, California* could only have been written before that disastrous day.

"Tomorrow Is Coming, Children" was published in the second issue of *TREK*, which came out in February 1943. It embodied the confusion and displacement felt by Issei, in particular, although it did so under a veil of patriotism. The main character was based on Mori's mother, and the story itself provided the kernel around which he built his 1979 novel, *Woman from Hiroshima*. On the surface, "Tomorrow Is Coming, Children" appeared to be a classic immigrant narrative recounting the successful Americanization of an Issei grandmother. Consciously or unconsciously, Mori appeared to follow the formulaic conventions of nineteenth-century Americanization or assimilation narratives that were popular during the late nineteenth and early twentieth centuries.

In these immigration stories, the narrators first characterized life in the "Old World" and the dilemma over whether to go to America. Next, they recounted the perils of the long journey by sea, typically characterized by illness, hunger, and crowded quarters. The text then described the immigrants' reactions to the United States as they approached Ellis Island on the East Coast or Angel Island on the West. In East Coast stories, impressions of the Statue of Liberty figured prominently; in West Coast stories, Lady Liberty was replaced by passage through the Golden Gate, the strait that connects the Pacific Ocean to San Francisco Bay. This was followed by a portrayal of the reunion between the immigrant and the family member who preceded him or her, and in these vignettes, the importance of clothing and money as tools of assimilation (and therefore also protection against discrimination) was nearly always highlighted. Finally, the conventional tales presented images of immigrant housing, most often in the form of ethnic neighborhoods or multiethnic tenements, followed by a portrayal of the challenges and rewards of finding work. In most instances, a rags-to-riches transformation took place in a city where the streets were metaphorically "paved with gold."[35]

Mori's immigration narrative, "Tomorrow Is Coming, Children," adheres to but also importantly departs from these formulaic conventions of the genre to offer a compelling commentary on the peculiar plight of Japanese Americans in the 1940s. Mori first deviates from the formula in his portrayal of the setting: he stages the tale within the confines of a relocation center, using the ruse of an Issei grandmother telling stories to her Sansei grandchildren to alleviate their boredom in the barracks. This in itself signals that "Tomorrow" will not be a stereotypical immigration tale. So, too, does the accompanying illustration by the contributing artist, Tom Yamamoto. In it, the oba-san sits in front of what appears to be a barrack window, outside of which stand a telephone pole, mountain-like images, and the snowy roof of a building next door. Picking up on a symbol often used by Miné Okubo in her camp illustrations, Yamamoto clads the grandmother in a blouse covered with miniature plus signs, which some argue Okubo used to indicate the barbed wires enclosing the community. As the two grandchildren look up to their grandmother, the boy is notably concerned.

The setting notwithstanding, Mori opens the story with the expected reminiscences of life in the "Old World" of Japan:

> Long ago, children, I lived in a country called Japan. Your grandpa was already in California earning money for my boat ticket. The village people rarely went out of Japan and were shocked when they learned I would follow your grandpa as soon as the money came. "America," they cried! "America is on the other side of the world! You will be in a strange country. You cannot read or write their language. What will you do?"

Despite these warnings, the oba-san elects to emigrate because, "in my dreams," she told her grandchildren, "I saw the San Francisco your grandpa wrote about: San Francisco, the city with strange enticing food; the city with gold coins; the city with many strange faces and music; the city with great buildings and ships."[36]

TOMORROW IS COMING, CHILDREN

Topaz inmate and artist Tom Yamamoto's illustration for the English version of Toshio Mori's story "Tomorrow Is Coming, Children" ran in the February 1943 edition of *TREK*. The illustration for the English version, which was read by many Nisei, portrays a grandmother telling her life story to her grandchildren from within the confines of the Topaz prison camp, thereby visually highlighting the incarceration above all her experiences.

TREK, *February 1943, p. 13, Topaz prison camp, Delta, Utah. Densho, ddr-densho-142-426, courtesy of the Library of Congress*

Next, Mori follows convention and offers a description of the sea voyage: "the sea was rough and I was sick almost all the way. There were others in the room just as ill. I couldn't touch the food. I began to have crazy thoughts. Why was I going to America? Why had I been foolish enough to leave my village?"[37] (*TREK* 2:13). Eventually, the oba-san's fear abates when she sees her "new world":

> When the boat finally passed the Golden Gate, I had my first glimpse of San Francisco. I was on deck for hours, waiting for the golden city of dreams.

> I stood there with the other immigrants, chatting nervously and excitedly. "America! America! We are in America!" someone cried.[38]

Mori then works in a reference to the trope of donning new clothes in order to become a "real" American:

> "What was I wearing, Annabelle? My best kimono, a beautiful thing. But do you know what your grandpa did when he saw me come off the boat? He looked at it and shook his head. He hauled me around as if he were ashamed of me. I could not understand."
>
> "Never wear this thing again," he told me that night.
>
> "Why?" I demanded. "It is a beautiful kimono."
>
> "You look like a foreigner," he said. "You must dress like an American. You belong here."[39]

Mori portrays the oba-san as, in time, coming to feel as though she does indeed "belong" to the United States, and it, to her. "Ah, San Francisco, my dream city. My San Francisco is everywhere. I like the dirty brown hills, the black soil and the sandy beaches. I like the tall buildings, the bridges, the parks and the roar of the city traffic. They are of me and I feel like humming."[40]

The reality, of course, was that by 1942, Issei and Nisei had learned that others did not think Issei "belonged" in America. While on one hand, the story appeared to be an affirmation of "American" ideals, an altogether different interpretation was possible when one considered that it was composed from behind bars. When read from this perspective, different themes in the story rise to the fore—those of loss, of discrimination, of disenfranchisement. "I lost grandpa. I lost my boy. I lost my mother and father. Long ago, I lost my friends in Japan," the oba-san laments.[41] She recalls the poverty and hostility she and her husband experienced shortly after her arrival:

> We had a small empty house and no money. We spread our blankets on the floor and slept. We used big boxes for tables and small ones for chairs. The city of my dreams began to frighten me. Rocks were thrown at the house and the windows smashed to bits. Loud cries and laughter followed each attack, and I cowered in the corner waiting for the end.
>
> "Oh, why did I come? Whatever did we come for?" I asked your grandpa.
>
> He only looked at me. "Just a little more time . . . a little more time," his eyes seemed to say.[42]

Although Tom Yamamoto drew the illustration for the English version of the story, the artist and writer Miné Okubo provided the one for its translation into Japanese. (Portions of the literary magazine were translated into Japanese for the benefit of Issei whose reading skills in English were limited.) Okubo's drawing emphasizes the losses described by the oba-san. Rather than depicting the camp, she portrays the kimono-clad grandmother on the ship departing Japan, framed by Mount Fuji and waving a white kerchief to those she is leaving behind.

Ultimately, Mori's fictional oba-san makes a place for herself and her family. But all of this is upended when she and her American-born children and grandchildren are evacuated and confined: "Yes, Annabelle and Johnny, we are at war. I do not forget the fact. How can I ever forget? My mother country and my adopted land at war! Incredulous!" At this point in the tale, Mori becomes curiously ambiguous about the national allegiances of the grandmother. Although earlier in the story the oba-san repeatedly affirms to her grandchildren her faith in America, Mori provides no national identifiers in the final paragraphs. He portrays the oba-san as seeing clearly the costs of the war:

> If there were no war we would not be in a relocation center. We would be back in our house on Market Street, hanging out our wash on the clothesline and watering our flower garden. You would be attending school with your neighborhood friends. Ah, war is terrifying. It upsets personal life and hopes.

She then concludes that during war, "you must choose sides. War has given your grandmother an opportunity to find where her heart lay. To her surprise her choice has been made long ago, and no war will sway her a bit. For grandma, the sky is clear. The sun is shining."[43] She never explicitly states, however, which side she chooses.

This same ambiguity characterized Mori's contribution to the June 1943 edition of *TREK*. The story, ironically titled "One Happy Family," recounts the very unhappy separation of a father, mother, and son as a result of Executive Order 9066. In the story, the father is arrested by the FBI on the night of December 7, 1941, and imprisoned in a DOJ detention facility while the mother and son are sent to an unnamed assembly center and then to Topaz. Okubo illustrated this tale, and she creates no uncertainty about the setting. She very clearly locates it in a prison camp by portraying a guard

子供たちよ　明日と言ふ日は
きっと來ますよ

子供たちよ。遠い遠い昔に私は日本といふ国に住んで居たんだよ。おまへたちのおぢい様は私をアメリカに呼ぶ船の切符を買ふために早くからカリホルニヤへ来て働いて居た。その頃私の村の人たちの中には、日本を出て外国で働いて居るものなどはあまりなかった。だから、お金が来次才私がおぢいさんの後について行くのだと聞いた時本当におどろいたものだよ。

「アメリカ！」と村の人たちは叫んだのだよ。「アメリカは世界の向ふ側にある所ではありませんか。外国ですよ。言葉もわからず読んだり書いたりすることも出来ないのに一体どうするつもりなのですか？」 私はただ微笑んで夢の中におまへたちのおぢいさんの手紙にあった桑港を見てゐたのだよ。美しい、珍らしい、おいしい食物のある町。金貨がころがってる町。異人さんのゐる町。ふしぎな音楽の聞える町。高い建物の並んだ町。大きな船のある町。さうしてゐるうちにおぢいさんの手紙が来た。それにはお金が入ってゐて、「すぐおいでなさい、ぐずぐずしないで」と書いてあったのだよ。さうすると近所隣の人たちが家にやって来て大きな声を出して「行ってはいけませんよ。こちらにいらっしゃい、日本とアメリカに必ず戦争がありますよ。太平洋の真中でつかまってアメリカにはどうしても行かれないやうになりますよ」でも私の気持はもうきまってゐた。お隣の人は遠い向ふの異国に行ってゐる移民のお話をしどんなに淋しく困るやうになるかも知れないと言って肩をなでて泣いてくれた。「切符も買ひ、荷物も出来て居るんですもの、どうしても私は行くつもりです」と私は云った。それからひと月の間と云ふもの村の人々は私を招待しておわかれのパアティをしてくれた。それを思ふと行くに行かれぬ心持にはなったけれども、一旦心を決めたのだもの。いよいよ出発する日が来ると、村の人は汽車まで見送りに来てくれた。みんな元気よく手を振ってくれたがその眼はみんな悲しさうだった。だけど私は悲しくはなかったよ。私はただ一図に桑港とあなた方のおぢいさんの事ばかりを考へて居たのだよ。神戸まで一所に来てくれたのは兄さんだった。さうして船が動き出すと初めて胸をさすやうなかなしみがせまって来たのだった。

Topaz inmate and artist Miné Okubo's illustration for the Japanese version of Toshio Mori's story "Tomorrow Is Coming, Children" was published in the February 1943 edition of *TREK*. The illustration for the Japanese version, which was read primarily by Issei, portrays a kimono-clad Japanese woman waving good-bye to her family in the shadow of Mt. Fuji as she embarks for the United States. It thereby visually highlighted the act of emigrating, rather than being incarcerated, and above all emphasized the grandmother's experiences.

TREK, *February 1943, p. 44, Topaz prison camp, Delta, Utah. Densho, ddr-densho-142-426, courtesy of the Library of Congress*

This illustration by Topaz inmate and artist Miné Okubo accompanied Toshio Mori's story "One Happy Family" in the June 1943 edition of *TREK*. The image of an incarcerated mother and son reading a letter from the boy's father, who has been held as an enemy alien in a Department of Justice prison, lays bare the sarcasm of Mori's title of the story.

TREK, *June 1943, p. 12, Topaz prison camp, Utah. Densho, ddr-densho-142-427, courtesy of the Library of Congress*

tower through the window. A mother and her son are framed by a barracks window and the mother is reading a letter while her son, also in the shadow of the guard tower, looks up, with worry, at his mother's face.

The boy's worry results from his confusion about the absence of his father. Mori identifies the boy in the very first line of the story as "the little American Japanese boy," inverting the terms, Japanese and American, which were most commonly used to refer to Nisei, so as to emphasize the boy's birthright and citizenship. The boy attempts to guess where his father is because his mother, obviously deeply sad, tells her son that this father is "on vacation." When he asks, "Mama, did he do something bad? Is he a bad man in America?" the mother responds,

> "He is innocent, daddy is. Please remember that, Ben. Don't ever be ashamed of him. Believe in him."
>
> "Why was he taken away, mama?" he asked.
>
> Mother shook her head slowly. "He was taken as a suspect but he is not guilty. He was taken because America doubted him and he had no explanation."[44]

Mori's repetition of "America," first as a place in which a Japanese American man can be defined as "bad" and second, as a collective entity that has the power to judge a person's guilt or innocence, emphasizes the nation-state as a judicial force that can give or take away a person's freedom.

Not surprisingly, his mother's explanation frightens the boy:

> All of a sudden his eyes opened wide, and he knew why his father was not home, why his mama must suffer and become sad. He remembered the headline of the city papers, he recalled that day when a strange group of older boys at school called him a Jap and chased him home. America was at war with Japan, but he could not understand. What has war to do with their home, with his quiet father who had worked hard for a living?[45]

Mori's portrayal of the young boy's logic painfully illustrates the confusion experienced by so many incarcerated children. While some memoirs and narratives about the event create the impression that the impact of the imprisonment was not as severe on the youth, this is not necessarily the case. Children witnessed their parents suffer, worry, and grow depressed without a clear understanding of why. Patterns of behavior and parenting that got solidified in the artificial environment of the camps were quite different from those adhered to both before and after the war, in more typical home settings. Transgenerational trauma is one of the more tragic aspects of the incarceration.

In an attempt to guard against her son's potential resentment, the mother encourages the boy to "never become bitter. America is for us plain people. Believe in America. Bitterness is not for the common man. When you grow up you will realize that this war was fought to destroy bitterness, sadness, and fear." But tellingly, the boy does not understand what his mother means. Wishing "for the world to turn out right," and "realizing his helplessness," the boy sobs in his mother's lap.

Mori closes the tale with an uncharacteristically somber tone. The mother assures the son that his father will return "when the government investigates his case. He will be back free," but "the world swam before [the boy's] closed eyes as he clung tightly to her skirts. The little boy continued sobbing because even a mother cannot soothe and comfort one at times." Mori once again poses and then leaves unanswered important questions: Would the government act justly? Would the father be freed? Could the wounds of the incarceration ever be healed?[46]

An equally somber tone is reflected in Toyo Suyemoto's poem, "Promise," which Mori's tale frames on the page. *TREK* was typed by hand and then mimeographed, so the layout of the magazine was clearly intentional. "Promise" echoes the themes of "One Happy Family":

Here is the seed nurtured
Through a long winter spell,
Now new-sprung to the warmth
Of sun from its dark shell.

A promise yet, will mine
Flower fulfill its leaf
And bud, and thus annul
Remembered frost and grief?

When these pieces were written, the future was unknown to Mori, to Suyemoto, to all who were incarcerated. They did know that they had already lost their freedom, their autonomy, their homes, and businesses. But they, like the boy in the story, did not know what lay ahead.

"Resettlement" turned out to be the next step in the detainees' futures. Mori's story "The Travelers," which appeared in *All Aboard*, the final literary magazine produced by Topaz writers and published in the spring of 1944, simultaneously celebrated and lamented the effects of this policy.[47] On one hand, the movement of detainees to cities east of the Rocky Mountains represented a degree of liberation from their captivity. On the other, however, the dispersal of people to parts unknown, with the explicit intention of breaking up Japanese American communities on the West Coast, also meant the destruction of long-standing relationships. This brought with its own level of loss.

Mori depicts "The Travelers" as a crew of shoppers, "relocatees," and Nisei soldiers on a bus bound first for the train station in Delta, Utah, the town closest to Topaz, and then to multiple resettlement destinations. One man is going to Akron, Ohio; another, to Madison, Wisconsin to study at the state university. An Issei mother and her daughter are embarking for Kansas City to secure a good education for the daughter. Another young woman is headed to Chicago to be a stenographer, while her friend is "getting married in Philadelphia." A soldier is going first to Camp Shelby in Mississippi for training and then to the warfront to serve in the all-Nisei combat unit.[48] In the tale, Mori uses two metaphors to suggest the double-sided coin characterizing this groups' impending "freedom": a bird signifies liberation from confinement, but scattering seeds signifies the dispersal of communities and even family members from one another.

One member of the group, for example, upon seeing a bird flying alongside the bus, interprets it as "an idyl." " 'How lucky the birds are. They can live in spite of a war-torn world,' " cries a detainee. Another character in the story, however, refers to the travelers as "like seeds in the wind," landing randomly. They might land in the fertile soil of a welcoming city, but they also might land in parched earth, like the desert which they were fleeing. Would these "seeds," the detained themselves, be able to find success and a community in Akron, Madison, Kansas City, Chicago, or Philadelphia? Or would they be choked by ongoing discrimination and denial of their rights? The only character Mori portrays as being at peace with this question is the "aged woman" accompanying her son to the train station to send him off for military duty:

> The aged woman continued gazing at her fellow travelers. Once, twice, she smiled to herself. She noticed the solemnity and independence of the relocatees and the boisterousness and companionship of the shoppers' group. "On the way . . . our journey," she whispered softly to herself. "Travelers . . . we are all travelers on the earth."[49]

Mori suggests that, in the face of an unknown future, one must find contentment in the journey.

Mori developed this theme in more depth in "The Trees," which was published in the December 1942 edition of *TREK*. It is, perhaps, the most cryptic of all his stories. While the plot is simple, its meaning is complex. It may very well have been intended, in fact, as a parable for Mori's imprisoned peers. In the story, two friends, Hashimoto and Fukushima, walk together in the dawn through Hashimoto's *bonsai* garden. Fukushima seeks to learn Hashimoto's "secret of happiness," but when Hashimoto is unable to explain it to Fukushima's satisfaction, Fukushima becomes enraged: "when I leave here today I shall never see you again," he shouts at Hashimoto.[50] Fukushima is frustrated because he assumes that Hashimoto's happiness derives from whatever it is that Hashimoto "sees in the trees."

Hashimoto responds to his friend's repeated queries about what he sees by stating variously, "Why, I see the trees," "I simply see the trees," and "I cannot explain the trees, Fukushima." As Fukushima angrily and desperately demands another explanation, Hashimoto tries a different approach:

> "Did you not say you were cold a few minutes ago?" Hashimoto said.
>
> "Yes, I was cold," Fukushima admitted.
>
> "Look at yourself now," Hashimoto said. "You are warm and perspiring. You are very warm."
>
> "What of it? That is a fact," said Fukushima. "What are you talking about?"
>
> "The difference between warmth and cold is movement," said Hashimoto. "And movement makes warmth and cold."
>
> "Hashimoto, I do not want to hear about warmth and cold," pleaded Fukushima. "I want to share your happiness. I want you to explain the trees you see."
>
> "I cannot explain the trees, Fukushima," Hashimoto said. "But listen, friend. The warmth and cold I talk about is in the trees."
>
> Fukushima shook his head. "You are not my friend. You do not want to tell me your secret."

Hashimoto avers: "You are my friend, and the secret you mention is the most exposed of all."[51] Mori leaves it up to his readers to determine the secret of happiness, but he provides pointed clues throughout the story.

First, he describes Fukushima as attributing his chill to the fact that "the sun is not warm enough," as opposed to his own failure to dress appropriately, thereby suggesting that we do have some control over our own equanimity, even in the most desperate of circumstances. Then, he describes Fukushima as interpreting his life as controlled by "fate": "You know what happened to me. A year ago I was fairly rich. I owned stock and properties. And then fate overtook me and I lost all. I am a defeated man but I want to fight on, and

I come to you. . . . Why are you so happy?" Here again, Mori seems to suggest that outlook rather than "fate" actually determines one's "happiness." Mori portrays Hashimoto as "not always happy, . . . I am cold and warm too," indicating that a constant state of bliss is unrealistic and unattainable, but so, too, is a constant state of misery.[52] In short, through "The Trees" Mori suggests that the secret of happiness is dependent on how, not what, one truly "sees," in a Buddhist sense. That is, for the incarcerated Mori, "happiness" was dependent on those things about which he had obtained true insight.

Mori himself seriously considered becoming a Buddhist missionary, and his spiritual beliefs and training are evident in this tale. The Buddha taught four Noble Truths: that life is inescapably filled with suffering; that suffering results from our desire for or attachment to things, people, and ideas; that we can reduce suffering only by reducing our attachments and desires; and that the way to alleviate attachment and desire is to follow the Noble Eightfold Path, or Middle Way. The Buddha himself came to the Middle Way after first, a life of luxury and indulgence and then, one of austerity and deprivation. Rejecting both extremes, he sought a more balanced and simple way of being by learning to integrate the elements of the Noble Eightfold Path into daily life: Right Understanding (*Samma ditthi*), Right Thought (*Samma sankappa*), Right Speech (*Samma vaca*), Right Action (*Samma kammanta*), Right Livelihood (*Samma ajiva*), Right Effort (*Samma vayama*), Right Mindfulness (*Samma sati*), and Right Concentration (*Samma samadhi*). Though no evidence proves that "The Trees" was based on Mori's understanding of Buddhism, the central tenets of the practice seem clearly embedded in it.

Fukushima suffers because of his strong desire for the "secret" of happiness, which he equates with the wealth he lost. Hashimoto, on the other hand, demonstrates "right understanding" by seeing the world and everything in it as it really is, not as he believes or wants it to be: "I simply see the trees," he says. For one gifted with Right Understanding, "the secret" Fukushima desires "is the most exposed of all." Hashimoto seems to embody Right Intent, as well, in that he seeks nothing in his walk through the trees except exactly that: mindfully experiencing walking through the trees:

> They walked among the trees. They crossed many times the little stream running alongside the path. The sparrows chattered noisily overhead. The two circled the garden several times, crisscrossed, and finally sat down to rest on an old stone bench.[53]

Central to Right Intent is the ability to accept life simply as it is, to persistently and patiently pursuing the path one is on. The circuitous route of the men's walk through the garden frustrates Fukushima because his need to understand the secret of happiness is not fulfilled by it. For Hashimoto, the movement itself—a movement that brings warmth from cold but is not directed toward a specific goal—and only the movement, matters.

Finally, Hashimoto practices Right Speech by not reacting in kind to Fukushima's words of hostility and rejection. Right Speech involves a recognition of the ways in which words cause suffering, division and dissension. Hashimoto's repeated attempts to explain his happiness to Fukushima demonstrates a sincere wish to communicate with him, but because Fukushima remains locked in his attachments and desires, mutual understanding between the two friends is impossible. Mori found miscommunication both tragic and dangerous: "misunderstanding causes war," he states in another of his stories.[54] Because misunderstanding exists on both sides of this friendship, Hashimoto and Fukushima part.

Perhaps Mori offered "The Trees" as a salve for his imprisoned peers; perhaps not. But through it, he created a valuable analogy to their collective experience, showing that letting go of the past and accepting and living in the present, no matter how dismal, is the only way to not cause further suffering to oneself. This is not to suggest, however, that Mori advocated a passive acceptance of captivity. On the contrary, the one nonfiction piece Mori published in camp was titled "Topaz Station," and through it he made a very political statement about the injustice of the incarceration. He grounded this in his extensive knowledge of American literary history and traditions. In "Topaz Station," Mori employed styles and themes central to notions of American exceptionalism and to mythical ideals of American progress to emphasize the very "Americanness" of the incarcerees. In so doing, he highlighted the degree to which the rights of Japanese Americans had been violated.

Mori begins "Topaz Station" by describing Topaz as a "city of glimmering lights in the darkness between the mountains [that] wailed its birth cry on September 11, 1942." Intentionally or not, Mori's evokes Puritan notions of the "city on a hill" that served as the foundation for building a democracy on the American frontier. Topaz's 10,000 inhabitants, confined to a mile square area, are, he states, "here to continue living" because Topaz Station is just that—merely "a station" for Mori and his fellow detainees, a "stopping-off place on the way to progress as good Americans for a better America."[55] Mori follows this nationalist progressive vision with one of three passages that evoke the literary style of the quintessential American author, Walt Whitman, namely the literary catalog. In this, Whitman lists workers of all kinds, one no more prominently than another, as representative of the nation:

> The pure contralto sings in the organ loft,
> The carpenter dresses his plank, the tongue of his foreplane whistles its
>   wild ascending lisp,
> The married and unmarried children ride home to their Thanksgiving
>   dinner,
> The pilot seizes the king-pin, he heaves down with a strong arm,
> The mate stands braced in the whale-boat, lance and harpoon are ready,
> The duck-shooter walks by silent and cautious stretches,
> The deacons are ordain'd with cross'd hands at the altar,
> The spinning-girl retreats and advances to the hum of the big wheel,
> The farmer stops by the bars as he walks on a First-day loafe and looks at
>   the oats and rye.[56]

Whitman's purpose in using the literary catalog was to bring all members of American society into equal standing, both in spirit and also metaphorically on the page. Throughout the poem, he embraced rich, poor, men, women, gay, straight, all races and ethnicities, immigrant, enslaved, prostitute, and president, identifying each as equally central to the sustenance of the nation.

Mori does the same when characterizing Topaz. "Doctors, lawyers, domestic workers, gardeners, farmers, schoolboys, artists, florists, clerks, housewives, and all, are here. Nothing is missing here, people of America," Mori writes. Throughout the essay, he emphasizes the fundamental similarities between those inside and outside the camp, despite the barbed wire that separates them. All people wish "to live out [their] days in the most pleasant way possible, and Topaz people are no different," he states.[57] Capitalizing on the ever-optimistic vision of "morning in America," itself an evocation of American national mythologies of innovation and progress, and implicitly challenging any association with the "land of the rising sun," Mori describes "the cold and the dark greyness of dawn in the east [as] a clarion call to the new and young Americans."[58]

> This is the home front of a new day. Aged Japanese people, living twenty to fifty years in America, cannot erase their years in America. They have hope in the American way of life, they know no ease but by their participation in

> the struggle on the American frontiers [*sic*]. They seek pleasures of life, they enjoy music, songs, drama, liberty, glamor, and ham and eggs. More than ever, the young Americans of Japanese ancestry see the world of movies, ice cream, milkshakes, Broadway, Buicks, Saturday Evening Post, electric refrigerators and hot dogs.[59]

Mori highlights the loyalty of the Issei who had lived in Japan but chose to move to the United States and had been shaped by decades of living there to emphasize their allegiance to their adopted nation. Through cataloging stereoptypical American consumer goods that have shaped the lives of Nisei just as they have shaped the lives of all other young Americans, Mori demands recognition of the injustice being inflicted on patriotic Americans of Japanese descent. In poignant ways, Mori exposes just how very American "Topaz Station," a prison in the desert for ethnic outsiders, truly is.

All Aboard was intended to provide useful information to readers who would soon begin the process of leaving camp. Mori was let out of Topaz on October 31, 1945. Needing to support his family after the war, he returned to the nursery business and put his literary aspirations on hold. Hisaye Yamamoto, in her 1979 introduction to a collection of Mori's works titled *The Chauvinist*, describes this: "there Toshio Mori has dwelt ever since, amongst the sweet peas, stocks snapdragons, dahlias and zinnias."[60] He did continue to write, but his son, Steven, recalls the challenges work posed for the artist:

> Being a writer is one of the hardest professions one can choose for a living, my father used to tell me. He knew from experience, since he struggled all of his life to make ends meet, supporting his writing and his family by running a nursery and later working as a salesman for a wholesale florist.[61]

After the incarceration, Mori resumed his practice of running the floral business by day and writing at night, but the writing career to which he aspired was never achieved.

Mori's prewar masterpiece, *Yokohama, California,* was eventually published by Caxton in 1949, but it was a different book, in both tone and content, from the original that he had submitted to the press in 1940. Mori added two stories, both of which commented directly on the war. The first was "Tomorrow Is Coming, Children," the immigrant narrative of the woman's journey from Japan to California, which Mori had published in *TREK*, while he was incarcerated. The poet Lawson Fusao Inada suggested this tale was inserted as the opening story to demonstrate to postwar readers that Issei and Nisei were just like any other American immigrants: they, too, through hard work and sacrifice, achieved success in the United States. "The inclusion and placement of 'Tomorrow Is Coming, Children,'" explained Inada in his introduction to the 1985 edition of *Yokohama, California*, "can be seen as Caxton's attempt to soften history, to start with bygones and get into the book in a positive way; the nondiscerning reader might even think that the bulk of the book takes place *after* the war, with the people having made a remarkable recovery."[62] "Tomorrow Is Coming, Children," when interpreted as a classic American rags-to-riches immigration tale, was intended to serve as an antidote to the reality of the incarceration.

The second story added to the postwar version of *Yokohama, California* was titled "Slant-Eyed Americans," and it recounts a Japanese American family's reactions to the bombing of Pearl Harbor. The story opens on the morning of December 7, 1941. The family in the story, like so many other Americans, was portrayed as eating brunch and listening to the radio when the news of Pearl Harbor broke and, like so many other Americans, this family reacted with fear and disbelief. "It couldn't be true," says the Nisei protagonist, incredulously, to his parents. His mother hopes the radio is just putting on "one those plays" intended to "scare people about invasion," presumably referring to Orson Wells's 1938 "War of the Worlds" hoax. When the bombing is confirmed, however, this Japanese American family begins to realize the implications it will have on them, in comparison to their white neighbors and friends. "This is very bad for the people with Japanese faces," the son laments. "Since Japan declared war on the United States it'll mean that you parents of American citizens have become enemy aliens."[63]

"Slant-Eyed Americans" lacks the literary nuance that marks Mori's style and craft in his prewar stories. The fine subtlety that demands the reader's thoughtful engagement is replaced in "Slant-Eyed Americans" with jingoism. As the family's fellow Japanese American flower distributors worry about their livelihoods, for example, the protagonist admonishes one of them: "Buck up, Tom, . . . You have a good future, don't lose hope."[64] The mother echoes these platitudes. She tells Tom to "cheer up, . . . This is no time for young folks to despair. Roll up your sleeves and get to work. America needs you. . . . You young men should work hard all the more, keeping up the normal routine of life."[65] She expresses her faith that "America is right. She cannot fail. Her principles will stand the test of time and tyranny. Someday aggression will be outlawed by all nations." Tom's response is perhaps the least convincing: "Yes, if the gardens are ruined I'll rebuild them. . . . I'll take charge of every garden in the city. All the gardens of America for that matter. I'll rebuild them as fast as the enemies wreck them."[66] This portion of the story merges into a sort of modern-day morality tale as it preaches the good old Franklinian gospel of hard work done by self-made men. "Good for you!," the speaker says to Tom. "Tomorrow we'll get up early in the morning and work, sweat and create. Let's shake on it."[67] No need to fear the Nisei, Mori seems to insist.

Only when the story turns to a subject close to Mori himself—the departure of the narrator's brother for the warfront—does the language return to the precision and sensitivity characterizing his prewar stories. Mori's own brother, Kazuo, fought for the all-Nisei 442nd Regiment. As the war in Europe heated up, the US government recognized that soldiers fluent in Japanese would be an asset. At the same time, Nisei—who were, of course, American citizens—were coming of age for induction into the military and in 1940, when the draft was reinstituted, Nisei were included. At the time of the bombing of Pearl Harbor, approximately 5,000 Japanese Americans soldiers were enlisted.[68] Mori's brother, Kazuo, was wounded on May 5, 1945 and returned home permanently paralyzed.

"Slant-Eyed Americans" tells the story of a Nisei solider visiting his family during a quick trip home for Christmas in 1941, before he ships out to battle. When the narrator picks up his brother at the train station, the narrator finds himself unable to express his innermost thoughts: "On the way I tried to think of the many things I wanted to say. From the moment I spotted him waiting on the corner I could not say the thing I wanted to." His parents faced the same difficulty:

> Mother could not say anything. . . . Father sat in the room reading the papers but his eyes were over the sheet and his hands were trembling. Mother scurried about getting his supper ready. I sat across the table from my brother, and in the silence which was action I watched the wave of emotions in the room. My brother was aware of it too. He sat there without a word, but I knew he understood.[69]

The silence stems from the family's fear of what is to come for the brother/soldier. Though they may face economic uncertainty in the United States (Executive Order 9066 was not issued until February 19, 1942), there was no doubt that their brother/son would be on the front lines of war—that he would be going, as Mori writes, "beyond life and death matters, where the true soldiers of war or peace must travel"—and there certainly was doubt about whether he would return.[70]

The final scene of "Slant-Eyed Americans" depicts the family's farewell at the train station. A friend of the mother says to the Nisei soldier,

> "Give your best to America. Our people's honor depend [*sic*] on you Nisei soldiers." My brother nodded and then glanced at Mother. For a moment her eyes twinkled and she nodded. He waved good-bye from the platform. Once inside the train we lost him. . . . We stood and watched until the last of the train was lost in the night of darkness.[71]

Mori expresses so much in the unsaid, here: what will be literally lost through the soldier's participation in war?[72] Will he be able to give his "best to America," given the incarceration to come for his family at home? What is the role of "Slant-Eyed Americans," who are equally as Japanese and American as they were the day before December 7, 1941? Whereas the majority of stories in *Yokohama, California*—all but two written before World War II—portray Japanese Americans comfortably situated within their communities, this story definitely does not.

Communities like that described in *Yokohama, California* were ruined by the war. The type of Japanese American towns whose residents happily watched baseball and lived ordinary lives of birth, marriage, illness, and death before the war were forever changed after it. The incarceration split up families and friends. College-aged children who ordinarily would have lived at home and gone to a school nearby were sent to unfamiliar universities in the Midwest and on the East Coast while their families were confined to prison camps. The resettlement campaign, designed with the explicit intention of breaking up "concentrated" communities of Japanese Americans on the West Coast, did just that. While Philip Roth's Jewish American, William Saroyan's Armenian American, and Jerre Mangione's Sicilian American immigrant enclaves continued to thrive, the type of Japanese American immigrant sanctuary cities, or "Little Tokyos," exemplified in *Yokohama, California* were grievously altered, if they re-formed at all.

Mori's literary career was a war casualty as well. The modified version of *Yokohama, California* that was published in 1949 received little critical attention. Mori continued to write after the war, but his primary occupation involved supporting his family financially and raising his son, Steven. During this time, according to his son, Mori experimented: he tried to write greeting cards but was rejected by Hallmark. He wrote some song lyrics but they were plagiarized and "became a moderate hit for a major recording star." He tried his hand writing articles for *Playboy* because of its reputation for publishing the best writers at the time, but his focus was on his family. Steven Mori describes his father fondly:

> As a father, he was as idyllic as any all-American dad on television could be in the fifties. He played ball with me, took me to movies, encouraged my reading, watched TV with me, and was stern but understanding when I got into mischief, which was often. Since he worked at home [in the family nursery business] during my childhood, he was always there when I needed him. I know that the literary world is probably missing some great stories because of his presence, but I don't think either of us would have traded those years for anything.[73]

Steven Mori is correct: the world would surely benefit from more of the gentle, nuanced, and subtle depictions of American culture that are found in Mori's stories.

Fortunately, among the many accomplishments of the redress movement in the 1970s was the rediscovery and resurrection of Mori's writing, as well as that of other incarcerated authors. Many are included in the 1974 collection, *Aiiieeeee! An Introduction to Asian American Writing*, edited by Lawson Fusao Inada, Shawn Wong, Jeffrey Chan, and Frank Chin. This led to a Mori renaissance, of sorts. In 1978, his novel, *The Woman from Hiroshima*, was published by Isthmus Press in San Francisco. In 1979, the Asian American Curriculum Project, generated by the Asian American Studies Center at the University of California at Los Angeles—an organization to be commended for its remarkable work in preserving Asian American writing in the United States—published *The Chauvinist and Other Stories*. In 2000, Mori's son released the collection *Unfinished Message: Selected Works of Toshio Mori* through Santa Clara University and Heyday Books. Unfortunately, Mori died in the midst of this recognition, in 1980, but like other great American writers whose work did not garner appropriate attention during their lifetimes, Mori's legacy lives on. Who knows what more he might have accomplished had his literary career not been derailed?

4

Miné Okubo

An Aesthetic Life Launched

Just as the careers of Nisei writers were on the rise in the late 1930s, so, too, was that of the artist Miné Okubo. The cataclysmic cultural disruption caused by war, however, knocked all of them off their paths. Toyo Suyemoto, Toshio Mori, and Miné Okubo were sent to Topaz, and all contributed to *TREK*. Oddly, however, the effects of incarceration on their careers were strikingly different. Suyemoto's and Mori's hopes for a literary life were more or less derailed, but Okubo's career took off. *Citizen 13660*, Okubo's graphic memoir depicting her experience in captivity, was published in 1946 and during the immediate postwar years it came to be seen, in the eyes of the government at least, as the nation's most accurate and objective chronicle of the incarceration. There was more beneath the surface of Okubo's images, however, than many realized at the time. Okubo's career trajectory sheds light on the impact of the incarceration on Japanese American literary history, as well as on the cultural roles that the white majority in the United States expected Japanese Americans to occupy before, during, and after the war.

Prior to the war and for most of her career after it, Okubo considered herself first and foremost an artist rather than a writer. She earned a Master of Fine Arts degree from Berkeley in 1936 and was already recognized as a skilled painter by the late1930s. In 1938, she received a fellowship from the University of California, which enabled her to travel throughout Europe to study art. The outbreak of the war in 1939, however, forced her premature return to the United States, and she moved back to the San Francisco Bay area. In 1940, she was selected to assist the Mexican muralist Diego Rivera in creating his monumental work, *Pan-American Unity: The Marriage of the Artistic Expression of the North and South of this Continent*, for the Golden Gate International Exposition on Treasure Island in the San Francisco Bay.[1]

The goal of the exposition was to showcase and revitalize the state's economy following the Depression, and the recent completion of the Golden Gate Bridge in 1937 provided the celebratory occasion through which to do

That Damned Fence. Heather Hathaway, Oxford University Press. © Oxford University Press 2022.
DOI: 10.1093/oso/9780190098315.003.0005

so. Rivera was commissioned to lead the "Art in Action" part of the exposition, which was a project designed to allow the public to observe artists actively practicing their crafts.[2] Sculptors, woodcarvers, lithographers, and ceramicists occupied the Fine Arts Palace, but Rivera's ten-paneled mural, 22 feet high by 74 feet long, was the centerpiece of the exhibit and towered over all. He and various assistants, including Okubo, worked on the mural while the public watched.[3] Upon the exhibition's close, Rivera's mural was supposed to hang in the new library of San Francisco Junior College (now City College of San Francisco), but the war interrupted this artist's life as well. The new library was never built and Rivera's masterpiece was mothballed, first on the exposition grounds and then at the college, until it was placed in the lobby of the campus theater in 1961.[4]

Rivera's leftist political leanings were well known at the time: he had just been fired from painting a mural in Rockefeller Center in New York City because he refused to remove a positive image of Lenin.[5] By 1940 Rivera, along with so many others, grew increasingly alarmed by the fascism of Hitler and Mussolini, however, and he believed that the only way that North and South America could challenge it was to work together against authoritarianism. But first, Rivera believed, the United States had to rid itself of the racial prejudice at its root.[6]

Perhaps this view influenced Miné Okubo's decision to join the group of apprentices who were recruited to help execute Rivera's grand vision. Though Okubo's participation is regularly overlooked in mainstream works on Rivera and his mural, she certainly was there. Okubo joked years later, in fact, that when people watched her, a petite, female, Japanese American apprentice positioned on a scaffold parallel to and directly underneath the rather rotund Mexican maestro, they mused "that she must be 'Diego's sixth child by a third marriage,' poking fun at Rivera's proclivity to wed and procreate."[7] A brief film of the artists in action seems to offer a glimpse of Okubo herself at work, in fact. Produced in 1940, this short film portrays the range of works artists created during the second year of the exposition.[8]

The optimistic political and cultural unity embodied in both the exposition and Rivera's mural, however, was short-lived. On December 7, 1941, when Pearl Harbor was bombed, Okubo was working on mosaics for Fort Ord, a US Army post on Monterey Bay, and for the Servicemen's Hospitality House in Oakland, California. "I was too busy," she recalled, "to bother about the reports of possible evacuation. However, it was not long before I realized my predicament."[9] Okubo's predicament proved to be detainment in the Tanforan Racetrack and then in Topaz. In Topaz, she joined the writers Toyo Suyemoto, Taro Katayama, James Yamada, and Toshio Mori, along with fellow artists Chiura and Haruko Obata, George and Hisako Hibi, Byron Takashi Tsuzuki, and Charles Erabu Mikami, among others. As part of this talented cohort, Okubo found a way to continue to produce her art.[10]

While detained in the Tanforan racetrack, Okubo assisted Chiura Obata, a Berkeley art professor, set up a makeshift art school for incarcerated children. Obata was a gifted painter and committed educator who was greatly concerned about how children would fare under the circumstances of confinement. He recalls:

> While I was waiting for the bus [to Tanforan] there was a soldier with a gun. There was a little child, five or six years old, not knowing anything, with childlike innocence, playing with the soldier—playing hide and seek at the edge of the street trees. . . . Seeing that scene in a situation where we were being forced into an unreasonable evacuation, to kill the burning heart, burning determination of these young people was very bad. Somehow we had to support the active, learning minds of the young people and provide them with a place where they could learn. . . . We had to do something about it. My first thought was to open an art school and start teaching everyone.[11]

Accordingly, just three days after arriving in Tanforan, Obata requested permission from the assembly center's administration to create an art school that would be a branch of the Tanforan Adult Education Program. Okubo worked for Obata there and also in the school he later established in Topaz.

On the day the Tanforan school was set to open, a raging rainstorm consumed the assembly center. As Obata trudged across the muddy racetrack toward the mess hall that had been converted to an art studio, he worried about whether any student would come to his school. When he got there, though, he "saw three tiny girls standing on the doorsteps."

> I ran to open the door. I noticed their little rubber boots and raincoats were drenched. In the mess hall art building there is an enormous cooking stove but no heating facility. I was afraid that maybe these little ones may catch colds. I ran out and went to a nearby friend who lived in a stall and asked for a couple of towels and wiped their cold heads and hands to warm them up. I asked the youngest girl (six years old), "Do you like to learn to paint?" With smiles and sparkling eyes she responded, "Sure I do!" "Who is

> your teacher?" I asked. "Miné Okubo," she replied. The older girls standing by remarked, "Yes, she's pretty. I want to learn from her too." In my heart, I thank the mothers for their bravery in sending their beloved children even in such storms. I thanked Heaven for having started this movement.[12]

Despite its rocky first day, the Tanforan Art School developed into a booming success. More than 600 students, children and adults alike, took ninety classes a week, ranging from figure painting to mechanical drawing to cartoons and tempera, fulfilling Obata's belief that "education is as important as food to a human individual whether young or old."[13] He established a similar art school when he was transferred to Topaz because he held to the tenet that "anywhere and anytime, take up your brush and express what you face and what you think without wasting your time and energy complaining and crying out. I hold that statement as my aim, and . . . the aim of artists."[14]

Okubo shared the need to use art as a form of expression under duress, as is illustrated by the scenes she sketched of life around her while in Tanforan and Topaz. Eventually these constituted her graphic memoir, *Citizen 13660*, published by Columbia University Press in 1946. This provided the first insider's account of what took place behind the barbed wire of the camps during the war itself. *Citizen 13660* interested readers because the government gave the American public so little insight about the incarceration. The War Relocation Authority (WRA), in fact, capitalized on this interest by using Okubo's memoir to demonstrate that those who had so recently been defined as dangerous agents in the American social fabric were now sufficiently rehabilitated to become valuable contributors to the new communities in which they were resettling. Okubo's postwar graphic memoir was considered by the government to be such an excellent illustration of the virtues of the recently incarcerated, as they accepted their plights and demonstrated their good citizenship, that it was appropriated as a form of soft propaganda for the resettlement campaign.[15]

How could this be? How could one of the most allegedly "objective" chronicles of the incarceration be celebrated by those who imagined and implemented the tragedy?[16] Two factors explain this. The first is historical, the second is literary. First, once the catastrophe of the incarceration became clear to the government in terms of its economic, political, and social costs, the imperative to close the camps and disperse the detained in new communities on the East Coast and in the Midwest followed closely behind. Ironically, whereas the government sought to break up the Little Tokyos of

Issei and Nisei that allegedly threatened the safety of the United States after the bombing of Pearl Harbor, it now argued that it had inadvertently recreated these concentrated communities in the camps, thus necessitating a resettlement program. Consequently, a primary goal of the program was to disperse Japanese Americans across a broad array of cities and states outside the West Coast so that predominantly Japanese American communities did not form anew. For this campaign to succeed, however, the government had to ensure white Americans that Japanese Americans were neither dangerous nor embittered by their incarceration.

Okubo and her memoir were considered evidence of both. Even after incarceration she remained active in California art circles, exhibiting two drawings, *On Guard* and *Evacuees*, in the spring 1943 show at the San Francisco Museum of Art. *On Guard* is a black and white mural showing two armed guards on a hill, towering over the barracks of a prison camp in the distant background. *Evacuees* portrays a Japanese American family grappling with the baggage and other belongings upon being evicted.[17] Neither directly depicted Japanese American suffering or images from inside the camp (where cameras, if not drawings, were prohibited); nor did they overtly criticize the incarceration itself. Nevertheless, pacifist groups who opposed the incarceration found Okubo's camp drawings compelling and printed and publicized both these and some of her other works.

Based on these drawings, as well as on her reputation in the Bay area art world prior to her incarceration, Okubo was asked by *Fortune* magazine in New York to illustrate a forthcoming issue on Japan. The WRA, which was now looking for ways to empty the camps, released her, and Okubo left Topaz for New York in early 1944.[18] This move proved pivotal in Okubo's career. In New York, she further developed her reputation by presenting her art in diverse venues and, in so doing, became known to the WRA as an artist on whom the government could rely to present images of the incarceration that did not explicitly condemn it as unjust. She also was used by the WRA as a success story that demonstrated the efficacy of resettlement on the East Coast.[19] Okubo's memoir was similarly heralded by the WRA as a literary work that, in its alleged objectivity, told the "truth" about the incarceration.

The WRA did not necessarily understand, however, the nature of *Citizen 13660* as a political document. Although Okubo's personal life-story may have been co-opted by the government to reassure the American public that the incarceration did no harm to Japanese Americans, Okubo's own writings and illustrations tell a different story. Many readers see in *Citizen 13660*, for example, a form of literary bilingualism in which the author speaks to two different audiences—typically, insiders and outsiders—at the same time. A writer whose first language is Spanish, for instance, may write an English-language novel but will insert phrases or words in Spanish that non-Spanish speakers will not understand. This strategy establishes a privileged and private line of communication with one group of preferred readers. This objective can be achieved in works that are written entirely in English as well. In Henry Roth's 1934 novel, *Call It Sleep*, rather than writing in actual Yiddish, Roth translates a mother's statements to her young son literally, using syntax that indicates to the reader that she is speaking in Yiddish even though we are reading it in English. Roth establishes an intimacy between parent and child, between those who speak Yiddish and those who do not, while holding others on the periphery.[20]

Okubo does something similar, but not by using two different languages at once. Rather, she develops her own form of literary bilingualism in her juxtaposition of image and caption in ways that allow for multiple interpretations of the scene being portrayed. The captions in *Citizen 13660* are typically understated; they merely describe what is taking place. The images, on the other hand, tell a more pointed story. In them, Okubo embeds subtle clues that suggest nuanced meanings to the attentive reader—and especially to readers who experienced the events themselves.[21]

Okubo's representation of her registration at the Civil Control Station in Berkeley provides one illustration. All Japanese Americans were required to report to civil control stations to be assigned their family number, in her case 13660, and an assembly center. Okubo's caption to her drawing depicting this scene neutrally states the basic facts of the situation:

> Civil Control Stations were established by the Wartime Civil Control Administration in each of the designated areas. One member of each family was asked to register for the family; people without families registered individually. On Sunday, April 26, 1942, I reported to Pilgrim Hall of the First Congregational Church in Berkeley to register for my brother and myself—a family unit of two. Soldiers were standing guard at the entrance and around the buildings.[22]

Her caption is straightforward and informational. There is, indeed, a Pilgrim Hall in the First Congregational Church in Berkeley that was used as a civil control station for Japanese Americans during the war, at the behest of pastor

Vere Loper, who thought it was more respectful than requiring the community to report to the fire station.[23]

Through the graphic drawing accompanying this caption, however, Okubo speaks on another level to those who shared her experience. She plays on the ironies of circumstance. In the caption, she specifically identifies that she must report to a Pilgrim Hall, a place that, one would assume by the name, offered a safe haven for spiritual seekers and political refugees like the Pilgrims. She states that the hall is located in a Congregational church, a place in which one would expect a Christ-like welcome. But through her drawing, she deliberately undercuts these connotations as she portrays herself having to pass by two large military men wielding oversized and intimidating rifles, staring her down as she tries to enter the building. She looks with scorn at the soldier on the right, while holding her hand up, seemingly to keep a distance between herself and the soldier on the left. Though Okubo's caption is detached and descriptive, her image clearly captures her disdain for the situation.

Okubo's pattern of creating an ironic dissonance between caption and image can also be seen in her depiction of herself reading the "'funnies'" while waiting to be registered. Again, a rifle-bearing soldier looms pointedly in the foreground. Obviously, there is nothing funny about the situation at all. Part of the caption to this image states, "As a result of the interview, my family name was reduced to No. 13660." This caption is more pointed than many in *Citizen 13660* in that it expresses, through the use of the term "reduced," the denigration of human beings to things. A central of tenet of racism involves establishing the "other" as the utter opposite of oneself. If I am a person, you are a thing; if I am a human, you are an animal or an insect or a monster. The reference to Jews as vermin in Nazi propaganda is just one illustration of this. While Jews had dehumanizing numbers forever tattooed on their forearms, Japanese Americans had them tagged to their clothing—a difference in placement and permanence but not in intent.

The theme of dehumanization continues in Okubo's portrayal of the bodily inspections of the imprisoned. Okubo explains:

> I was asked to enter one of the slightly partitioned and curtained compartments and was ordered to undress. A nurse looked into my mouth with a flashlight and checked my arms to see if I had been vaccinated for smallpox. When I rejoined my brother I asked him what they made him do. 'They made us strip,' he said.[24]

Okubo made this illustration of herself registering at the Civil Control Station at Pilgrim Hall of First Congregational Church, Berkeley, California, in 1942. Though she is flanked by two armed guards, she does not hide her disdain.
Miné Okubo Collection, Japanese American National Museum (Gift of Mine Okubo Estate, 2007.62.19)

The image depicting this experience, however, reflects a level of disorder and humiliation not captured by the words. Women's and girls' mouths are inspected and temperatures are taken by taller, more imposing medical personnel. Okubo depicts herself as awkwardly holding on to her clothing while being handled by a nurse and she emphasizes the vulnerability of the experience by portraying a young girl in the next stall, all alone, as another nurse grabs her head and shoves a thermometer in her mouth. These images might evoke, for those who know the history of slavery in the United States, inspections of enslaved people by potential slave owners, though admittedly the circumstances differ considerably.

A visual bilingualism characterizes others of Okubo's drawings as well. Consider her portrayal of Tanforan as it existed upon her arrival. In Okubo's drawing, captioned only by the simple statement that "the camp was a mess," we see barracks in disarray with wood planks scattered about and Okubo herself looking on and sketching the scene. Compare this to the photograph

Okubo's illustration of people waiting to register at the Civil Control Station in Berkeley, California. She highlights the injustice of the situation by portraying herself reading the "funnies" in a newspaper while a gun is effectively pointed at her head.

Miné Okubo Collection, Japanese American National Museum (Gift of Mine Okubo Estate, 2007.62.20)

taken by Dorothea Lange, which makes far more real the dank mud, water-filled moats, and splintered wood out of which inmates were expected to craft living spaces. To outsiders, Okubo's sketch pales in its portrayal of the depravity of the conditions, but to those who actually lived through the event, her drawing would undoubtedly trigger a full-sensory recollection of the smells, sights, and other sensations of the moment.

Given Okubo's strategic bilingualism and the WRA's apparent ignorance of it, it is not surprising that the organization found Okubo's renditions of life in the camp to be a useful tool through which to represent the incarceration to the postwar public. *Citizen 13660* was, and remains, Rorschach-like: one can see or read whatever one wishes to as it speaks one language to insiders who experienced the incarceration and another to outsiders who wished to downplay its traumatic significance. Okubo created a body of other work during

Okubo documented the medical exams given to women and children upon entering the Tanforan Assembly Center. Having to strip down and be examined in front of others was a humiliating experience for many of the inmates.
Miné Okubo Collection, Japanese American National Museum (Gift of Mine Okubo Estate, 2007.62.32)

her detainment for the covers of Topaz's literary magazine, *TREK*, however, and these tell a very different story about her own carceral experience. The *TREK* covers bear no captions, so the images speak for themselves. They are directed toward Okubo's fellow incarcerees rather than toward the American public. In their tone and style, they resemble works, and the leftist political leanings, of her one-time mentor, Diego Rivera.

Whereas the images in *Citizen 13660* are fairly fluid, the drawings in *TREK* are stark and stiff. Each is framed on the bottom by the large block lettering she designed for *TREK*; each lacks dimensional depth; each portrays an event in the camp engaged in by multiple people at a time. All recall Rivera-like blocky portrayals of the body that can be seen in the murals on which Okubo worked for the Golden Gate International Exposition. Most importantly, all three invite comparisons to drawings she included in *Citizen 13660*.

Okubo's drawing of the exterior condition of the living quarters at Tanforan. The buildings were still under construction, and residents had to use wooden planks to cross over mud troughs to enter each unit.

Miné Okubo Collection, Japanese American National Museum (Gift of Mine Okubo Estate, 2007.62.49)

Okubo's first image, created for the inaugural edition of *TREK* in December 1942, commemorates Christmas of that year, as it shows a family of five attempting to be festive within the confines of the camp. Sitting in front of one of the infamous potbelly stoves that were supposed to provide warmth in the quarters, the father is the largest figure in the drawing and, along with this son, occupies the left third, vertically, of the plane. The father holds his arms out stiffly, apparently trying to amuse the family with what appears to be a homemade button spinner toy that he holds in his hands. Button spinners imply motion, but Okubo makes this one static. The mother and the son appear to be looking at it, while the baby on the lower left is reaching for a bonsai tree that substitutes for the typical evergreen the family would likely have used outside of camp. No one in the image appears to be engaging directly with another. The "stockings" are, clearly, worn socks that are draped above, on a close line that also holds other laundry. Without the Santa suit that the father wears, the candy cane that the girl is eating, and the

At the newly assembled barracks at the Tanforan Assembly Center, the buildings were only partially completed when inmates arrived.
Densho, ddr-densho-151-19, courtesy of the National Archives and Records Administration

star the boy is holding, one would not know it was Christmas. No one bears festive expressions of any sort.

Compare this to the Christmas 1942 image Okubo used in *Citizen 13660.* Many of the features are similar, but the overall composition of the plane is far less condensed and claustrophobic. In the *Citizen 13660* rendition of a Christmas scene, the potbelly stove again more or less centers the image, but the distance between it and the family is greater. The father again holds a button spinner, but his arms are relaxed rather than extended and he looks down to his son as he spins. Okubo uses a broken line to illustrate that the string in this image is in motion, infusing the scene with action and vitality that is missing from the *TREK* cover. The son reaches up to the father and the spinner, while the tree—not clearly a bonsai but again, not an evergreen—sits at the edge of the image with the star already on it. In this rendition of Christmas 1942, the mother, toddler, and daughter all look toward the activity of the father and son, suggesting engagement among the family members. Finally, a few more domestic touches create warmth: the mother holds a tray of mugs of tea or hot chocolate, perhaps; a cat is curled up in

Miné Okubo's illustration of a family trying to celebrate Christmas in the barracks appeared on the cover of the December 1942 edition of *TREK*. Gathered around the potbelly stove that was used to heat each unit, the family strives to find joy under the bleak circumstances of their first Christmas in captivity.

TREK, *December 1942, cover, Topaz prison camp, Delta, Utah. Densho, ddr-densho-142-425, courtesy of the Library of Congress* front of the stove; and the daughter and toddler are playing together with a large book or newspaper on the floor.

These differences are significant. The image conveyed in *Citizen 13660*, intended as it was for outside audiences, reflects an animated family in its domestic sphere, albeit a barrack in the middle of the Utah desert, where parents are trying to create the best holiday for their children that the circumstances allow. The *TREK* cover, by contrast, intended as it was for those inside the prison camp, is both more somber and more sobering. To convey frivolity in a time of despair would be disingenuous and insulting to those for whom Christmas 1942 was filled with foreboding. Okubo's drawing echoes the sentiments of journalist Taro Katayama in an article in this same edition of *TREK*: to greet "the annual holiday," he stated, "to mouth its traditional merriness would be, we felt, a painful mockery both of our plight and of our actual feelings."[25] This attitude, and its expression in Okubo's illustration, is

Okubo's illustration of the first Christmas at camp was published in her memoir, *Citizen 13660.* In comparison to the drawing that appeared in *TREK* in 1942, this re-creation, published in 1946, softens the portrayal of the event, adding a bit of warmth to the scene through rounder shapes and the family's more direct interaction.

Miné Okubo Collection, Japanese American National Museum (Gift of Mine Okubo Estate, 2007.62.155)

clearly demonstrated in the *TREK* cover, despite her modification of it for *Citizen 13660.*

The second cover Okubo created, for the February 1943 edition of *TREK*, portrays a mess hall scene. Before the war, dining together as a family may have been a time of connection and catching up on the day's events; in the mess hall, the family meal is a wholly different experience. Teenagers were often employed as servers and thus ate away from other family members. Multiple people, many of whom were unknown to one another prior to the incarceration, shared a table. Okubo captures, in a flat single-dimensional plane on the page, this discordant group in her drawing of eight people who sit eating. On the top right a man reaches out for a piece of celery from a communal plate that sits in the center of the table. Next to him, a mother holds a baby and beneath her on the page, a boy stands on the picnic-table style bench, reaching for the drinking glass of the man sitting across from him. The man appears to be swatting away the boy's hand. The man wears getas, which are elevated, wooden Japanese sandals that were repurposed in the camps to keep people's feet above the mud, muck, and silt that developed in the streets following rainstorms.

There is no doubt that this is a scene from camp, not a family gathering. Next to the man is a teenaged girl drinking a beverage, eyes seemingly focused only on her glass. Above her is a man slurping soup out of a bowl, and next to him sits a scarved female eating a spoonful of something. No one in the image engages the eyes of another. Aside from the man protesting the boy's infringement on his space, no one is communing at all in what is typically considered a communal activity, the breaking of bread and sharing of a meal. The monodimensional angularity and emptiness of the illustration itself parallel the blank and vapid life in the gridded and barren square mile of Topaz.

By comparison, in *Citizen 13660* Okubo portrays a similar dining scene but again, like the revised version of Christmas 1942, it is more animated than the *TREK* cover. Okubo's image of diners in *Citizen 13660* runs horizontally rather than vertically across the page. Again, a child is misbehaving as he drops food onto his head. Next to him a man slurps his soup, while another, seemingly in a suit jacket, looks at the mischievous boy with apparent amusement. Okubo portrays herself in the lower right corner, in a sort of visual stand-off with the woman next to her, and perhaps also with the man and child to the woman's left, over what, we are not certain. Her caption reads:

Okubo's cover illustration for the February 1943 edition of *TREK* depicts a typical mess hall scene. The loss of a quiet family dinner took a toll on many incarcerated families as this routine was replaced by cafeteria lines and communal tables.

TREK, *February 1943, cover, Topaz prison camp, Delta, Utah. Densho, ddr-densho-142-426, courtesy of the Library of Congress*

> Table manners were forgotten. Guzzle, guzzle, guzzle; hurry, hurry, hurry. Family life was lacking. Everyone ate wherever he or she pleased. Mothers had lost all control over their children. Before mess tickets were issued, most of us were hungry after one meal, so we would dash to another mess hall for a second meal. Some managed to get three meals this way.[26]

Again, in the *Citizen 13660* drawing the figures are engaged with one another, even if somewhat contentiously as Okubo portrays herself, while in the *TREK* version the flat figures each seem to be isolated in their own worlds.

Citizen 13660's mess hall dinner is also very different from another that Okubo includes in her memoir that portrays her return to Berkeley from Europe. The drawing runs angularly across the page from lower left to upper right, and portrays ten people from a variety of ethnic or racial backgrounds sitting at a dining a table. Okubo sits at the head. All but one of the guests are looking at her, appearing to listen intently. The group is actively enjoying their meal and one another. She captions this: "I had a good home and many

In her memoir, *Citizen 13660*, Okubo included multiple drawings of mess hall scenes in Tanforan and Topaz. All portray overcrowded tables with discontented diners at them.

Miné Okubo Collection, Japanese American National Museum (Gift of Mine Okubo Estate, 2007.62.90)

friends. Everything was going along fine" (*Citizen 13660*, 7). This image immediately precedes her portrayal of the family breakfast table, when they heard the news about the bombing of Pearl Harbor, after which, obviously, everything stopped "going along fine."

Most interesting about the *TREK* mess hall cover, however, is the way it echoes two of Diego Rivera's "mealtime" paintings—*Our Bread* and *Wall Street Banquet, 1928*—both painted as part of the extensive mural he produced for the Ministry of Education in Mexico between 1922 and 1928.[27] *Our Bread* portrays the "noble poor" breaking bread in a celebration of solidarity. At a rustic table sit young and old, dark-skinned and light-skinned, who are looked upon by peasants and proletariat leaders, all of whom benefit from the fruit of their labors working the land. The bounty of the earth frames the image as a figure seemingly symbolizing indigeneity holds on

Okubo's illustration of dining with friends in Berkeley, before the war, was published in her memoir. In contrast to the images of dining in camp, here Okubo and her friends are relaxed and enjoying themselves in her own dining room.

Miné Okubo Collection, Japanese American National Museum (Gift of Mine Okubo Estate, 2007.62.11)

his head a large basket containing squash, pineapple, and other agricultural products. *Wall Street Banquet, 1928*, by contrast, presents eight well-clad, wealthy individuals who, though seated at a table as though ready to eat a meal, are instead linked together by the golden ticker tape woven among them that signifies their capitalist wealth.[28]

Okubo's mess hall meals in both *TREK* and *Citizen 13660* compare to Rivera's images in multiple ways. First, in contrast to *Our Bread*, in Okubo's drawings no beneficent father-figure sits at the head of the table and breaks bread for all to share. Rather, everyone is out for themselves in the mess hall. She indicates this in the accompanying text: "Before mess tickets were issued, most of us were hungry after one meal, so we would dash to another mess hall for a second meal. Some managed to get three meals this way."[29] The *TREK* cover, however, given its nondimensional, vertical layout on the page that directly parallels Rivera's, tells more. The two round plates at the top of the plane recall the eyes of the dark, grim-reaper-like image in Rivera's *Wall Street Banquet*. The eight people are analogous to those in Rivera's painting as well, but whereas the Wall Street woman on the lower left wears heels representing her wealth, the imprisoned man wears camp-made getas, demonstrating his lack of it. Whereas the Wall Street diners sit at a linen-clad table and on comfortable formal chairs, those in Topaz are seated at a wooden picnic table. The Wall Street diners are famous industrialists, but Okubo's figures are unnamed inmates. Rivera condemningly casts the Statue of Liberty in the form of a lamp, but Okubo does not echo that theme, probably because it would be too objectionable to camp administrators and too painful a reminder of their nation's betrayal for incarcerated camp readers. The only thing in "Wall Street Banquet, 1928," that Okubo does not portray ironically is the facial expressions of the diners: in neither painting is anyone happy.

To insiders, this cover represents a different type of Okubo's strategic bilingualism. Though not all who were incarcerated likely recognized Okubo's allusions to Rivera or even knew of *Wall Street Banquet, 1928* itself, some certainly would have given the class demographics and educational levels of Topaz residents generally, combined with Rivera's prominence at the Golden Gate Exposition. Surely at least some of Okubo's fellow artists would have seen the similarities. If they did, they would undoubtedly appreciate her critique of capitalism from the confines of her life in an American concentration camp and her condemnation of those in power who govern the lives of those lacking it.

Okubo's third and final cover, for the June 1943 edition of *TREK*, is more interactive than the first two. Though rendered in the same geometric and stark style as the previous two covers, this one presents human connections in the form of a mother bathing her child in a communal washroom. Neither smiles, but the woman's arm cradles the child's back as she washes his torso with a cloth. To the left stands another woman, hand raised, who is speaking to the mother. Their gazes do not lock, however; only the mother and the child appear to be truly interacting with one another. Two men stand in the background: one, presented in profile, is shaving, using a handheld mirror as his guide, while the other, whose face is shrouded by his hat's brim, is washing clothes in one quarter of the same laundry tub in which the mother bathes her child. Although Okubo's drawing shows engagement between the women and the nurturing of a child, the dissonance of this scene resonates loudly. In the midst of a communal wash house, private acts of personal grooming become public, suggesting the degree to which systems of familial intimacy as well as formality and etiquette have deteriorated after two years of camp life.

Again, this *TREK* cover compares to a bath/laundry scene in *Citizen 13660*. In this, Okubo portrays the bathhouse from a broader vantage point, depicting a mother with a child on her back, washing clothes in the foreground, and a father bathing a boy opposite her. Two other sets of washtubs are pictured in the background. In one, a man is doing laundry; in another, a woman appears to be washing dishes; in the third, someone is washing his feet, and it is unclear what activity is taking place in the fourth. What makes this image distinctive in comparison to the *TREK* cover is the inclusion of Okubo herself, looking out of the frame to the reader, in the lower left corner. Additionally, she draws a smiling child playing with a bucket and also looking out at the reader from the lower right. Again, Okubo's *Citizen 13660* image is softer than the same scene depicted in *TREK*. The winsomeness of the child on the right, and the humanizing of the audience's gaze through projecting it as being seen through the eyes of Okubo herself, combine to add a familial and familiar tone to the scene.

Miné Okubo's artistic rendering of scenes from inside the camps, whether those created for *TREK* or those published in her postwar memoir, valuably document her experience of the incarceration. But a comparison of analogous images in *TREK* and *Citizen 13660* suggests how prewar and postwar influences and audiences shaped her work. When depicting the challenges of living in camp explicitly for the eyes of her fellow inmates on the *TREK*

Okubo's cover illustration for the June 1943 edition of *TREK* depicts a mother bathing a child in the laundry tubs in Topaz. Like dining, the ordinarily private domestic act of bathing became a public event in the prison camps.

TREK, *June 1943, cover page, Topaz prison camp, Delta, Utah. Densho, ddr-densho-142-427, courtesy of the Library of Congress*

covers, Okubo seems to have drawn on both the aesthetic style and leftist politics of her prewar mentor, Diego Rivera. But when packaging her memoir for the larger reading public, Okubo seems to have been keenly aware of the need to present an image of postwar Japanese Americans that was palatable to white Americans, especially to those in whose communities' former detainees resettled.

Okubo's drawing of the laundry room at Topaz was published in her memoir, *Citizen 13660.* Again, the scene is less stern and harsh in comparison to the original rendition she created, while incarcerated, for the cover of *TREK.*
Miné Okubo Collection, Japanese American National Museum (Gift of Mine Okubo Estate, 2007.62.158)

Whether Okubo felt her memoir was co-opted by the WRA or whether she, instead, used the government's interest in her work to her advantage matters not. Model postwar Japanese Americans were expected to have accepted and seemingly forgiven the nation for the tragedies inflicted on their lives and livelihoods by the incarceration. They were to assimilate quietly into their new surroundings and not look back negatively. Though this social coercion would prove to take a significant psychological toll on both those who were incarcerated and their descendants, at the time it became Okubo's responsibility, in many ways, to convey this ideal citizen in *Citizen 13660.* If she wanted to further the well-being of Japanese Americans after the war, using her art as a political tool was a wise and well-orchestrated way to do so.

PART II

WRITING ELSEWHERE

5
The *Pulse* of Granada/Amache

A silkscreen image of the Amache/Granada camp shows its distinctive red and white water tower. The silkscreen shop at Amache/Granada produced posters for the war department, calendars to be sold in the camp, and holiday cards, among other materials.
Densho, en-denshopd-i206-00001-1, courtesy of the Amache Preservation Society

The authors and artists held in Topaz were professionally trained and skilled, making *TREK* and *All Aboard* not only the "most serendipitous" of publications, produced by "real writers," as their fellow authors Hisaye Yamamoto and Wakako Yamauchi later described them, but also of unusually high quality. The literary magazines of the other camps, however, all run by nonprofessionals, contain equally valuable material. The journals produced

That Damned Fence. Heather Hathaway, Oxford University Press. © Oxford University Press 2022.
DOI: 10.1093/oso/9780190098315.003.0006

in Amache, Tule Lake, Jerome, and Rohwer demonstrate just how different the cultures were that developed in the various confinement sites depending on the camp's population, physical location and geographical features, and administration. In Amache, the administration's healthy respect for the incarcerated created a comparatively calm environment in which writers felt free to comment more explicitly on their incarceration.

The Granada Relocation Center, as it was officially titled, was located in southeast Colorado and was more commonly known by its postal address, Amache. Several features distinguished it from other camps. It was the smallest, holding a peak population of 7,318 inmates. Initially, those held came solely from California: the northern coast, southwest Los Angeles, and entire farming communities from the Yamato Colony in the Central Valley. This skilled farming population and Amache's location on federally owned land that previously had been used for agricultural purposes led it to become the War Relocation Authority's (WRA) self-acclaimed "farm stand," supplying food to the other camps and to the war-rationed nation more generally. A unique industry also developed in Amache: a high-volume silk screen shop produced posters and other materials for the war department. Perhaps the most distinguishing characteristic, however, was the critical candor with which evacuees commented on their plight.

These thoughts are expressed in Amache's literary magazine, *Pulse*, which ran for just one issue. Reading this single issue is, in itself, revealing. Reading it alongside the diary of the Stanford professor Yamato Ichihashi and the memoir of Lily Yuriko Nakai Havey titled *Gasa Gasa Girl Goes to Camp*, however, offers a valuable cross-generational perspective on Amache that further enriches our understanding of the camp. Finally, augmenting this with poetry produced by Lawson Fusao Inada, another Amache survivor, breathes life into yet another temporary wartime "city" that suddenly appeared on, and then was as suddenly erased from, the American landscape during World War II, this time on the Colorado plains.[1]

Yamato Ichihashi had migrated to the United States in 1894, at sixteen, and by World War II had established himself as a leading academic and community leader in Palo Alto, California. Though he feared an eventual conflict between the United States and Japan, he was as shocked as everyone else by the bombing of Pearl Harbor. He knew immediately what it might entail for the Japanese and Japanese American community in California. On Monday, December 8, 1941, despite his stellar reputation on the Stanford campus, Professor Ichihashi cautiously approached his classroom and, looking in from the hallway asked, "Shall I come in?" His students responded with resounding applause, but this anecdote demonstrates how quickly fortunes turned for people of Japanese descent living in the United States on December 7, 1941. The *Palo Alto Times* commented on this, if equivocally: "We are at war with Japan but not with our Nipponese neighbors, many of whom have proved their loyalty and most of whom can be counted on for self-sacrificing devotion to this country, which they have adopted or where they were born."[2]

Ichihashi was acutely aware of the hostility that might be directed toward Issei, so he approached both his department chair and his dean at Stanford about how best to proceed with his career. They suggested a sabbatical, but when the government ordered a mandatory evacuation on May 26, 1942, the Ichihashi family's fate was sealed. He and his wife, Kei, were required to report for detention in the Santa Anita Racetrack. A member of the local chapter of the American Friends, the Quaker service organization that lent moral support to the evacuees, recalled how Ichihashi sat quietly and alone on the bus ride to the center. She described him as "very disciplined and remote from his fellow passengers. We thought how he was from a different social class than most of them, how he was the most distinguished of all."[3]

Amache was rumored to be less fractious than other camps, and this may have been due to the fact that all who were incarcerated there came from only two assembly centers, Santa Anna and Merced. Santa Anna was the largest of the fifteen assembly centers, holding nearly 19,000 people at its peak, and it was also among the most primitive.[4] Ichihashi's diary entry documents the disorder and confusion surrounding the move to the racetrack:

> We assembled at the Japanese Language School . . . [in Palo Alto]. We were supposed to leave there at 12:00, but due to the inadequacy of trucks to carry luggage, we were detained until after 1 p.m.; we did not reach San Jose until 2:00. A medical examination was held and we did not get on the train until 3:00. It was a hot day, but we had to walk quite a distance with heavy luggage; it was cruel hardship on old people like ourselves.[5]

When the Ichihashis boarded the train, they were discouraged by the condition of the cars. Ichihashi recalled "old day coaches [that were] dirty and smelly—no light in the lavatory which people, especially children, dirtied in no time." He continued:

> Upholstered chairs showed moth-eaten spots. . . . At night, heat was turned on and it got too hot, so that electric fans were turned on; thus passengers suffered either from heat or draft. This was the worst-managed train [I] experienced in the U.S, in addition to the above characteristics.[6]

The train was also running behind, further taxing the patience and the stamina of the Ichihashis. This made for a long night: the train was supposed to arrive at Santa Anita early the next morning but it did not reach the racetrack until 12:30 p.m.

After a trying trip, the Ichihashis found themselves exhausted by the effort to find their luggage and take it to their living quarters, which Ichihashi described as a "woodshed." "We had to stand in heat 2 ½ hours," he wrote. "When we got to our dwelling-to-be after 3 hours, we were shocked to discover that it was empty except [for] *mutsuki* [diapers] drying which belonged to the [people] next door."[7] At 5:00 p.m. the hungry couple, who had run out of the food they had packed for themselves on the train, was called to the mess hall where they learned that the thousands of inmates ate in three shifts. The meal consisted of unripened cherries, spaghetti, boiled potatoes, and rice. The nutritional value of the food served to detainees, especially during the early phases of the evacuation, was marginal. Like the Ichihashis' meal, it was often overloaded with carbohydrates and lacking in fruits, vegetables, and proteins. Ichihashi commented on the psychological toll the setting and the food took on his spirit:

> Thus far we saw the shed and food, both of which made us feel very sad; it was an awful come-down. But when we returned to the shed, we found two dangerous wooden cots and we were told to pack bags with straw for mattresses. This was too [much].[8]

He did not mention the odor of the stall, but this left a lasting impression on many Santa Anita evacuees. Horse urine, manure, and hay stench, intensified by the heat, could not be disguised by the white-wash paint. "I don't know which was worse, the size of the rooms or the smell of the horses," remembered a Santa Anita detainee. "No matter how you clean it up, a stable's a stable."[9]

The experience was no less trying on the young. Ten-year-old Lily Havey reacted to Santa Anita with similar despair. In her memoir, *Gasa Gasa Girl Goes to Camp*, Havey recalls believing that she actually *was* going to "camp," like those attended by her friends in the Boy and Girl Scouts.[10] When she arrived, however, she looked out the bus window to find only soldiers, barbed wire and "row after row of black shacks but no tents." She wondered to herself: "Where are the tents? The mountains, the trees? So many boxes, suitcases, black-haired people. Who are they all? Are they all camping with us?" Havey's confusion continued when she got to the family's living quarters: "My mother and brother hurry into Room 6. No, I'm not going inside this dirty-looking building. I put down my suitcase and I sit on it. I hate camping."[11]

Havey's description of her first night and morning in the assembly center captured how difficult the transition was for both adults and children:

> It was a strange night. Searchlights swept our window. Sometimes the light flooded the room, outlining our cots against the slatted walls; then they drained away, leaving ghostly images. Sometimes the light seeped in slowly, probing like a gelatinous creature. Sometimes the streams of light appeared red, resembling blood washing the walls. Light—dark, light—dark, over and over again throughout the night. Footsteps passed by, some marching angrily, some shuffling quietly. Voices from all directions disturbed my sleep. They mumbled. They cried. Babies wailed. Skeletons lay beneath the barrack. A bony hand thrust up a white surrendered flag. Pine sap oozed from the fresh-cut lumber, and its sharp tang enveloped me. When I awoke, I found beads of pitch tangled in my hair.[12]

Morning was no better. A cacophony of "banging doors, bawling babies, shouts in Japanese and English, a search for toothbrushes and towels, and a dash for the bathroom" welcomed her to her new home. "Clangs and bongs assaulted us. Each mess hall had its own signal; Morse codes rang from all sectors of the camp. Our mess hall was a beehive."[13]

Most poignant, however, was Havey's recollection of the abrupt contrast between her pre- and post–Santa Anita lives:

> Before the war . . . we had lived in Hollywood—a poor section, to be sure, but Hollywood, home of the movie stars. Hollywood meant glamor—all those blonde-haired, red-lipped, leggy women wrapped in furs waving cigarette holders. Our house was in walking distance of Monogram Studios.

Only a few miles away from her home stood the famous Hollywood sign, promising fame, beauty, and elegance. She and her best friend vowed to climb to the top of it together some day, but she notes that this "never happened.

And now it never would. Never. Look at us. We lived in a barrack at a racetrack. Would anything ever be normal again?"[14]

Those held at the Merced assembly center, formerly the Merced County Fairgrounds, were similarly shocked by their new surroundings. Merced was much smaller than Santa Anita, housing only 4,500 people at its peak, but the center's facilities were no better. Evacuees lived in cramped quarters in tarpaper barracks: "if you wanted to get to the bed on the other side of the room you had to crawl over the other beds—It was that crowded! There wasn't even room to stand up. I ended up outside most of the time," recalled on Merced resident.[15] Merced detainees also suffered stifling heat and were served starch-laden food. But the latrines at Merced caused the most dismay. The women's toilets were simply boards with holes cut into them, placed about a foot apart, with no partitions or walls. The men's urinals consisted of long, slanted, tin troughs that drained into cesspools in the corners of the buildings. One Merced detainee described the women's latrine as disgustingly crude:

> At the end of this thing, there was this water gushing down . . . it just poured down into this [large bucket] until it got heavy and then it would tip over and go "swish." That was how they flushed it. The first night we got there—Oh, there were women trying to pound up sheets for some sort of partition. Because this was really bad—from a home, to something like this.[16]

Another remembered it as "a flume under 4 holes . . . every 2 minutes there was water running down the inclined flume. I had to make sure I sat on the topside so I wouldn't get splashed. Ugh, just the thought of it."[17]

Eventually, inmates at Santa Anita and Merced were transferred to Granada/Amache, a place that the Ichihashis found much more tolerable than the Santa Anita racetrack. Ichihashi observed:

> Amache is famous . . . for its variable climate richly interspersed with heat and cold, gales and sand-storms, lightning and cloud-bursts, etc., most of which we have already experienced. Nevertheless, it is not an intolerable place to live; in fact, Kei and I have become very much attached to our new "home."

That took some work, however. The first "apartment" to which they were assigned was situated near the sewage containment ponds and, depending on the wind's direction, foul odors wafted in the couple's direction. They were actually prepared for this, but they were not prepared for what came next: the realization that the previous occupant of their "apartment," an elderly man, "had lost the control over his body" and this "made the room intolerably odorous." After a series of other housing mishaps, the camp's director, James G. Lindley, gave the Ichihashis the right to choose from the remaining rooms. The couple's final space was not ideal—"the walls [were] scratched all over, and the ceiling too for no apparent reasons; dust and junk were so piled up on the floor so as to fill five wheel-barrow fulls; the windows were so dirty that their transparency was gone"—but they cleaned it up and tried to make a home for themselves for the duration of their incarceration.[18]

By this time, Ichihashi had begun to write a history of his evacuation and relocation. From Santa Anita the couple was first sent briefly to the Tule Lake facility and then to Amache. Ichihashi was struck by the differences between the two centers. In a "research essay" titled "Relocation from Tule Lake to Granada," he wrote:

> There exists [*sic*] a number of pleasant phases which were conspicuously absent at Tule Lake: the camp is smaller and more compact, and yet spacious because of the skillful arrangement of barracks; the inhabitants are quiet and sensible, . . . the administrative personnel is decidedly more understanding and sympathetic towards the residents.[19]

The most notable difference Ichihashi noticed between Tule Lake and Amache, however, was the tenor of the camp overall. Whereas Tule Lake was filled with agitation, Amache felt much less tense. Ichihashi attributed this contrast to a number of factors.

First, he noted that in Amache detainees were "allowed a large degree of freedom of movement; they can go outside for pleasure or shopping without restrictions." This may have been because Colorado's governor, Ralph L. Carr, was one of the few officials to welcome the construction of a camp in his state when the decision was made to isolate Japanese Americans in the interior. The governors of Arizona, Wyoming, and Idaho disagreed. Idaho's attorney general, Bert Miller, argued that "all Japanese [should] be put in concentration camps, for the remainder of the war, and that no attempt should be made to provide work for them." Reflecting the virulent racism of the time, he added, "We want to keep this a white man's country." But governor Carr thought differently. "If Colorado's part in the war is to take 100,000 of them, then Colorado will take care of them," he stated.[20]

Second, Ichihashi observed that the "age-composition and sex-distribution" in Amache appeared to be quite different from Tule Lake. He noted that Amache's population consisted of a significant number of elderly men and women, some young Nisei women whose husbands were in the military or working on sugar beet farms, and a group of adult men whom he found "quiet" and "passive." He rather disdainfully commented that other academics, entertainers, and musicians were all "conspicuous by their absence." Whether accurately or not, he attributed the placidity of the camp to a lack of intellectual interest among the incarcerated. "Passivity in general" characterizes the group, according to Ichihashi: "They are not active in work, play, hobbies, intellectual pursuits. . . . They may be philosophers or just plain dumbs. In either case, they make no noise, and retire very early. The whole camp is dark, as outside lights are few and dim and far between; there is not night life in the camp, and it is a paradise for old people who love quietude."[21]

Ichihashi himself was not wholly comforted by these qualities, however. He lamented how the malaise engendered by incarceration was particularly dangerous for the young people in the camp.

> There may be other reasons for human passivity in general at this camp, but the foregoing appear to be more important ones as far as I can see and feel. In a sense, it is too bad that we should be forced to live such a life; it is particularly bad for those who have to prepare themselves for the future. Young people need strong stimuli to prevent [themselves] from succumbing to inactivity; how such needed stimuli can be created requires hard thinking on the part of those who are endowed with active brains.[22]

Reflecting his training as a college professor, Ichihashi set a goal of challenging himself mentally throughout the duration of his incarceration and of trying to provide outlets through which young people might do the same.

The treatment of detainees by the camp's administrative officers proved to be the most striking difference between Tule Lake and Amache. Their offices, Ichihashi observed,

> are easily accessible to the residents, and formality is absent; the director himself occupies a simple office, and meets every caller very informally. His example seems to be followed by all the other members of the administration. Thus the relationship between the administration and the residents

is not only informal, but even intimate, reducing to a minimum any irritation.[23]

Project Director Lindley's letter to the camp on December 24, 1942, which was published in the camp newspaper, the Granada *Pioneer*, corroborates this. He thanked the evacuees for maintaining a "peaceful" rapport that had not drawn "undesirable" attention from the press or the public. "You are not here because you wanted to come, or because I wanted you to come," Lindley states outright. "But you are here . . . and we want you to go out from the center believing in a democracy that you have lived under [in Amache]. Pass your own laws and enforce them—we will help you. Take over the responsibilities as well as the rights of a democracy."[24]

The more tolerant tone in Amache, especially in comparison to Tule Lake, may have been due to the administrators' lack of "the California-type of anti-Japanese prejudice," as Ichihashi described it. Camp director Lindley's final report bore this out.[25] "It is hard for me to visualize any other group of people who would be so well behaved under similar conditions," Lindley wrote. As part of the WRA and well aware of its agenda to present the incarcerated as model citizens during the resettlement period, Lindley emphasized the very pacifism that Ichihashi found somewhat grating: "in close contact with them over three years, I can only admire their cheerful acceptance of unfair treatment; their overcoming of fear, resentment and frustration; their willingness to give their time and effort to make various phases of the WRA program work." They were, he insisted, "people—even as you and I." Although Lindley's assertion that the incarcerated accepted their circumstances "cheerfully" is inaccurate and his recognition of their shared humanity, even if well-intended, is condescending, Lindley's praise appears to have been sincere. He hoped that resettlement would result in a mutually beneficial relationship between Japanese Americans and their new neighbors in East Coast and Midwestern communities so that "something good will come out of this 'piece of wartime folly.' "[26]

Reports officer and camp photographer Joe McClelland equally respected and was respected by Amache detainees. This was exemplified in the way he managed the production of Granada/Amache's newspaper, the Granada *Pioneer*, and its literary magazine, the *Pulse*. The *Pulse* was issued sometime during the spring of 1943 (the publication itself is undated but the May 25, 1943, edition of the *Tulean Dispatch Daily* refers to the magazine's impending debut) and spanned only eighteen pages. The journal contained a "short novel," three stories, three feature articles, six poems, and two "vignettes." McClelland, described by the *Pulse* editor Suyeo Sako as a "publication advisor" rather than an administrative officer or supervisor, was known for his leniency when it came to censorship. In the foreword to the single edition, McClelland identified his commitment to allowing the publication to be an unfiltered expression of the thoughts and desires of the detainees:

> With this issue we introduce *Pulse*, a magazine supplement to the [camp newspaper, the] Granada *Pioneer*. To Amache, a city cut into the dry prairie and fully populated in a period of one month, we dedicate this publication. It is our purpose and desire to feel and report the pulse of our city through the medium of story, essay, and poem. May *Pulse* express truly our thoughts, our plans, our happiness, our sadness. May it record the heartbeat of Amache.[27]

McClelland's use of "we" and "our" suggests that he saw himself in league with the imprisoned, and his personal photos bear this out. Several, for example, show WRA officials playing cards with detainees. John Embree, the WRA community analyst for Amache, confirmed in early 1943 that relations between officers and inmates were "infinitely better" than at the other WRA facilities.[28]

Within this comparatively harmonious context the May 15, 1943, Granada *Pioneer* invited submissions for the inaugural edition of the *Pulse*. Apparently, submissions were not forthcoming, because the July 14 edition of the *Pioneer* featured a cartoon sketch of the *Pulse*'s editor waiting in vain for contributions. "Pictured above is a broken, dejected man. You see, he is the editor of the PIONEER magazine PULSE. He waits and waits for people to send in stories, poems, features, gags and things for the PULSE but people don't cooperate. So what are you gonna do about it, huh?"[29] Though enough material was generated for one edition of the *Pulse*, the call for additional material went unheeded and the *Pulse* never saw a second issue.

One cause of the paucity of writers in Amache, especially in comparison to Topaz, involves the differing demographics of each camp. Ichihashi's assessment of his fellow Amache detainees as "just plain dumbs" was unfair because those incarcerated in Amache were highly skilled, if less formally educated, farmers who came from California's Central Valley. The entirety of the communities of Yamato, Cortez, and Cressey, all farming colonies near Livingston, California, were sent to Amache, and this group was among the few who were able, through careful planning, to retain and return to their farmlands after the war.[30]

Yamato, Cortez, and Cressey were collectively known as the Yamato Colony. The area had been established by the Japanese-immigrant newspaperman and philanthropist Kyutaro Abiko in 1904 to encourage the development of a permanent settlement of Japanese farmers in central California.[31] Abiko envisioned farming as the surest path to success for Japanese immigrants in the state. With the proceeds from his highly successful vernacular newspaper, *Nichibei Shinbun*, which he founded in 1899 and which became one of the two major San Francisco–based Japanese newspapers, Abiko purchased 3,000 acres of land in the Central Valley. He then sold forty-acre parcels to Japanese immigrant farmers. Just before World War II, in 1940, nearly 4,000 acres were being farmed by nearly seventy families.

When it became clear that the Yamato Colony communities would be evacuated—and that their property would likely be usurped by land-grabbers during their absence—the farmers responded aggressively and strategically. The group pooled their resources to hire a land manager to care for and continue to farm their properties during the evacuation and detention. This was a rare instance of Japanese Americans being able to retain their property throughout the war and to return to it after they were released. Although President Truman signed the Japanese Evacuation Claims Act in June 1948, the Act provided next to no compensation for loss of property and none for the suffering and trauma of incarceration. Of the approximately $132 million worth of claims filed, only $38 million were eventually paid by the government—and the last claim was not settled until 1965.[32] The wise move by the families constituting the Yamato Colony resulted in another distinctive feature of Amache: because there was land to return to and farm, Amache experienced a comparatively low rate of resettlement to the Midwest and East. Much of the Yamato Colony land continues to be farmed today by the descendants of the imprisoned, in fact.[33]

The majority of those held at Amache used their skills and experience to grow food for the war-rationed nation, including for the inmates at the other camps. The first WRA director, Milton Eisenhower (Dwight D. Eisenhower's younger brother), envisioned Amache as a sort of WRA food generator that would cultivate sugar beets, alfalfa, and various truck crops.[34] His vision was possible for two reasons. First, Amache was one of the few camps that was located on reasonably arable land, thanks to the natural irrigation provided by the nearby Arkansas River (the other high crop-producing camps were Gila River and Heart Mountain). Second, the agricultural knowledge and abilities of its occupants ensured that the land was cultivated successfully.

The buildings and barracks of Amache were confined to the single square mile typical in most camps, but the entire acreage of this particular center topped 10,000. On this land, detained farmers produced hay, barley, sorghum, potatoes, lima beans, spinach, sugar beets, celery, mung beans, and daikon radish—several of which had never been farmed before in southeastern Colorado.[35] WRA Agricultural Enterprises data from June 1944 indicated that Amache was ranked first among the camps in terms of the numbers of acres (2,690) producing vegetables or field crops; first in the numbers of chickens farmed; and third in combined livestock production.[36] So productive was the camp farm, in fact, that Amache had its own slaughterhouse, poultry plant, butcher shop, and food processing facility.[37]

Amache, in effect, doubled as a prison camp and a self-sufficient, large-scale working farm. This had its pros and cons. On one hand, the detained farmers were exploited and severely underpaid for their labor. On the other, the opportunity to work the land, nurture produce, and provide for others allowed inmates a degree of physical freedom and psychological reward that may have contributed to their resilience as they awaited their freedom.[38]

The *Pulse*, however, gives a much less bucolic image of Amache's landscape than does its image as the WRA's farmstand. Numerous articles comment on the brutal wind that swept the prairie during arid months, as well as the damage caused by the dust that came along with it, and they suggest the degree to which detainees there, like Toyo Suyemoto in Topaz, felt as defeated by the terrain as by the barracks perched on it. "Amache in Retrospect," an anonymous contribution to the *Pulse*, for instance, focuses on the omnipresent and oppressive dust:

> It's not so wonderful how this thing called dust could find the smallest crevice in the haphazard structure that we call home and fill it up so evenly all around the room. One can sweep and dust in the morning. The wind blows again in the afternoon. Housekeeping does become a too frequent monotony.[39]

Shigeko Hirano remembered "the dust storms of Amache" as "just awful. We had to put something over our heads. It would hurt us, the sand would blow into our faces—it would actually hurt us. You could hardly breath [*sic*]."[40]

Lily Havey recalls a dust storm so severe that it actually risked students' lives. One day during school, she recalls, an "ominous gray air blotted the sun." This was not alarming at first given the regularity of such events, and the teacher told students that they would be dismissed "as soon as the wind dies down." But that time never came.

> Sand rasped again the windows, sounding like mice scratching for shelter. It spun in around the window frame, mounded on the sill, then streamed to the floor, where it puffed into hills. *What if the sand and dust blew in all night? What if they kept coming and coming and buried us? We'd smother to death. We would try to claw our way out of the choking mounds the way those ants must have tried when we poured dirt into their mazes. "Oh, those poor ants, those poor children! How they must have suffered," the mourners would lament.* I shook my head to get rid of this daydream. I realized I was very thirsty.[41]

As the wind continued to howl and night fell, Havey, her classmates, and even her teacher grew fearful. Eventually, two men, covered in dust and looking like ghosts to the children, came to take them to their homes. The men instructed the class to form a chain, holding hands with one another, with the teacher at the end. Havey recalls: "We grabbed hands that were grimy with sweat and dust and stepped into the storm, leaning into the wind and trying frantically to stay upright. Sand scraped my face and arms. I scrunched my eyes, peering at the shoes in front of me and following blindly."[42]

Their first stop was in a large hall that was closer to the barracks. They used this as the base from which to take individual children to their parents:

> Banks of candles sputtered in Terry Hall. Some Coleman lanterns sat dark on desks, their mantles having given up the struggle against shifting drafts of wind. Opaque light strained through the windows. Children hunkered on the floor or slumped on folding chairs. Heads on their knees, arms wrapped around their legs, they looked like baby bears settling in for winter in their caves. We took turns sipping cloudy water from a bucket. It tasted like mud.[43]

When Havey returned home, in a rare display of affection her "mother threw open the door. Sand billowed into the room, but she didn't notice. For a second, she stretched out her arms as if to hug me, but she checked herself and said, 'You are back safely,' and handed me a bottle of warm orange Nehi" that she had saved "for a special day."[44] Surviving a dust storm surely could have been seen as a special day for parents of incarcerated children, given how little control parents could actually exert over the children's present and future.

Other weather similarly wreaked havoc on Amache's occupants. A short essay in the *Pulse* titled "Amache in the Rain," by Fumi Takata, documented the dual sides of a downpour, noting that it at once brings life to the "yellow and barren landscape" while also a poignant memory of springs past to the farmer who recalls standing on the "crest of a hill under California skies overlooking his vast truck fields."[45] Havey remembered, through her child eyes, the simultaneous fascination and fear caused by an unexpected deluge in the middle of July.

> Without warning the sky—clear and blue one minute—gathered huge angry clouds with black underbellies. The raindrops pelted the ground and pocked the dry sand, and within seconds the rain was falling in sheets. I sprinted for cover beneath the roof of a tiny porch between two rooms and watched, fascinated, as the water poured around my feet and was momentarily dammed by the doors on either side of me. Suddenly, the doors burst open, and the churning water, roiling with mud, flooded the rooms.[46]

Amid the crashing thunder and pelting rain, Havey felt as if she "had been flung into violent ocean waves."[47] Then, as suddenly as it began, the torrent stopped. The blazing sun of the hot Colorado summer blasted through the clouds and baked away the rivulets filling the walkways. The steamy fog, she remembered, made the barracks look like they were "smoldering from an aborted fire."[48]

All seasons were taxing at Amache. Summer temperatures regularly soared beyond 100 degrees during the day and drew forth insects ranging from grasshoppers to spiders and centipedes. Winter proved to be just as harsh. "Winter nights," Havey remembered, "tested our endurance, our bodies, and our spirits."

> Snowstorms blew in from all directions in southeastern Colorado. From Kansas the snow bonded with the dust and sand of the Great Plains and fell heavily, tinged with a tawny hue. The barracks and the desert mutated into darker shades as if God had dipped a giant brush into a paint pot and flung it across the land. Even the sky turned a threatening brown. . . . If the storm pushed in from the north, the snow fell crystalline as if to prove that the vastness of Canada, Wyoming, and Montana was pure and virginal. Those storms brought crisp falling temperatures, sometimes hovering around zero for a week at a time. We stuffed paper and strips of cloth around the windows to seal out the cold, but they were useless against the relentless onslaught. We woke to find miniature mounds of snow on the windowsills with tiny icicles dangling below.[49]

Nearly every snowstorm brought with it a notorious wind that whipped inmates as they navigated their ways to the mess hall or latrines. Even Ichihashi found the weather a preoccupation; each entry of his extensive diary begins with a reference to it. "The climate here," he lamented, "strikes me as energy-sapping; I feel tired all the time; I sleep as I have never slept before. . . . There is no noise created by man, though there is plenty of what nature makes: thunder and gale."[50]

Suburbanites like Havey and Ichihashi seemed to have suffered the most from the desolate conditions. Toshiko Aiboshi, a Los Angeles teenager who had been sent to Amache along with a large portion of the Seinan (southwest Los Angeles) community, remembered her considerable confusion about how to live in this new and decidedly different environment:

> It was so desolate. I had never, ever been in a country situation, and there was nothing but dirt. No, it just, I said, "Where are we?" If you're in Los Angeles, even in those days it was a city, and so I'd never, ever gone to the country. The only time we ever went to anyplace it was to the beach, and so we were not used to a rural community and we said, "Where are we? They have stuck us into, I don't know." [Laughs] And, "are we going to stay here forever? Is this, how long is this going to last?" We had no idea. We had no idea whether we were gonna [get] food, we had no idea where we're gonna sleep. . . . It was bleak at . . . best. And so when we went to the barrack there was nothing in there except a stove, and we said, "What is that?" We had never, ever seen a stove like that. And I [said], "How does it work?" And

> nobody knew. [Laughs] And they said, "Oh, you'll be getting charcoal." And we said, "What's charcoal?" [Laughs] To make fire, and we had no idea.[51]

Los Angeles residents, coming from a climate that was temperate and lush year round, especially suffered in the cold and windy flatlands surrounding the Arkansas River valley. George Hirano recalled that "you were on a ridge. Amache is sort of located slightly higher than the area where the Arkansas river is, so it was like a gradual decline. Boy, did that expose you to a northern wind. It used to really hit us there. We got a lot of snow, which we had never experienced before."[52]

The misery and isolation of the climate and camp were captured in one of the more bitter contributions to the *Pulse*, Yoshio Abe's long poem titled "Imperfect Prairie." Abe was born in Portland in 1911 and at ten years old, he traveled with his Issei parents to Japan where he remained for fifteen years. His writing career began during this period. A member of the Alliance of Japanese Proletarian Writers, he published a novel titled *Ossan hitotsu tanomuze* (*Would You Do Me a Favor, Mister?*) in 1932.[53] Just a few years after his return to the United States in 1936, however, he was incarcerated. He was confined at the Santa Anita Racetrack and Amache.

In "Imperfect Prairie," Abe articulated his anger about the incarceration:[54]

> A watchtower lonely on the prairie
> Goggled its gray monocle in the high wind.
> Watching the slowness of the changing color
> Of winter day, from deep purple of dawn
> To yellow noon and to dark brown of dusk,
> The prairie knew no strangers from the West Coast
> Who from the corner of America
> Uprooted into the Center of America
> To slip between military-cup and politico-lip.
> But the prairie was yellow from the beginning
> And was still yellow,
> Tho' the winter has beaten her with
> The white of snow and the black of frost.
> The wind changed, and hollowed
> Its direction every day.
> But the prairie stood unmoved,
> Nonchalant of the rise and fall of life
> As though a heave of her abundant breast.

In this first stanza, Abe captures the powerlessness of the "yellow" incarcerees against both the omnipresent, controlling gaze of the government and the imperviousness of the desolate, yellow prairie.

In stanza two, Abe describes the emotional toil that is required to fight the oppression of the incarceration. He suggests that inmates may be tempted to surrender to the "fireside of the meekness / under the cover of the yellow prairie," but implies that to do so would be cowardly (the color yellow has long been associated with cowardice). One young man, however, defiantly resists:

> One snow-is-coming day
> Stripped cottonwood trees ripped
> The shoulder seems of the prairie,
> —Don't carry high you chip.
> The wind is sharp, 'nough to blow you down
> You, down-and-outer!
> And the low diving clouds menaced the wounded homage.
> There a wise old man said, "Seek the fireside
> Of the meekness, under the cover of yellow
> Skin of the prairie." (like cattle safe in the corral)
> Defied a young man –Stand high against
> The wind of hatred, and shout the very battle-cry of the War,—
> The expanse of the winter desolation
> Seeped away their voices,
> As frost thawed under the sagebrushes
>   And the earth was as black as it could be
> Yet the prairie was yellow from the outlook.

The young man stands against "hatred," shouting "the "battle-cry of the War," which, though undefined by Abe, surely involved resistance to totalitarianism.

The final lines of the poem, however, seem to question the degree to which resistance is possible among people who are confined behind guard towers and search lights:

> A watchtower lonely on the prairie
> Goggled its gray monocle in the high wind.
> —Under it, a corral of shipped Japanese.

Abe's resentment about the imprisonment is clear in this poem. He calls out the "corralling" of innocent people for what it is: a violation of their inalienable rights. Abe shows how an open and wild prairie that was once "perfectly" free has been rendered "imperfect" by the government's crime.

The negativity of "Imperfect Prairie" pervaded Abe's writing about his incarceration long after the war. In 1960, he and his wife returned to Japan, and there Abe completed a three-volume novel titled *The Man of Dual Nationality* about a young Kibei like Abe himself. He published this with the Toho Publishing Company in 1971. Abe wrote the novel in Japanese but an excerpt, translated into English, was published in 1985 in an academic journal focusing on ethnic studies. It embodies a similar anger and resentment found in "Imperfect Prairie."[55]

The translation, from volume one of the work, focuses on the experiences of the protagonist, Takeshi Iwamura, who is held in the Santa Anita Racetrack. (Volume two concentrates on experiences of the incarcerated in Amache; volume three is based on Abe's experiences in India during the war.)[56] Kibei, which literally means "returned to America," were Nisei (Japanese Americans who were born in the United States) who had spent an extended period of time in Japan, often having been sent there by their Issei parents to learn the language or experience immersion in Japanese culture.[57] Through the words of the protagonist, Abe raises an issue of considerable tension in many of the camps: mistrust of the Kibei by the Nisei.

> Issei and Nisei, one born in Japan, the other in America. This generational distinction, he understood and accepted. But he could not accept the distinction between Kibei and Nisei. After all, a Kibei was a Nisei who had been sent to Japan for educational purposes and then had returned. Why were they separate from the so-called "pure" Nisei? Iwamura shut his eyes and mouth tightly at [his girlfriend's] reminder that he was a Kibei.[58]

Abe's protagonist takes umbrage at his girlfriend's implication that the Kibei were somehow less American or less loyal to the United States than were the Nisei. The girlfriend, Sumiko, like many Nisei, wished to emphasize her "Americanness" and insisted on being called Sue. She was frustrated by being identified as "Japanese" when she was a US citizen. Takeshi, by contrast, was frustrated that, as a Kibei, his allegiances were called into question.

Bias against Kibei was based on a variety of misconceptions about the approximately 10,000 to 20,000 (among roughly 50,000 overall) who had returned to the United States after traveling to Japan prior to World War II. While in the 1930s Kibei had been valued by the Japanese American community as transnational cultural brokers, during the anti-Japanese fervor leading up to the war they became stereotyped as potential traitors. In the camps, members of the Japanese American Citizens League (JACL) considered themselves "true" Americans, in contrast to the Kibei. None of this was justified: the Kibei were also American citizens. They did not function as some type of political group or block either before the war or in the camps.[59] But the damage done by these misconceptions was another harmful legacy of the racism that caused the incarceration.

In addition to "Imperfect Prairie," Abe also contributed a short novel titled "Pipe Sand and Moon" to the *Pulse*. It, too, focuses on feelings of marginalization and entrapment. In it, Abe draws a parallel between the helplessness detainees felt and the position of Indigenous Americans.[60] The protagonist, a young male Nisei, expressed his fear of "becom[ing] domesticated" in camp, likening his plight to that of "a fat yellow Indian, if you like to call it. It's dangerous. Disintegration of morale. Day by day, we eat the wind and blow the wind, and we know no direction of tomorrow's wind."[61] The racism underlying Abe's analogy is obviously problematic, but it is not clear whether he, himself, harbored these beliefs or simply attributed them to his protagonist. Regardless, the analogy points to two interrelated problems plaguing US history. First, it exposes a historical pattern of pitting oppressed groups against one other in ways that ensure the supremacy of a third group, which retains its status as the most powerful. Second, the analogy draws a parallel between the incarceration of Japanese Americans and the expulsion of Indigenous Americans from native lands to isolated reservations, thereby tracing across time the long history of the discriminatory treatment of nonwhite Americans by the ruling elite.

Abe recognizes the cultural and personal damage caused by the confinement of American Indians to reservations, and through his protagonist, he expresses a fear held by many Japanese Americans: that they, too, might be permanently detained in the camps. This risk was especially apparent to those detained in the Gila River and Poston camps in Arizona, which were built on the Chemeheuvi, Hopi, Mohave, Navajo, Pima, and Maricopa reservations. The tribes resisted the placement of the camps on their lands because they opposed the injustice of the incarceration, but the WRA paid no attention.[62] Though Abe's story sought to differentiate Japanese Americans from American Indians, their mutual mistreatment by whites created an affinity between the two groups.

Lily Havey's experiences embody the complexities of this cross-cultural alliance. The WRA named Amache after the daughter of a Cheyenne Indian chief whose tribe lived on the camp's site, land bordering the Arkansas River. This appropriation left young Lily Havey confused about where she was headed. Havey remembered learning about "Indians" in the third grade, where she was taught inaccuracies and stereotypes: "They were poor, lived in hogans, and kept flocks of sheep. They lived on reservations. Was Amache a reservation? It sounded like one. Were we destined to become another tribe in Colorado? No, the government called it a 'relocation center.' We were being relocated from California. But why?"[63]

Her confusion multiplied when, on the long train ride from Santa Anita to Amache, Navajo women unexpectedly boarded the car to provide fry bread for those being relocated.

> Somewhere in the middle of [Arizona], the train lurched to a stop, and two dark women heaved themselves onto our coach. We stared at these creased and bronzed apparitions. Their black braids snaked down to their hips. Silver necklaces glinted on their breasts.
>
> "Who are they?" "Look at their clothes." "Get the police," echoed from those sitting around us. Dumbfounded, we sat and stared. Then one of the women smiled, revealing great gaps in her teeth and boomed, "Na-va-jo. You Ha-pa-nee." She dug into a basket slung over her arm and offered squares of something puffy and brown.
>
> "Fry bread," she said. . . . "Eat, eat," she urged.[64]

This offer both alarmed and tempted the young girl. "Were they poisoned?," she wondered. "Were these women agents sent to kill us?" Given what she had been taught in school, her questions were not unexpected.

Upon gaining her mother's approval, however, Havey accepted the gift of food:

> I hesitated but hunger won. I nibbled one. It oozed delicious fat.
>
> My mother tasted one. "Ah, *oishii*, delicious," she commented.
>
> The women walked through the car, dispensing their bread.
>
> "One more? Plenty here."

> "Yes, thank you." Both my mother and I accepted seconds. I savored mine as the women descended into the vast desert and waved us away, arms arcing good-byes, velvet skirts swirling. They were still waving as they dissolved into the gray landscape.[65]

As in this scene, the relationship between Indigenous Peoples and Japanese Americans in the United States improved, in some instances, during the war, because of their shared oppression.

Amache detainee and poet Lawson Fusao Inada noted the parallel between the two communities' circumstances in the introduction to his 1993 poetry collection, *Legends from Camp*. Inada described an experience, while traveling through the southwest, of providing a ride to two Navajo women whose car had broken down. In trying to explain who he was to their elderly grandmother who was sure he was not Japanese but rather "Delbert Yazzie's son, from up by Shiprock," he reflects on the bonds forged by ethnicity in the United States:

> I've heard it said that the Japanese are "one big tribe." Well, I don't know about that—it's a convenient generalization—but for the sake of convenience I'll stay with the generalization, because I do know this much: Wherever, whenever we may meet, or simply encounter one another, there's something in the air between us, a "spark of recognition" that might be termed a "tribal connection."
>
> It runs deep, and is just there. It doesn't have to be mentioned. Call it kinship, if you will—something shared by "kindred spirits"—because to me, it's more of a feeling than anything—like meeting a relative, or even meeting an ancestor. It runs deep, this sense of "our people."

Inada goes on to establish a broader concept of "our people" by linking Indigenous Americans to Japanese Americans to Jews liberated by American soldiers in Europe. In trying to explain his personal history to the grandmother, he sketched out geographical locations on the sand, using rocks as place-markers. Pointing to "this smooth one where we're standing," Inada defined it as "Amache Camp, in the Colorado desert, not all that far from here."

> While we're at it, let's let that little stone by your foot stand for Leupp—a "mini-camp" right here on the Navajo Nation. (And yes, we had major camps on other reservations; you might say that it makes sense that the

> chief camps administrator went on to become chief of the Bureau of Indian Affairs, where he "re-deployed" his policy of "relocation." Which included, yes, "termination." Which reminds me—down the ridge, in Europe, our relatives had base camps in Italy, France, Germany, and some of them liberated a camp called Dachau.)[66]

By loosely linking all those persecuted during World War II, Inada effectively established a kinship or "tribal" membership among the Navajo grandmother, himself, and those who were murdered in Europe because of their "lineage." Obviously, the circumstances and outcomes were different for all involved, but the root of their subjugation was the same: racism.

Inada's most powerful statement about this tragic connection can be found in his poem, "Healing Gila."

for The People
The people don't mention it much.
It goes without saying,
it stays without saying—

that concentration camp
on their reservation.

And they avoid that massive site
as they avoid contamination—

that massive void
punctuated by crusted nails,
punctured pipes, crumbled
failings of foundations . . .

What else is there to say?

This was a lush land once,
graced by a gifted people
gifted with the wisdom
of rivers, seasons, irrigation.

The waters went flowing
through a network of canals
in the delicate workings
of balances and health . . .

What else is there to say?

Then came the nation.
Then came the death.
Then came the desert.
Then came the camp.

But the desert is not deserted.
It goes without saying,
it stays without saying—

wind, spirits, tumbleweeds, pain.[67]

The eloquence and poignancy of Inada's poem is unmatched, but the writers of Amache's *Pulse* expressed similar feelings of uncertainty and despair. When read alongside work produced by Yamato Ichihashi, Lily Yuriko Nakai Havey, and Inada himself, the writing in the *Pulse* reflects the immediate realities of camp life and anticipates long-standing legacies of the incarceration and dislocation of Japanese Americans during the war. Their candor provides clear evidence that a quality often attributed to detainees, *gaman*, a stoic endurance of the unbearable, was complemented by clear and outspoken resistance and critique. If Amache was renowned for its placid camp culture, as both inmates and administrators agreed it was, it appears that the very right to speak freely was a crucial factor in this. By giving inmates their rightful freedom of expression, camp director James Lindley and reports officer Joe McClelland actually fostered the most harmonious of prison communities.

6

Dispatches from Tumultuous Tule Lake

Tule Lake was unusual among the ten camps for a variety of reasons. Whereas Amache's administrators worked well with the detained, for example, circumstances in Tule Lake tended to be much more tumultuous. While Topaz consisted of a fairly static population of inmates from a specific area in California, Tule Lake's population fluctuated considerably over time, thereby inhibiting the development of a stable community culture. Tule Lake's distinctiveness was most obviously due, however, to its designation on July 15, 1943, as the official "Segregation Center" for all whom the War Relocation Authority (WRA) wished to keep apart from their allegedly more "loyal" peers.

Initially, when Tule Lake opened on May 27, 1942, it was similar in form and function to the other nine relocation centers. It, too, was isolated on fairly desolate lands. The camp was located just south of the Oregon state line (approximately forty miles southeast of Klamath Falls, Oregon) on a dry lake bed situated in a volcanic corridor of the Cascade Range. Like at Heart Mountain in Wyoming, prominent geological markers broke the flat horizon of the inmates' views: to the west loomed an 800-foot basalt bluff designated "Castle Rock" by the incarcerated; to the east stood a domed hill which inmates referred to as Abalone Mountain.[1] Tule Lake's initial population was a hodgepodge of people from three primary regions: the largest number of inmates—nearly 5,000—came from the Sacramento area of California. About half as many, roughly 2,700, came from King County in Washington, and just over 400 were sent from the Hood River area in Oregon. At its peak, Tule Lake ballooned to a population of nearly 19,000 people who were packed into an area of roughly one and a half square miles. By comparison, just over a third of that number—approximately 7,000 individuals—were housed in Amache's one-square-mile.

Unlike other camps, however, Tule Lake was set on ancient lava beds produced by volcanic fissures, and fissures are an appropriate metaphor to describe the camp's cultural climate. The hope and optimism that surfaced occasionally in other camps was hard to come by in Tule Lake. From the

That Damned Fence. Heather Hathaway, Oxford University Press. © Oxford University Press 2022.
DOI: 10.1093/oso/9780190098315.003.0007

outset, area chambers of commerce resisted locating a camp in the region, unabashedly giving racism as the reason: community leaders stated that they preferred to maintain "the present character of the population [with] no orientals or negroes among its residents."[2] Tule Lake was the only relocation center referred to as a "colony" rather than a "city," as Topaz was described, and Tule Lake was indeed, at times, run much more like a penal colony than a camp.

Almost immediately after the center opened in late spring of 1942, unrest arose. Mess hall workers struck in July and waged a campaign for higher pay in August. Two other labor strikes took place in August and September to protest being incarcerated and then required to work to produce their own food for wages of sixteen dollars a month.[3] These acts of resistance were grounded specifically in the issue of the moment, in that prisoners of war could not be exploited as laborers per the rules of the Geneva Convention. At the same time, however, these acts were part of a long history of Asian American resistance movements on the West Coast.[4] After Tule Lake's function shifted to become an even more carceral state than when it opened, interaction in the camp was marked by a consistent assertion by inmates of their civil rights and an equally consistent crackdown by the camp authorities. At various points in its existence, the center was governed by martial law and guarded by military police, resisters were imprisoned either in the concrete jail or the infamous "stockade," and tear gas and tanks were used by the army when inmates undertook acts of civil disobedience.

The *Tulean Dispatch Magazine*, the literary accompaniment to the center's newspaper, the *Tulean Daily Dispatch*, provides a window into life in this particular relocation center prior to its conversion into a segregation facility. Upon that conversion, both the camp newspaper and the magazine ceased publication. The *Tulean Dispatch Magazine* was published in eleven editions between August 1942 and July 1943. The early issues reflect the tensions in the camp and the ensuing bitterness they created. A dark tone permeated all. The opening editorial of the inaugural August 1942 edition, for example, written by the editor George J. Nakamura, was titled "Let's Face Reality." That reality, he asserted, was undeniably life-altering:

> The current evacuation undoubtedly marks the turning point in the lifetime of thousands of young men like John Nisei. He is being drawn resignedly into a future enveloped in darkness and assailing uncertainties. . . .

> Today, he is experiencing a transition which, unless extreme care and fortitude and understanding are exercised, may prove disastrous for him.[5]

The potential disaster Nakamura identified was twofold: the prototypical "John Nisei" could either develop an "unhealthy distrust in democracy" or become a man "blinded with illusions." (The African American writer Ralph Ellison would develop his monumental novel, *Invisible Man,* around these two themes ten years later.) Neither was a good option. Only through accepting, Nakamura states, that "in an evacuation center, he . . . ceases to become an individual," only through pledging to work collectively and to look "to the future . . . with the strength that is derived from an indominatable [*sic*] inner spirit," would John Nisei emerge from the experience of eviction and incarceration whole.

Nakamura's October 1942 editorial was similarly ambivalent. While in some camps, the Christmas season lifted spirits temporarily, Nakamura anticipated it with caution. Christmases in the camps were regularly topics of interest in all the literary magazines and, although obviously an annual reminder of the uncertainty surrounding the Christmas that fell so soon after the bombing of Pearl Harbor, the holiday was commonly treated with a bit of frivolity. But Nakamura's piece contained none of the optimism that often characterized such articles. When asked by a child whether Santa Claus would be coming to Tule Lake, Nakamura thinks:

> Santa Claus? I swore under my breath. Does she mean the fat bewhiskered clown etched on Christmas cards garbed in resplendent red coat and black boots? The poor forgotten old fellow created out of imaginary notion [*sic*] of men to represent the ideals of brotherhood and good will?"

Nakamura tells the child that "men are blinded by hatred" and have "hearts . . . so cold as not to understand the suffering of [their] fellow men. . . . Christmas and Santa Claus do not live in the hearts of these men. They simply ridicule the idea that people can conceive such childish ideals." He closed the editorial by assuring the child that Santa would, indeed, come and might even bring her a doll, while he himself desperately yearned for "a new force of hope to push aside the dark, frozen surface of our human scene."[6]

Many inmates, however, were unable to muster this strength. The bleakness of Nakamura's early editorial was matched by other contributors to the fall 1942 issue of the *Tulean Dispatch Magazine.* Constance Murayama's

Santa Claus pauses on top of a barracks, puzzled by how to descend into the smokestack to deliver his Christmas presents. This cartoon was printed in the *Tulean Dispatch Magazine*. Christmas was a particularly challenging time for inmates with children.

Tulean Dispatch Magazine, *August 1942, p. 1, Tulean Dispatch Magazine collection. Densho, ddr-densho-65-9, courtesy of Library of Congress*

short story, "Pattern of a Coda," signaled the profound impact that living in overcrowded barracks among thousands of people, while simultaneously experiencing little emotional or physical intimacy, had on detainees. The narrator reflected that

> perhaps she was born to be lonely, . . . that the moments that ripped her were the only aware moments she could have. . . . But the words were meaningless; drip, drip, drip. If they dripped a hundred years, perhaps a little hole would appear and the loneliness would pour out. . . . Anger, sudden annoyances slipped in like a stone slipping sideways into a lake of oil. A lethargic bubble, then nothing.[7]

Murayama seemed to be characterizing depression, a condition that must have been nearly universal among adult detainees, but the incidence of it in the camps is difficult to track. It was not commonly diagnosed, and few records charting mental illness among inmates exist, though occasionally evidence of an inmate being sent to a psychiatric facility pops up. The writer Hisaye Yamamoto provides a fictional rendition of a mental breakdown and hospitalization in her story, "The Legend of Miss Sasagawara."

The *Dispatch* editor Howard M. Imazeki's article titled "My Blood," also published in the November issue, likewise projected despair but added a tone of defiance. Imazeki referred to feeling "overwhelmed . . . with bitterness and frustration" during the eviction. He described that period as a time "when our sense of perspective and our faith in American Democracy were completely darkened by the feeling of persecution and humiliation." Though people "smiled as [they] tucked away the Bible and a couple of 'non-dangerous' books in our suitcases to get ready for the 'E Day,' [evacuation day] . . . those were the smiles of a ghost." In reality, he claimed: "we wept as children romped around with joyful excitement as though they were going on a picnic, not mindful of the fact that their parents were losing everything to meet the military demands. We wept also when the children began whimpering about "going home."[8]

Imazeki's tone then shifted, however. He challenged his community to reject "the quagmire of racial discrimination, criticism, hatred, and persecution" they faced because of their "blood." "I am proud of the blood that is sustaining me," he stated, "be it Type 2, Japanese, Mongoloid or call it whatever you will. It is this blood that has created in me what I am: my color, my feature, my feeling and my thinking. With this blood I eat, I hear, I smell, I touch, I feel and I think." He then lays claim to his future and that of his descendants in his native land: "with this blood, too, I procreate and perceive the future and God. . . . With this blood, then, I aim to create my destiny while I live. I pray that the blood of my people in America will never lose an ounce of humility, humanity and virility."[9] The anger underscoring Imazeki's article is compelling, and even a bit threatening.

"This Is Our Colony," written by Yoshimi Shibata and published in the December 1942 issue of the *Dispatch*, by contrast, preached a perhaps overly determined optimism: "this is our Colony and we can make this into a modern Shangri-la of life and happiness by developing a sound mental attitude."[10] He made rather heroic efforts to emphasize the individual's power to determine the outcome of the experience of incarceration:

> Many of us are dissatisfied with life in this Colony, but let us not be dismayed. The ambition which fired many great men did not come to them ready made. They learned them [*sic*] by being dissatisfied. We can never desire anything better unless we are dissatisfied with what we have. But here is the big difference between the great man and the weakling. The weakling sits idly, groans and whines about his troubles; the great man sets about to change things.[11]

Though Shibata acknowledged that the "present circumstance is a rare experience unparalled [*sic*] in American History, placing the will of man to an acid test," he nevertheless bought into the propaganda that referred to the inmates as pioneers:

> We are pioneering an immense project; the first of its kind in American history. The success depends greatly upon the use of our brains. . . . It is important that our thinking be positive and constructive, not complaining and destructive.[12]

In the end, Shibata sees hard work and the right attitude as indicators of true American spirit: "Let us make this Colony a growing concern with life and happiness, to prove now and forever, that we are worthy of being loyal Americans. Thus proving in action that our proclamation of being good Americans is sincere."[13]

Battles over who were "true" Americans seem to have been endemic to the land on which the Tule Lake camp sat. This land, after all, had been stolen and colonized from the start. Whereas the Poston and Gila River camps were built on Indian reservations where tribal members were living and farming in 1942, Tule Lake was located on the ancestral home of the Modoc tribe, which the US Army had defeated in the Battle of Lost River in 1872.[14] The beaten Modocs were expelled from the lava beds of northern California and sent to a reservation in Oklahoma at the end of the nineteenth century, only to have their original territory become a confinement site for Japanese Americans a half century later.[15] But the Modocs' presence lingered. In August 1942, in fact, a group of boys, digging under their barracks, unearthed an ancient skull. It was presumed to belong to a Modoc warrior, according to the *Tulean Dispatch*.[16] The regular reminders of what happened to the Modoc in the very same location was sobering for detainees, sparking fears of being permanently confined to Japanese American reservations.[17]

At the same time, some inmates took courage from the fortitude of Modoc Chief Kintpuash, also known as Captain Jack, and his warriors, as an article in the *Tulean Dispatch Magazine* suggests. Tom Seto, in recounting the history of the battle of Lost River, expressed admiration for the Indians who fought "one of the last and most stubborn conflicts in American frontier history," and claimed that more US soldiers were killed in this battle than in the Spanish–American war.[18] Perhaps hinting toward a call to arms among the incarcerated, he ended the essay by noting that the land on which the Modocs fought for their freedom was unchanged:

> To this day the lava beds are practically in the same condition as they were in that year 1872. They are located southwest of the project and were set aside as a national monument in 1925. The Black Ledge is situated directly across [from] the main entrance.[19]

Seto seemed well aware that the very land on which Japanese Americans were currently segregated was bloodied with a history of expulsion and removal, just like their own.[20]

All of these pieces were written before the crises that arose in the camps over the "loyalty questionnaire." On February 9, 1943, the government initiated a process to determine the "loyalty" or "disloyalty" of all colonists, in conjunction with the initiation of the resettlement program.[21] The WRA originally created the questionnaire as a litmus test to determine male Niseis' willingness to serve in a Japanese American combat unit, now that the need for Nisei soldiers became clear. Part of the goal was to assess the potential allegiance of Nisei to Japan versus the United States, were they to enlist or be drafted.[22] By the fall of 1942, however, when the government realized that resettlement of the imprisoned was more cost-efficient than holding them at the government's expense, the questionnaire morphed into a mechanism by which to determine detainees' suitability to move to "friendly cities" (those in which Japanese Americans had been reasonably well received) away from the West Coast.[23]

This initiative was sloppily planned and executed, however, as Shuji Kimura's April 1943 article in the *Dispatch Magazine* sarcastically pointed out:

> "Fix up the questionnaire for the Jap concentration camps; ask them if they're loyal to the U.S."—and so the form must have been written in 10 seconds of an afternoon in an office in Washington D.C., teletyped and sent

A cartoon drawing of boy playing under a barrack and discovering ancient skulls, printed in the *Tulean Dispatch Magazine.* Tule Lake was located on the grounds of a battle for land that took place between the Modoc Indians and the United States government in 1872–1873. The remains were assumed to be of casualties of that battle.

Tulean Dispatch Magazine, *November 1942, p. 20, Tulean Dispatch Magazine collection. Densho, ddr-densho-65-429, courtesy of the Library of Congress*

> to the 10 relocation camps in the West. Allegiance—United States—. Did the person who phrased that question ask himself and really try to understand what he was asking? Did he ask himself what allegiance means, what United States means? If he did, he could not have asked this question lightly, for this question can only be asked humbly, and only to one's own self.[24]

Kimura continued,

> loyalty doesn't mean saying 'yes' or 'no,' or extending one's hand to the flag, or raising a hat or standing up when one hears the 'Star Spangled Banner'; anyone can do these things. No, loyalty has to be in our hearts and in our memories; it has to be in our fibre and in our bones. Loyalty comes from having lived in America, and having lived deeply."[25]

Kimura then recalled images that signified his own allegiance to the United States, ranging from memories of fishing trips and picnics to the smell of bacon, pork, and beans. Loyalty, he stated, came from "knowing the beauties" of the American countryside, and from "having worked in America, . . . plowing, . . . chopping, . . . spraying, . . . and harvesting" it. Loyalty also transcended the negative, according to Kimura: it meant "having known the bitterness of contempt," the "helplessness against men who sit in legislatures passing laws to drive us from our farms, from our jobs . . . the pain of auctions before pitiless spectators," while also and "above all, affirming and re-echoing in our hearts the American dream" in which "black and white and red and yellow men shall be considered equal as men."[26]

Other writers in the *Tulean Dispatch Magazine* similarly called out the injustices they were experiencing, but, like Kimura, many found this challenging because doing so clashed with their own profound patriotism. In "Nisei America: Entrails of a Thought," for example, Riley O'Suga recorded his thoughts just after he had been rejected from the army, despite his 1-A classification. "Sorry," he was told, "no more Japanese." He deliberately cataloged American surnames from a wide variety of ethnicities, suggesting that these groups enriched America just as deeply as did Japanese Americans.

> To think of America. Of its teeming, yearning, colorful cosmopolitan masses; blond, brunette, titian, and black-haired people; the white, red, black and yellow-skinned people. I see names: from Smith, Robeson, Dos

> Passos, Kaiser, Goldberg, La Guardia, Fields, Bok, MacArthur, Chang, Sullivan, Yamamoto, to Jones. I see the country-side and a simple farmhouse, the city and gigantic skyscraper, the broad river and a steaming showboat, the lofty mountain and a rushing stream, the national park and a pleasure resort, the flower garden and a cozy home.[27]

Next, he highlights the unique vernaculars, cultures, and practices developing across the nation.

> I hear colloquial and provincial peculiarities of tongue. A Texan and his herd, a New Yorker and his night club, a Georgian and his julep, a Californian and his movie, an Oklahoman and his dusty plains, a New Englander and his tea. I hear voices of discord and harmony. An Italian fisherman sings and Joe DiMaggio smacks a baseball, an Irish policeman whistles and George M. Cohen composes, a Negro bootblack taps rhythm and Marian Anderson sings spirituals, a Chinese laundryman laughs and James Wong Howe shoots movies, a German machinist guzzles beer and Wendall Wilkie orates, a Japanese farmer sighs and Mike Masaoka fights and champions, a Jewish merchant changes and Eddie Cantor cracks jokes, a Russian makes music and Alexander P. de Savorsky designs airplanes, a French check exclaims and Charles Boyer emotes, a Slavic laborer grins and Louis Adamic writes America.

The pan-ethnic nature of the nation, O'Suga believed, was responsible for the best of the United States, for the "benevolence, the protection, the indifference and that beauty that is America."[28]

In the end, however, as a Japanese American during World War II, O'Suga could not escape the "scorn" and discrimination that also gripped the nation, exemplified by "the countless who point at me and hiss, 'You dirty Jap.'" At this, O'Suga describes that "bitterness, contempt and loneliness gripped [his] soul." Having been rejected from the military because of his ancestry, the author ponders his past, present and future:

> What am I doing in an internment camp? Why must I be separated and confined within a barb-wired enclosure? Why must I be shunned and shackled—I, who was born, weaned, educated, played, worked, fought and lived with and for America? What have I done?"[29]

A conflicting sense of patriotism and betrayal pervaded the tenor of Tule Lake even before it was designated a segregation center.

These same sentiments were expressed metaphorically in a February 1943 piece titled "Johnny's Uncle," written by Hama Akashi. Told from the perspective of a young boy, Johnny, the tale appears, at first, to be a chronicle of the breakdown of a family relationship. The child is portrayed as loving his uncle deeply, enjoying the freedom of the city life they shared, missing him while studying abroad, and doing all the uncle asked upon his return, even though that meant moving away from the uncle to work the fields and raise crops. When the boy returned home, the uncle asked for further proof of the nephew's love for him, something that stunned and deeply hurt Johnny. He tried to prove it, nonetheless, but "thoughts kept pounding in Johnny's head. Words kept ringing in his ears. 'If you want to show your loyalty' . . . . Johnny resented" even being questioned.

In the final paragraph, Akashi breaks the narrative conceit by bringing readers to the discovery that Johnny is actually incarcerated:

> Johnny was walking on the gravel road beside the central fire-break. He did not know how long he had been walking and thinking. Suddenly he looked up and saw the Star Spangled Banner waving against the sky which was unusually blue. He couldn't check the tears that streamed down his cheeks, not the same kind of tears he experienced in a foreign land but something mingled with pain, deep down in his heart. He uttered a whimpering, appealing cry—for he missed him just the same.
>
> "Uncle Sam! Uncle Sam!"[30]

All of these pieces reflect not "disloyal" Americans but rather those who so deeply held to democratic ideals that compromising them in any way, including acquiescing to the idea that simply checking boxes on a questionnaire could somehow "prove" or "disprove" that commitment, was the ultimate betrayal.

The infamous questionnaire asked thirty-three questions. Many seemed innocuous on the surface—name, address, date of birth, previous residences—but others held the potential to entrap respondents. What is the citizenship and race of your immediate and extended family members? Are you a registered voter, and if so, for which party? Do you have relatives in Japan and, if so, where do they live? Have you traveled abroad? Where, when, and why? Simply providing factual answers recounting one's personal history of marrying an Issei or visiting one's grandparents in Japan could create cause for suspicion.

Other questions were trickier and subject to additional scrutiny. What religion are you? Of what organizations are you a member and how much money have you contributed to them? What magazines and newspapers do you read? What are your sports and hobbies? Do you speak any foreign languages and how proficiently? These questions needed to be answered thoughtfully. If one practiced Buddhism, spoke some Japanese, or read the local *nihonmachi* (Japanese community) newspaper, one might be perceived as potentially disloyal.[31] After all, many Isseis' involvement in community organizations was considered cause enough to arrest them the night that Pearl Harbor had been bombed. The incarcerated understandably wondered whether the questionnaire was some new type of crucible that would be used to determine their futures, either inside or outside the camps. The ambiguity of the questions and the absence of clear information about what, exactly, it would be used for left many people apprehensive and confused about how to respond.

Two questions, numbers 27 and 28, proved to be especially contentious. The first asked if the respondent were "willing to serve in the armed forces of the United States on combat duty, wherever ordered." The second asked if the respondent were "will[ing] to swear unqualified allegiance to the United States of America and faithfully defend the United States from any or all attack by foreign or domestic forces, and foreswear any form of allegiance or obedience to the Japanese emperor, or any other foreign government, power, or organization." For Nisei men who volunteered to serve in the military, these questions were easily answered. Of course they would defend their country against foreign antagonists. Of course they held no allegiance to the emperor of the land that they, too, saw as "the enemy."[32] Indeed, the all-Nisei 442nd division of the United States Army, formed in March 1943, was among the most decorated units fighting in the war.

When the loyalty test was adapted for general use among all the incarcerated, however, its flaws became readily apparent. Issei had no country but Japan in which to claim citizenship: as "nonwhites" they were prohibited from becoming US citizens by the Supreme Court's 1922 decision in *Ozawa vs. United States*.[33] To renounce Japanese citizenship would mean becoming nationless and thus relinquishing the protections that nationality conferred including being granted a passport to allow international travel or the right to appeal to one's consulate, for example. Consequently, question 28 was revised to read: "Will you swear to abide by the laws of the United States and to take no action which would in any way interfere with the war effort of the United States?" This revision thereby allowed Issei the possibility of answering affirmatively, if they chose, without surrendering their Japanese citizenship. But as WRA director Dillon Myer himself stated, by the time the revision was made to the question, "much confusion had already been produced" and both Issei and Nisei were wary.[34]

Moreover, the idea that two answers on a questionnaire would be sufficient to measure patriotism or allegiance, particularly since there was no way to qualify one's responses, was both illogical and naïve. Answers could range from "yes-yes"—I am willing to serve my country and I will follow the law and support the war effort—to "no-no," but what about all those in between? "Yes," I am willing to serve my country but "no," I will not commit to following the law or supporting the war effort? Or "no," I am not willing to serve in the military but "yes," I will be law-abiding and support the war effort? In the latter case, if one were to be drafted and refused to serve, then one would implicitly *not* be following the law and supporting the war.

A number of factors that had nothing to do with one's loyalty to the nation necessarily dictated peoples' responses. Obligations to stay with or care for Issei elders, or even to follow them in their wish to repatriate to Japan, influenced some Nisei who were simultaneously loyal to their families and to the United States. Having a brother already serving in the military affected others whose parents did not want to sacrifice more than one son to war.[35] Peer and parental pressure to show one's "red-blooded" Americanness by fighting for the nation shaped another set of responses, while an opposing group sought to show the very same quality by refusing to serve in a Nisei-only military unit that perpetuated "Jap Crow," along with its standing policy of Jim Crow segregation.[36]

A large percentage of Block 42 at Tule Lake refused to answer the questionnaire at all to protest the denial of their civil rights as incarcerated American citizens. Threatened with $10,000 fines, twenty years in prison, or both, this group was first sent to Alturas and Klamath Falls county jails. Because they had committed no actual crime with which they could be charged, however, they were sent back to Tule Lake. Here, in a no-person's land in which the Constitution had already been violated, the WRA was able to confine the men in a prison within a prison—the "isolation center"—for as long as it deemed appropriate. Finally, Nisei like Riley O'Suga who had volunteered to serve in the military immediately after the war broke out but who had been rejected precisely because of their Japanese ancestry, found the turn of events painfully ironic. If the army had accepted their original applications, they would already be contributing to the war effort. Given their incarceration, however, many of these men were no longer willing to put their lives on the line. Then, as now, acts of resistance that actually demonstrated one's commitment to the democratic principles on which the nation was founded, such as standing up against injustice, were misinterpreted as signs of disloyalty though, in reality, they embodied the very best of American ideals.

Throughout the tumultuous spring of 1943, the loyalty questionnaire had made a bad situation only worse in all the camps. One year into Tule Lake's existence, there was absolutely nothing to celebrate. In the special "Anniversary Edition" of the *Tulean Dispatch*, issued on May 27, 1943, an editorial written by then editor-in-chief, Tsuyoshi Nakamura, made this painfully clear. Titled "Not a Day for Celebrating," Nakamura observed:

> [The occasion] is not one which calls for boisterous celebration for the events of the past year, the mental anguish and heartache experienced by the evacuees do not make a proper theme for celebration. The word anniversary connotes some sort of an accomplishment over a given period of time. It usually implies success. This term then is not a fitting one for us since we are not accomplishing anything by our isolated existence here. A second anniversary would be tragic for it would be an indication that we are gradually becoming accustomed to this purposeless life. During an anniversary event, one usually receives congratulatory messages; on this our anniversary date, messages of condolences would be much more appropriate.[37]

Nakamura emphasized instead the resettlement program: "Messages of congratulation should be addressed to those who have successfully relocated and are now a part of a normal community life. On this date then we should firmly resolve to follow in their footsteps so that a year from now will not find us still living behind barbed wire fences."[38]

The final issue of the *Dispatch Magazine*, published in July 1943, similarly focused on whether to remain in camp or resettle as promptly as possible. In a sermon he preached in the Tule Lake Union Church, Reverend Shigeo Tanabe encouraged resettlement, but also called into question whether becoming part of a "normal community" was likely for Japanese Americans while the war raged on because of the "rising tide of racial antipathy over the country against us in these Centers."[39] Nonetheless, Reverend Tanabe cautioned his congregants against fostering the "deep-seated habit" that could develop among the incarcerated to "blame somebody out there, sometimes the government, sometimes the army, sometimes the general public outside, for the plight [they were] in." Though Tanabe admitted that the "evacuation has been a terrible failure from every point of view," he also preached to his listeners that maintaining an "unforgiving attitude" about it will "warp your personalit[ies]."[40] Instead, he urged inmates to "fight for democracy and human freedom" where ever they resettle by being "prepared to live with all races" in "the brave new world" into which they would soon reenter.[41]

In hindsight, it appears that resettlement, despite its anxiety-inducing unknowns, may have been preferable to staying in Tule Lake, given the troubles that accompanied its transformation into the only official segregation center. Disputes between the "Old Tuleans," those who were sent to Tule Lake originally, and those transferred from other camps, were common. Many of the Old Tulean "disloyals" were already angry because of the questionnaire. The ballooning of the population of "disloyals" from other facilities, which further taxed scarce resources, only exacerbated negativity.

By September 1943, the camp newspaper published a "Farewell Issue," marking its own demise as the camp shifted from the Tule Lake Relocation Center to the Tule Lake Segregation Center. Over the course of that spring and summer, nearly 12,000 inmates whom the government deemed "disloyal" were moved into Tule Lake, while approximately 6,000 "loyal" prisoners were moved out and sent to one of the other nine camps. Once again, it was necessary for inmates to try to forge a new community among people forced to live together but who had little in common other than sharing Japanese ancestry. The *Tulean Dispatch* city editor, Kunio Otani noted in a front page editorial titled "The Final Chapter" that "segregation means that once again we are faced with the difficulty of parting from friends, relatives—even our parents, in some instances" and starting over from nothing.[42] The "loyalty questionnaire" proved to be a stateside government bomb thrown into already toxic circumstances that left permanent scars as it tore apart families, in some instances, and entire communities, in others.

7

Wartime Novels

Toshio Mori's *The Brothers Murata* and Hiroshi Nakamura's *Treadmill*

The first postwar literary work to address how the loyalty questionnaire affected Japanese American communities was John Okada's novel, *No-No Boy*. It was published in 1957 by a Japanese press which printed it in English and distributed in the United States because no American presses would accept it. Miné Okubo's *Citizen 13660* had been welcomed by the War Relocation Authority and was well received by the public as evidence of the virtue of the formerly incarcerated seeking membership in communities across the country. Few readers in the United States, however, either within the Japanese American community or outside it, were receptive to Okada's novel. As Okada's biographer, Frank Abe, describes, by 1957 a novel about war resisters in the camps was not something anyone—neither Japanese Americans nor the white majority—wanted to recall.[1]

Part of this disinterest was based in the collective national shame that surrounded the event, but part was also based in the painful realities of the subject matter: *No-No Boy* explored how the demand for proof of loyalty among Issei and Nisei irrevocably affected Japanese American families and communities. Okada himself had volunteered for the military from Minidoka, but his novel examines the fallout experienced by Ichiro Yamada, a fictional character who resisted the draft and was consequently imprisoned for two years following his two years of confinement in a relocation center. The title is a bit confusing: the phrase "no-no boys" actually refers to those who answered "no" to questions twenty-seven and twenty-eight on the loyalty questionnaire. These men were sent to Tule Lake for segregation. But Ichiro, the protagonist of *No-No Boy*, is part of a different group of actual draft resisters: those who answered "yes" to one or both of the two questions, but who still refused to serve to protest being drafted into the army from the very camps in which the government had incarcerated them. Men who were imprisoned for committing crimes could not be drafted into the military,

That Damned Fence. Heather Hathaway, Oxford University Press. © Oxford University Press 2022.
DOI: 10.1093/oso/9780190098315.003.0008

they reasoned, so how could those who were similarly imprisoned but had committed no crimes?

Led by a group describing themselves as the Fair Play Committee at the Heart Mountain, Wyoming camp, draft resisters saw their response as an act of civil disobedience, demonstrating their objection to the denial of their civil rights as defined by the First Amendment to the US Constitution. The First Amendment preserves the freedoms of speech, religion, assembly, and the right to petition the government for redress of grievances. For the draft resisters, refusing to serve in the United States military until after their rights as citizens were restored fell clearly under the protection of the right to petition for the redress of grievances. Unfortunately, however, the federal district court in Cheyenne, Wyoming, did not agree and in two separate court decisions in 1944, resisters were sentenced to up to three years of additional incarceration in two federal prisons: McNeil Island Federal Penitentiary near Tacoma, Washington, and Leavenworth Federal Penitentiary in Kansas.

Okada's novel explores the impact the loyalty questionnaire had on the Japanese American community. Draft resisters were judged by those who enlisted as unpatriotic. Soldiers who had been wounded in war bore hostility toward those who refused to serve, as did the families of soldiers who had been killed. Generational conflicts arose as well. Some Issei parents felt abandoned by their Nisei children who either volunteered or were drafted, while other Issei were ostracized by Nisei because of their continued allegiance to Japan. In *No-No Boy*, Ichiro's mother cannot accept that Japan did not win the war and retreats into delusion while Ichiro, embracing his identity as both Japanese and American, resents her views. *No-No Boy* teases out all these tensions and shows how the careless imposition of the loyalty questionnaire by the War Relocation Authority permanently altered social and familial bonds in postwar Japanese America.[2]

Two less well-known literary works, both written while the authors were incarcerated, illuminate the fear, confusion, and disarray the questionnaire caused when it was originally distributed in the camps, in the early spring of 1943: Toshio Mori's *The Brothers Murata* (2000) and Hiroshi Nakamura's *Treadmill: A Documentary Novel* (1996). *The Brothers Murata* focuses solely on the impact of the questionnaire on two brothers who take different stands on enlisting, to shocking ends. *Treadmill* provides the most comprehensive fictional rendering of life inside an American concentration camp and raises issues such as sexual assault and suicide that few writers were willing to address.

Mori dedicates *The Brothers Murata* to his own brother, "Kazuo, ex-sergeant, 442nd Infantry" and to his parents and family. Kazuo did serve in the military and was seriously wounded in the war while Toshio stayed in camp, and though the plotline of *The Brothers Murata* is similar, no evidence suggests that Mori's novel is autobiographical. In the opening scene, Hiro, the younger of the two siblings, returns to Topaz from his induction physical at Fort Douglas in Salt Lake City. On the train, other members of his group refer to a movement in camp among those who were evading the draft, led by Hiro's brother, Frank. Frank's role in the movement is news to Hiro. "Hiro shook his head. 'I can't see why a Nisei should refuse to fight for his country—unless he's a coward. . . . I won't believe it till Frank says so. It can't be my brother—not Frank.' "[3]

Eventually, however, Hiro learns that Frank is, indeed, refusing to serve, and the difference in beliefs between the two brothers sets up the main conflict of the novel:

> "You're smearing our name," [Hiro said.] . . . "Have you forgotten what Papa said to us? Please, Frank, remember his wish."
>
> Frank inhaled slowly. "I do remember Papa's words. I also remember his teachings. He was a man of peace—do not forget his philosophy of harmony. It was his dream that someday there will be harmony among the people of the world. And I am working for that harmony."
>
> "But your attitude is contrary to Papa's love for the United States," protested Hiro. "What good is your work if you destroy it?"
>
> "By fighting for our civil rights I show love for the American way of life, am I not?" asked Frank blandly. . . . "I don't like war which kills human beings and brings destruction to mankind. I don't want any part of this war or any other wars, and I'm willing to risk my life and freedom for this conviction."[4]

Hiro, the protagonist, supports the war, and that includes engaging in the violence of combat, if necessary. Frank, the antagonist, supports a pacifism that ironically and tragically, in the end, generates violence both within the camp and against himself. Their deceased father can simultaneously embrace American patriotism and a Buddhist-tinged pacifism, but his sons' inabilities to do the same results in disaster.

Mori portrays the men's contrasting views as microcosmically reflecting the macrocosmic divisions that pervaded many of the camps. Two oppositional groups emerged in many of the relocation centers, and violence between them was not uncommon. In the novel, Mori depicts this conflict through two scenes: one in which Hiro is mugged and beaten up by an unknown group as he walks back to his quarters late one evening, and another in which he and his mother are victims of a nighttime assault in their quarters, during which Hiro is seriously injured. Since Frank is a leader of the resisters and has moved into a friend's quarters by the time of the break-in, Hiro is painfully uncertain about the degree to which his brother might have been involved in the attacks.

Their widowed mother is caught in the middle. Because Hiro volunteered, his mother is shunned by fellow Issei. She defends her son publicly, to a packed mess hall:

> I have heard many times, both directly and indirectly, the harsh criticism coming our way. And why do we receive this treatment? Simply because my son here volunteered for the Army. Before that, you counted us as one of you. Now, we are ostracized."[5]

She explains that, as a mother, she certainly does not want him to go to war either: "I raised him so he could, in my old age, give me comfort and support. I did not want him to die. I wanted him; I need him. It was cruel that he must go."[6] But she accepts his reasons for enlisting:

> And what are his reasons for volunteering—volunteering from a concentration camp, if you consider it so? What makes him risk his hide when he does not have to? He volunteered, fellow people, because he does not know any country but this land. He does not know Japan; he does not know England nor Russia nor China. He does know the place where he was born and raised. He does know its familiar way of life, and don't tell me that that is unimportant. The way some of you Issei speak adoringly of your mother country shows what the early ties could do to individuals.[7]

She announced to the room, now stunned into silence: "It is not your business if my son wishes to serve his country. It is he who is risking life—not you. And if he believes it is worthwhile, you or anyone else have no right to stop him—not even his mother."[8]

Hiro's decision to serve also puts his girlfriend, Jean, in an awkward position. Jean chooses to stay with Hiro in Topaz against the wishes of her parents who are being transferred, along with other "disloyal" Issei, to Tule Lake and they want her to accompany them. As tensions rise in the camp, Jean threatens to leave Hiro unless he does something about what Topaz's community of army volunteers define as "the opposition's most powerful weapon. . . . Frank Murata."[9]

> "What are you going to do about your brother?' she insisted doggedly. 'I don't see how you can sit still and watch him toy with you like a baby. . . . Frank is making life miserable for me. . . . You must do something about him. I cannot remain with you unless you stop him."[10]

These competing allegiances force Hiro into a corner. When his friend Tad Aihara asks him how he will contend with his brother, Hiro cannot say:

> He was honest with himself. He did not know what to do; he did not see how one was to do what he must do. But he knew for certain that he must meet whatever is to come, whenever the day. And then he would have to act precisely, swiftly, wisely.[11]

At this point in the tale, Mori leaves Hiro's intentions ambiguous, but toward the end of the novel the two brothers again come together over the words of their father.

During a visit from Frank while Hiro is recuperating from the assault, Frank tells his brother that he has received induction papers from the local draft board. Frank tells Hiro that he will refuse to appear and Hiro urges him to think of their father.

> "I remember his sayings, Hiro," Frank said softly. He placed his hand on Hiro's shoulder. "Did he not say this: 'Man must fight for what is right to reach harmony, and God made us so each one of us has a spark capable of giving light to others.' "
>
> "You remember, yes," [Hiro responded]. "Are you following them?"
>
> "Yes," [Frank replied]. "I'm working for harmony just as much as you are. You said this war is a process for the coming harmony and that we are participants, did you not?"
>
> "Yes. And you said by refusing to participate you are working for harmony!"

"I did," Frank said, nodding in assent. "Did he not say, 'Harmony results from clashes of ideas'? It is a process with trials and errors. I may make mistakes on the way but fundamentally I shall be on the right road."

"Remember what Papa said about willingness?" [Hiro] asked in turn. "He said that it is the will to harmonize more than anything else which will save the people's world. That is what he told us, remember?"

"Yes." Frank rose to his feet and stretched his arms. "And where does this get us? We agree here and then disagree in action. Why can we not get together? We're both fighting for harmony."

"Yes. I will fight on the battlefield and you behind the front." Hiro looked squarely in his [brother's] eyes. Then his eyes softened.[12]

As in his story "The Trees," Mori creates two figures who cannot come to a mutual understanding. In *The Brothers Murata*, both believe in "harmony" but see different ways to achieve that. The consequence of this disharmony turns out to be deadly.

Frank's refusal to enlist results in his impending incarceration by the FBI. Prior to his departure, however, Hiro invites Frank for a weekend in Salt Lake City: "It'll be the last time together for a long while. . . . I can get the short-term leave for us right away. We can make it this weekend," Hiro urges. Frank agrees, figuring it "would be [his] last fling" for some time. Hiro is eager to take his brother to the top of the Alta building which, he tells Frank, "makes you almost believe you're in San Francisco again. The foggy mist over the city reminds you of the bay, and the lake looks like an ocean." He wants to "do the town red. . . . The city lights and traffic" are awakening, Hiro enthusiastically tells Frank. "It's a tonic."[13] The two appear at last to have found the harmony which their father urged.

Mori's ending to the story, however, is utterly unexpected. In the final scene, as the two men admire Salt Lake City from the top floor of the skyscraper, Frank leans out the window and Hiro pushes him to his death. "In one swift, surging moment, Hiro charged forward and pushed him out the window. Down below, screams and shouts froze the air. A police whistle blew shrilly. Far away, a siren began screaming."[14] Mori's portrayal of Hiro's reaction to what he just did, kill his brother, conveys the ambivalence about loyalty that underscores the novel as a whole. At first, "leaning heavily against the wall, [Hiro] violently shook his head. His legs, bent and trembling, buckled under him. He sat there, his eyes unseeing and staring, his mind racing with thoughts. Take a cut. Follow through. Go all the way.[15]

Throughout the story, Mori invests militaristic and masculinized clichés like the slogans here—"take a cut, follow through, go all the way"—in the willing-soldier-Hiro's mind as he struggles to reconcile with his brother. At another moment in the novel, for example, Mori portrays another of Hiro's interior monologues:

> You must time yourself. Timing counts a lot, my boy. You must work with time. You must be ready; you must be at the peak of efficiency at the momentous time. You must jive with time. Okay. Patience, my boy. . . . You are the butt now. You are the receiver of foul names. They spite you for what you have done. *What have I done?* . . . You're finished, through, according to them. They know you. They sized you. Not by a long shot, eh? They do not know you, bub. . . . They do not know this in you: You will not stand for it when they come to crush your spirit. *Yep, I am the bub who takes his spirit straight.* You need spirit. Spirit is you. Without spirit you are not you.[16]

Within the context of Mori's other writings, this language and its message sounds stilted and foreign. In *The Brothers Murata*, however, Mori uses it at moments when Hiro is trying to convince himself of something, based on stereotypical notions of masculinity—of enlisting, of protecting Jean, of outsmarting Frank. Like a good soldier, in these moments Hiro puts "the cause" before his own personal ethics. Mori leaves readers with this chilling final image of Hiro, seemingly now cool as a cucumber as he exits the building while his brother lies, dead, below: "Then slowly and deliberately, he rose to his feet. As he walked toward the elevator and before pressing the button for 'down,' he pushed back his hair and straightened his tie."[17]

In this deceptively complex modern morality tale, Mori deliberately challenges readers to question who is in the right? Hiro or Frank? The killer or the killed? The soldier or the pacifist? The conformer or the rebel? Most importantly, which brother fills which role?

Mori suggests that the trauma of being rejected and imprisoned by the only country one has ever known, through the fault of none of the incarcerated, can lead Hiro to justify harming others, including his own brother. The experience of incarceration and the pressure to prove one's allegiance to the United States has warped Hiro's morality and perspective. By contrast, Frank's response to the same trauma is empathy—to try to see the problem from his brother's perspective. He chooses to move out of his family quarters, for example, so the relationship with his brother is not destroyed by their contrasting views. He visits Hiro when he is injured, clearly suggesting that he was not involved in the brutality inflicted on his mother and brother. He is able to disagree peacefully with both his government and his brother. Considering the flawed reasoning of frightened human beings, however, this allegiance to pacificism mistakenly marks him as the conveyor of injustice. In reality, however, it is just the opposite.

In keeping with Mori's brilliant and challenging writing in his short story collection, *Yokohama, California,* and in *TREK, The Brothers Murata* is a masterpiece of subtlety. Mori presents a complex ethical dilemma without providing readers an easy solution. Frank's purist pacifism results in his followers perpetrating violence on those who disagree with them, as is illustrated in their beating of Hiro. Hiro's commitment to going to war in the name of the type of harmony urged by their father, distorts his thinking in a way that allows him to rationalize murdering his own brother. What path is noble, in a Buddhist sense? In the end, Mori places the burden of the decision on us, his readers.

If Mori's *The Brothers Murata* is philosophically abstract, Hiroshi Nakamura's *Treadmill: A Documentary Novel* is the opposite. It is a realist work directly based on Nakamura's own experiences in the Salinas Assembly Center, Poston, and Tule Lake. Little is known about the author beyond a brief biography provided by his wife and daughter. Nakamura was born in Gilroy, California, in 1915. By the time the war hit, he had attended San Jose State College and the University of California at Berkeley, graduating from the latter in 1937 with a major in zoology and a minor in journalism. He then took a job as an English editor and translator in the Manchurian branch of a Tokyo-based newspaper, but when international tensions heated up, he returned to the United States. According to his family, he was in the photography business when Pearl Harbor was bombed.

Treadmill is Nakamura's only novel, though he had written short stories prior to the war under the name Allen Middleton. Middleton, his wife and daughter explained, was a literal translation of Nakamura, and the writer thought that using this Anglo pseudonym might pave the way for publication. He was mistaken; none of his short stories made it into print. As for so many Japanese Americans, the war radically altered Nakamura's career path and forced him out of journalism. Unable to find employment in that field after the war, Nakamura, his wife, and several of their siblings opened a small grocery store after the war in Los Angeles. Nakamura did attempt to get *Treadmill* published during the 1950 but he did not succeed. As his wife, Mary Sato Nakamura explains, "several publishers liked *Treadmill* but wrote to him that they could not publish it because they feared publishing it could damage their reputation. They were probably afraid of being considered a pro-Japanese publishing house because of the pervasive anti-Japanese sentiment throughout the nation at that time."[18] With that, Nakamura gave up writing. He died prematurely at age fifty-eight, in 1973, of stomach cancer.

Fortunately, the sociologist Peter Suzuki discovered a typed manuscript of *Treadmill* in 1974 in a box in the National Archives. How it arrived there is unclear, but Suzuki recognized its significance immediately. As a sociologist, he was interested in the window into daily life in a camp that it offered and he compared various plot elements to the historical events that took place during the war to test its veracity. It came out as sound, as truly the "documentary" novel that Nakamura intended it to be. Suzuki praised the author's "acute ethnographic eye, . . . respect for historical accuracy, . . . and considerable courage" in writing the work while incarcerated. He also admired Nakamura's boldness in trying to publish a novel that presented the truths of the camps during a postwar era when many Nisei chose to be silent about or at least temper their discussions of the incarceration.[19] Not until 1996, however, was Suzuki able to bring the novel into print.

Suzuki's admiration for the historical accuracy of *Treadmill* is well founded: Nakamura's preface, which unfortunately was not included in the 1996 publication, is a harbinger of the realism contained within its pages.

> This is the story of Teru Noguchi, American daughter of Japanese ancestry. This is the record of a people in bewilderment forsaken by their land of adoption.
>
> We were forced from our homes. We were herded into confinement as a demonstration of loyalty. Yet we were denied the rights of loyal men. Not understanding why nor knowing where, with the whole of our worldly goods clutched tightly in our hands and trying desperately to keep together the ties of blood, we stumbled wearily through shocking heat and stifling dust—without liberty, without home, with uncertain future.
>
> We cheered in darkness on the dregs—of disillusionment, of bitterness, of hopelessness; we cheated, we lied, we were honest, we were brave, we

> stood on the hot burning sands and made our decisions, each according to his conscience.
>
> We were different, we were human. Even as you.[20]

Indeed, Nakamura left close to nothing out of his novel. *Treadmill* captures the full humanity of the incarcerated, both good and bad. Nakamura presented aspects of daily existence that have largely gone undocumented elsewhere and these provide a reminder of the individual tragedies that underlay this national nightmare.

Nakamura gives us rare portrayals, for example, of both sexual assault and unplanned pregnancy in the camp. In one scene, young women in the latrine discuss the difficulty of experiencing menstrual periods in a public bathroom and one-room family "apartments" without walls. "'Those times are the worst,'" says one character. "'I don't think the army took account of us. This is a man's world.'"[21] Someone follows up with the comment, "'poor Michiko,'" to which another replies, "'Who was it?'"—that is, who is the father of Michiko's baby, a conversation catalyzed by the talk of menstruation. Other women in the latrine respond that "no one knew. The night watchman who flashed his light in on the oblivious pair in a corner of the mess hall described him as being kind of hefty and wearing a bright plaid shirt. 'But no pants,' he said subsequently."[22]

Nakamura describes how the pregnant Michiko becomes the subject of both gossip and derision:

> The story spread fast and everyone who had ever noticed trim, sparkle-eyed Michiko . . . focused no further than 79-C where Michiko lived. . . . Teru stared curiously at Michiko after she heard the story at the office. . . . Michiko squirmed under [Teru's] innocently searching eyes. She thought in panic, God, even Teru knows. Why didn't I stop him?[23]

Nakamura characterizes unplanned pregnancies as being open secrets in the camp, given the lack of privacy: "There were always the four or more unfortunate 'incidents'" that were commonly known.[24]

Michiko's thought, "why didn't I stop him?," raises the painful question of whether she freely consented to the sex. Remarkably, Nakamura tackles this problem head on by providing what may be the only fictional presentation of a rape in the camps. A female character, Alice, is sexually assaulted by Pete, an acquaintance, in an empty barrack after a dance. At first, Alice willingly leaves the dance with Pete, but then she becomes nervous as they move into an abandoned block:

> "This is far enough. Let's go back," Alice unsuccessfully tried to keep the worry out of her voice. She looked around at the empty barracks and shivered.
>
> "What's your hurry?" Pete's hand slid around her waist and pulled her close. His heavy hand searched for and found her breast.
>
> Alice gasped and jerked away from his hold. She ran and stumbled and he caught up with her. He grabbed her.
>
> "I'll scream."
>
> "Don't be such a baby," Pete said hoarsely.
>
> "I want to go back," Alice sobbed.
>
> "Sit down here a minute, and rest first," Pete said. "You don't want to go back all out of breath."
>
> He was strong and he easily pulled her down on the doorstep with him. He tried to get her to look at him.
>
> "What's the matter?" he asked. "When we were dancing, I thought you felt like I did."
>
> He covered her firm breasts with his hands and cupped them tightly. "It won't hurt," he whispered urgently.
>
> "No," Alice said between sobs which grew more violent and audible.
>
> "People will hear you here," Pete said. "Let's go inside until you get over it."
>
> He eagerly supported her into the darkened barrack and carefully closed the door behind him.[25]

Nakamura's portrayal of this is striking given the sensitivity of the topic and postwar efforts to portray Japanese Americans in only the most positive light.

Because, in part, of the shame suffered by victims, very little has been written about sexual assault in the camps. One other novel, *City in the Sun*, published in 1946 by Karon Kehoe, a white camp administrator who worked at the Gila River camp, alludes to something similar when she depicts a young boy returning from an encounter with a soldier behind the barracks, bearing candy and a great deal of shame. Kehoe only hints toward a molestation probably because of the risks she would face, as a closeted lesbian, for exposing such abuses in the camps.[26] But it is not unlikely that such violations occurred, especially in settings of such great power differentials between administrators and incarcerees.

In *Treadmill*, Nakamura portrays Alice, like many sexual assault survivors, telling no one about the rape. Because she has no means by which to end the resulting pregnancy, Alice's trauma is ultimately exposed when she is unable to hide her morning sickness from her mother:

> Mrs. Sakaguchi called anxiously, "Alice, aren't you getting up this morning again?"
>
> There was no answer from the cot in the corner.
>
> "It will get to be a habit, so get up," she said and pulled back the blankets.
>
> Her daughter's scared, wide-awake faced peered up at her.
>
> "I don't feel like eating," Alice protested.
>
> "Don't you feel well?" Mrs. Sakaguchi asked, her mind frozen with the worry that had been in her ever since Alice had come home with her dress torn and immediately gone to bed without stopping to tell her about the dance.
>
> "I just don't feel hungry," Alice said. Her face was pale and blotchy.
>
> "Alice," Her [*sic*] voice was tight. "Something hasn't happened, has it?"
>
> Alice stared pleadingly at her mother. She didn't say anything.[27]

The frankness with which Nakamura documents this entire episode in the novel testifies to his boldness and bravery as an ethnographer revealing hidden truths of the incarceration. His portrayal of Alice's father's reaction is similarly bracing and tackles another taboo issue in Japanese American culture at the time: social discrimination among groups within the community itself.

When Alice's father is told about the pregnancy, the question of her consent is not even on his radar. Rather, he responds with anger because Pete is an "etta." "Etta" or "eta" is a derogatory term used to refer to descendants of Burakumin, people historically discriminated against in feudal Japan because of their ancestral birthplaces and professions. Those whose work involved touching dead animals—butchery, mortuary, and tanning, for example—were considered defiled and were ostracized.[28] This discrimination continued well into the twentieth century. As recently as the 1970s, in fact, a Buraku rights group learned of a 330-page handwritten list of Buraku names and community locations that employers could purchase in order to vet their employees.[29]

Nakamura explains in *Treadmill* that in camp, "*Etta* [was] indicated quickly by four uplifted fingers meaning fourth class following the nobility, middle class, and low class." Through the character of Teru's mother, he elaborates:

> The origin of the *Etta* is rather obscure but I was told that they came from Korea a long, long time ago. The rich ones were immediately absorbed into Japanese society but the poor ones were economically forced to accept the most menial position [*sic*], especially the butchering of animals and of condemned people. That, together with their habit of eating meat, which was taboo, set them apart.[30]

Sadly, Alice's father is worried primarily about intermarriage with an "etta," not her well-being or that of her baby. "[The pregnancy] cannot be undone so I will not say anything further. It is the future I am concerned with. I don't want you to do anything foolish like the Kato girl did," he tells her.[31]

Alice's father refers to another young woman in *Treadmill*, Doris Kato, who is described as having "run off" with Ray Minami, implying that he, too, was an "etta." By contrast, Pete, Alice's rapist, had taken flight for the sugar beet harvest shortly after he assaulted her, so she was on her own. When Alice's father asks her whether she has any thought of marrying Pete, she responds affirmatively, albeit with deep reluctance on her own part: "she wished there were some other way out than marrying Pete. She was afraid to go outside to him." Her father retorts:

> "I want you to give up that idea. You must think of the family. Your mother and I are old and won't live much longer but Emily and Paul [Alice's siblings] will have to find a husband and wife someday. If you go through with this, it will be impossible to find suitable persons for them."
>
> "But if go away, won't it be all right?," [Alice asks].
>
> "You cannot run away from this. It is the same wherever Japanese are. Have you ever stopped to think why go-between[s] are always necessary for marriage even in this country [?] They are to eliminate the possibility of *Etta* antecedents in the family."[32]

Alice's father's rejection of Pete as an "etta," coupled with Pete's abandonment of her, forces her to deal alone with her rape, the pregnancy, and the community's likely discrimination against her unborn child.

Nakamura portrays the outcome of Alice's sexual assault as deadly. Plagued by despair and shame, Alice "walked blindly out of the barrack. She walked past the site for the proposed school buildings where the adobe bricks lay baking in the sun and headed west into the thick mesquite bordering the camp."[33] As she becomes disoriented, dehydrated and further humiliated, Alice worries:

> How would she explain the impulse that made her walk so far away from camp? . . . What would she do when she got back . . . ? She couldn't stay there. People would wonder why she'd run away. Why couldn't people mind their own business? You couldn't even have diarrhea without people knowing.[34]

A few days later, Nakamura describes, "they finally found her bruised and blood soaked body on the second day near the river opposite Camp I."[35] Nakamura leaves it unclear whether Alice's death is a suicide or an accident. Did she choose to give up to escape her shame or was her death a consequence of getting lost in the brutal desert heat of Poston? Regardless, the devastating commentary remains the same: women's physical vulnerability in the artificially public environment of the incarceration camp results in Alice's death.

Nakamura also depicts other predictable, but similarly unspoken, realities of living under the conditions of confinement. Communicable illnesses, prostitution, sexually transmitted diseases, and the gossip that accompanied these, all classic characteristics of overcrowded living, are described in *Treadmill*. Protagonist Teru writes in a letter to a friend, "Saburo Miyake, two barracks down, died of the measles last week. Measles! I didn't think people died of that anymore. People are afraid to get sick."[36] Through Teru, Nakamura also expresses inmates' recognition that they are being held on Colorado Indian Reservation lands and their awareness of what else could befall them:

> the Indians told [the older residents] . . . that when this Indian reservation was first filled, over half of the total number of Indians who were earmarked for this reservation died either on the march here or within the first months after arriving. They are surprised that we don't die off like they did.[37]

In contrast to the article in the *Tule Lake Dispatch Magazine* that celebrated Modoc leader Captain Jack's tenacity in fighting off the army, a character in *Treadmill* expresses the opposite. Using the term common at the time to refer to Indigenous groups in the United States, he worries that "maybe [the government] is trying to make Indians out of us" by confining them to the camp forever.[38]

Nakamura tackles another taboo topic in the novel as he describes Teru's mother, Ayame, experiencing a psychological breakdown after apparently suffering some type of heat-related stroke on the long journey from the Assembly Center to Poston. His fictional tale is in keeping with inmates' recollections of the trip to Poston. Rudy Tokiwa, for example, remembers that the day he arrived at Poston it was 114 degrees: "people were fainting like flies, because none of us prepared for any of this."[39] Nakamura sets the physical catalyst for the mother's illness in the story as taking place on July 4, 1942, Independence Day, under temperatures reaching 122 degrees Fahrenheit, something that was not atypical in the Arizona camps:

> The Fourth of July found their train rattling through desert country. The windows were pushed up as far as their rusty grooves would permit. The hot, dry air fanned through their crowded coach. They sprawled and shifted uncomfortably on the lumpy seats. They looked at the soldiers guarding the exits. They eyed the barren, forbidding desert and felt the growing hotness. The vague uneasiness looked out of their eyes and at each other. Teru anxiously kept an eye on her mother. All night, she jerked helplessly to the steady clanking of the rails and twice she heard a suppressed gasp from where her mother curled restlessly on the seat they shared. Her eyes were closed and sunk deep in their sockets. "Is there something I can do?" Teru asked when [Ayame] opened her lusterless eyes to stare out the window.[40]

Nakamura's realistic depiction of a child's worry about the health of her mother during the evacuation is complemented by his equally realistic rendition of parents' concerns about their young children. He describes one infant's face, in the story, as so "red and blotchy" that "they avoided looking at him. His face was bloated and his ears were swollen to twice normal size. [They] were afraid he was going to die."[41]

In *Treadmill*, the group, upon exiting the train in Parker, is ushered into buses that are even hotter than the outdated rail cars. Just as they are finally allowed to disembark, they are forced back inside the boiling buses because of a blinding dust storm. Teru notices that her mother, Ayame,

> was mumbling something. Teru bent closer to hear and for the first time noticed how alarmingly red hot her mother's face had become. "Mother, are

> you all right?" There was no response from the limply slumped figure. The mumbling continued. Suddenly Ayame shouted "Father, *Anata*, why aren't you here?" Her eyes opened wide and she stared wildly at Teru. 'Where is Father?' "[42]

Teru's father was not present because he had been taken away by the FBI on the night of the bombing of Pearl Harbor but her mother, in a delusional state, does not remember this.

Teru grows increasingly frightened about her mother's "incoherent mumbling . . . she was breathing rapidly" and her "forehead . . . turning hot with fever."[43] In *Treadmill*, Ayame never fully recovers from this experience. Nakamura portrays her as refusing to eat because she believed they were serving her grass, as not recognizing her husband when he returned from his imprisonment by the FBI, and as withdrawing emotionally from the family. Through Teru, Nakamura explains the long-term physical and psychological consequences of the incarceration for many.

> Mother isn't quite the same. She's been acting a little differently lately. She does things I've never seen her do before. Maybe camp life is changing her. Mrs. Omada was sent to an asylum in Los Angeles yesterday. A few days ago, she took to running around in her underclothes and they had to have her locked up. It was terrible hearing her screams at night. As if that weren't too much for Mr. Omada, Fay broke down completely from the strain of worrying about her mother plus working in the sweltering kitchen and was hospitalized this morning. Dr. Katayama doesn't hold out much hope of her pulling through. . . . No one can say that the heat is killing these people, but our hygiene teacher at J.C. told us that the death rate definitely rises during a heat wave, and so, I myself believe that those people would be living today if they hadn't been forced to come to this awful place. The wind is getting worse. The whole barrack is shaking and rattling like it's going to fall apart. It's scary.[44]

Medical records of psychological problems in the camps are difficult to locate in the archives, but other literary portrayals also underscore their reality. One of the most poignant can be found in Hisaye Yamamoto's 1950 short story, "The Legend of Miss Sasagawara."

Yamamoto, a member of the San Francisco literati prior to the war, was detained in Poston. She published only one story in the camp newspaper while she was incarcerated, "Death Rides the Rails to Poston." This was the first entry of what was intended to be a serial mystery, but the series never came to fruition. After her release, however, she resumed her writing career. She published "The Legend of Miss Sasagawara," the only story she explicitly sets in a camp, in the *Kenyon Review* in 1950.

This powerful tale records the experience of Miss Sasagawara, a ballerina who is incarcerated with her father, a Buddhist priest who is intent on achieving Nirvana:

> Wherever he was headed, however doubtless his destination, he always seemed to be wandering lostly. This may have been because he walked so slowly, with negligible steps, or because he wore perpetually an air of bemusement, never talking directly to a person, as though, being what he was, he could not stop for an instant his meditation on the higher life.[45]

Yamamoto portrays Miss Sasagawara as suffering from her father's disengagement. She isolates herself from others in the camp, does not eat in the dining hall, uses the latrine only when the risk of running into others is low, and speaks to almost no one, as the narrator notes:

> If anyone in the Block or the entire camp of 15,000 or so had talked at any length with Miss Sasagawara (everyone happening to speak of her called her that, although her name, Mari, was simple enough and rather pretty) after her first and only visit to use Mrs. Murakami's sewing machine, I never heard of it.[46]

Again, the tight quarters subject Miss Sasagawara to rumor and gossip: "Well, if Miss Sasagawara was not one to speak to, she was certainly one to speak of, and she came up often as topic for the endless conversations which helped along monotonous days."[47]

This was especially the case after Miss Sasagawara went to the camp hospital one night complaining of pain. After the bathrobed, elderly Dr. Kawamoto, who had already retired before being incarcerated, finds her healthy, she flees, wearing only a hospital gown:

> [T]he orderlies chased after her and caught her and brought her back. Oh, she was just fighting them. But once they got her back to bed, she calmed down right away and Miss Morris asked her what was the big idea, you

> know, and do you know what she said? She said she didn't want any more of those doctors pawing her. *Pawing* her, imagine![48]

Yamamoto skillfully imparts her narrator with a tone of disbelief tinging on ridicule that misunderstood people typically experience in ordinary society. The compact confines of the camp, however, only exacerbated this negative attention on those who suffered mental illness.

Yamamoto depicts how such individuals tragically become specimens of others' scrutiny: "The whole hospital staff appeared to have gathered in the room to get a look at Miss Sasagawara, and the other patients, or those of them that could, were sitting up attentively in their high, white, and narrow beds." The narrator states that she knew that Miss Sasagawara had to be aware of her status as spectacle:

> With her head slightly bent, she was staring at a certain place on the floor, and I knew she must be aware of that concentrated gaze, of trembling old Dr. Kawamoto . . . of Miss Morris, the head nurse, of Miss Bowman, the nurse in charge of the general ward during the day, of the other patients, of the nurse's aides, of the orderlies, and of everyone else who tripped in and out abashedly on some pretext or other in order to pass by her bed. I knew this by her smile, for as she continued to look at the same piece of the floor, she continued, unexpectedly, to seem wryly amused with the entire proceedings. I peered at her wonderingly . . . [as] Dr. Kawamoto, Miss Morris, and Miss Bowman tried to persuade her to lie down and relax. She was as smilingly immune to tactful suggestions as she was to tactless gawking.[49]

Yamamoto echoes Nakamura's portrayal of how inescapably public life in the camps was, which in itself could cause a mental collapse among more sensitive inmates.

As a result of Miss Sasagawara's "immunity" to the intrusions of others, she is sent away to Phoenix for treatment. Yamamoto portrays this temporary leave as healing for Miss Sasagawara. She characterizes the ballerina as much healthier upon her return to camp. Miss Sasagawara speaks freely to others and even offers ballet lessons to children. But this equanimity is short-lived. Miss Sasagawara, again isolated and detained, unravels once more.

One day Miss Sasagawara is observed by others, sitting on her porch, watching the Yoshinaga boys roughhouse in the barrack across from hers. Yamamoto describes Miss Sasagawara's expression as "beatific" as she is fully absorbed in the boys' play. Recalling the description of Sasagawara in the camp hospital, Yamamoto again portrays Sasagawara's "head [as] bent to one side and she actually had one finger in her mouth as she gazed, in the manner of a shy child confronted with a marvel." Yamamoto then disrupts this innocent reverie with a neighbor who accuses the forty-year-old dancer of inappropriately fantasizing about the young men. Miss Sasagawara, stunned by the charge, retreats inside and is heard banging loudly on the walls of the apartment "wildly, for at least five minutes. Then all had been still."[50]

Finally one night, in the ultimate blow to her inclusion in the community, Miss Sasagawara is discovered in the Yoshinaga family's quarters, "sitting there on [an] apple crate, her hair all undone and flowing about her. She was dressed in a white nightgown with her hands clasped on her lap. And all she was doing was sitting there watching him, Joe Yoshinaga," sleep.[51] This unusual behavior, though utterly harmless, was beyond tolerance in the conforming and confining culture of camp, and shortly thereafter, Miss Sasagawara was sent to a "state institution" in California.[52]

Yamamoto provides, through "The Legend of Miss Sasagawara," insight into how the absurdity of unjust incarceration, combined with gossip in the camps, challenged the stability of those who were, perhaps, more fragile than the majority. She suggests that Miss Sasagawara suffers from emotional and physical deprivation rather than mental illness. She depicts the narrator, who had recently returned from college outside of camp, as musing about Miss Sasagawara's condition:

> I, who had so newly had some contact with the recorded explorations into the virgin territory of the human mind, sagely explained that Miss Sasagawara had no doubt looked upon Joe Yoshinaga as the image of either the lost lover or the lost son. But my words made me uneasy by their glibness, and I began to wonder seriously about Miss Sasagawara for the first time.[53]

The narrator's self-doubt is well placed.

After the war, the narrator discovers a poem in a poetry journal by a "Mari Sasagawara." The journal described the author as, at the time of publication, "an evacuee from the West Coast, making her home in a War Relocation center in Arizona." The narrator notes that it was a "*tour de force*, erratically brilliant, and through the first readings, tantalizingly obscure." The poem focused on "a man whose lifelong aim had been to achieve Nirvana, that saintly state of moral purity and universal wisdom." His quest for this was limited by his duties to support a family.

When "unusual circumstances," however, which felt to others like "imprisonment," freed the man from having to make a living, he also felt free to "extinguish all unworthy desire and consequently all evil, and to concentrate on that serene eight-fold [Buddhist] path of highest understanding, highest mindedness, highest speech, highest action, highest livelihood, highest recollectedness, highest endeavor and highest meditation."[54] The serenity of the father was not shared by the daughter. The narrator concludes:

> This man was certainly noble, . . . this man was beyond censure. The world was doubtless enriched by his presence. But say that someone else, someone sensitive, someone admiring, someone who had not achieved this sublime condition and who did not wish to, were somehow called to companion such a man. Was it not likely that the saint, blissfully bent on cleansing from his already radiant soul the last imperceptible blemishes . . . would be deaf and blind to the human passions rising, subsiding, and again rising, perhaps in anguished silence, within the selfsame room? The poet could not speak for others, of course; she could only speak for herself. But she would describe this man's devotion as a sort of madness, the monstrous sort which, pure of itself, might possibly bring troublous, scented scenes to recur in the other's sleep.[55]

Yamamoto's artful portrayal of the "madness" induced by losing one's possessions, profession, and personal space; of the terror experienced by some when forced into communal living; of the jarring disconnect between being surrounded by people but fundamentally alone, reveals the psychological traumas of camp as few other fictional works do.

The most painful record of this type of suffering, however, is a real one. Ted Nagata was incarcerated with his mother and sister in Topaz. When interviewed by the Densho Project, Nagata recalled his mother's pain:

> My mother had a very hard time in Topaz, and the stress of incarceration and being called the enemy, and why was the government doing this? She was a college person, so she knew her rights. It just affected her to the point where she couldn't carry on. She never did recover from that. So my mother was a real casualty [of the incarceration,] and I'm sure there were many others, too.

When asked how this affected him, Nagata explained,

> Well, it made my sister and I grow up fairly fast because without our mother to help us, we had to learn and do many things ourselves, and many things we went without. I mean, like brushing our teeth every day and taking a bath every day, some of those kinds of things we lost out on, because we didn't have people pushing us to do it every day. And even after the war, when we came to Salt Lake, we were, my sister and I, were put into an orphanage because my father couldn't quite handle us and finding a job and trying to find a place to live.[56]

Clearly, the psychological wounds inflicted by the incarceration lasted long after Japanese Americans were released from the camps. Though the nation wished to look away from the tragedy, the experience obviously left multigenerational scars.

While Nakamura's depiction in *Treadmill* of the psychological effects of the incarceration is rivaled by Yamamoto's fictional rendition and Nagata's lived experience, his documentary novel provides the single most comprehensive portrayal of nearly all aspects of life during the incarceration. Nakamura records generational cultural disagreements among Issei, Nisei, and Kibei. He documents labor unrest, strikes, and hostilities surrounding pay discrepancies. He captures the military occupation and the infamous "stockade" in Tule Lake, the violence enacted on members of the Japanese American Citizens League who were perceived to be working in consort with the administration, and the effects of evacuation, incarceration, and relocation on families. Not surprisingly, Nakamura also vividly portrays the tension that arose as a result of the loyalty questionnaire, showing the wide range of attitudes held among family members and friends.

The views of the Nisei about the questionnaire were all over the map, and Nakamura documents this diversity through the opinions of Teru's friends. Jiro, a Nisei from Gilroy, for example, rejects the call to volunteer for an all-Nisei military unit because he resists segregation for any reason: "Why don't they just draft us like anybody else? Give us a chance to mix with *Hakujin* and lose our identity as Japanese.' "[57] Kenji Hosada thinks he will volunteer, not because he is loyal to the United States but rather to advantage his family: he reasons that having a relative in the military will make their resettlement less difficult. Henry Kitano refuses to voluntarily enlist or be drafted because he believes that the government is acting unconstitutionally by imprisoning

Japanese Americans in the first place. He believes that, in taking this stance, he is most loyal to the ideals on which the nation was founded.

Issei and Kibei perspectives were equally strongly held. Some Issei elected to repatriate to Japan as soon as possible, based on the belief that the racial discrimination provoking the incarceration would never disappear. Mr. Itaya, an Issei, expresses this view, noting that skin color is the ultimate arbiter of inclusion in the United States:

> There's no use trying to delude ourselves that we're American. If our skins were white, it would be another matter. Look at the Indians around here. They say they're discriminated against even yet. Then look at the white-skinned immigrants. They don't even have to be born here to be considered full-fledged Americans.[58]

A Kibei backs up Itaya by describing how unusual he found living Japan, a place where skin color matters not at all if one is Japanese American:

> I'm not sure you can appreciate exactly what I mean when I say you haven't really lived until you've lived as Japanese in Japan. . . . Any one of you can walk into the Imperial Hotel in Japan and feel perfectly at home. You can expect obsequious service in the best restaurants and barber shops you can find in Tokyo. You can go to movies and project yourselves in the hero's role or wait at the stage door for your favorite actress to come out. If a sudden bolt of lightening [*sic*] tells you that the beautiful girl sitting across the streetcar from you is the only girl for you, you can follow her home and lay siege with telephone calls and flowers and candy—with fond expectations. Most important of all, you might be held back in life by inefficiency, or not having influential friends, or plan laziness, but never because you're Japanese.[59]

Teru soon experiences this herself when she follows her parents to Japan.

Teru's father applies for repatriation and, though she has been given a reasonably good job offer in Cleveland, Ohio, as well as a proposal to marry from a Japanese American doctor, she feels obligated to accompany her parents and to care for them and her younger brother as they age. Teru's sister Sally, in contrast, decides to marry her boyfriend and to try to make a life together in Detroit, Michigan, despite her own rage about the incarceration. These decisions come at a major cost. In the farewell scene, Nakamura illustrates the sacrifices made by families who chose to part as a result of their incarceration:

> Teru was conscious of the surrounding babble of farewells and Godspeeds only as a dull roaring in her ears. Her eyes were on Sally. Sally smiling hard through tears. . . . Sally stripped bare of all pretense. Looking too young without makeup and with her lower lip clenched white between her teeth. Too young to be getting married. It shouldn't have been time for her to marry. It shouldn't have been time to say goodbye. Not for as long as this farewell seemed to portend.[60]

As Sally sobs, Teru offers faintly reassuring words: "'We'll see each other again,' . . . but she was thinking, I'm going to Japan. You're staying here. This is our last moment together."[61] Nakamura leaves readers hanging about whether the two ever are reunited, putting readers in the same position of uncertainty experienced by the real people on whom his novel was based. The final words of *Treadmill* are from Teru, to her sister, in a letter:

> We who have passed through the evacuation have learned a lot. We mustn't forget.
>
> God willing, we'll meet again. When or where is uncertain but let's pray it's soon.
>
> Love,
> Teru

The decimation of Hiroshima and Nagasaki in August 1945 took nearly everyone by surprise and Nakamura depicts how it altered the plans of many, such as Teru and her parents, who had intended to repatriate to Japan. Those who had requested the move now had to determine whether returning was reasonable. A large portion of those held in Tule Lake were from Hiroshima and were forced to presume that their relatives were dead. For others, all the money they may have invested in Japanese stocks, bonds, and banks was of no value. "The future [so many had] hoped for is gone," Teru laments. "Many are saying that starting all over again in a beaten and crushed Japan is an impossibility."[62] But relocation within the United States held no more appeal. Nakamura's novel reveals that the status of all those who remained in the camps at war's end, but of the Tuleans in particular, was perhaps at its most precarious since December 7, 1941.

Tule Lake was the last of the War Relocation Authority camps to close, on March 20, 1946. Eventually, the camp emptied and detainees tried to get on with their lives. Tule Lake's footprint faded from the landscape, but its marks remained on the individuals involved. Nakamura invests Teru with offering an ominous warning: "Goodbye, America . . . don't do [this] again. Follow your heart and no few people can dictate a façade of greed, intolerance, or bigotry."[63] We would do well to heed this wisdom.

8
Jerome's *Magnet*

Jerome and Rohwer were built on Arkansas swampland in the pre-civil-rights-era South, which firmly adhered to the strict lines of Jim Crow segregation. The influx of Japanese Americans challenged the rigid racial structure, adding an entirely new dimension to the social and political dynamics that inmates had to negotiate with locals both inside and outside the camp. Daisuke Kitagawa recalled in the late 1960s that no one "wanted to be sent to the two Arkansas camps. . . . The fact that those camps were located south of the Mason-Dixon Line made them unpopular, and there were all kind of rumors rampant about them."[1] The journalist Larry Tajiri, who, along with his wife Guyo, edited the *Pacific Citizen* during the war from Salt Lake City which was outside of the evacuation zone, commented in a letter to Margaret Anderson, editor of *Common Ground*, that he couldn't "get out of the south fast enough." He had been in New Orleans on business and found "the sight of the Jim Crow cars and the white/colored segregation . . . nauseating."[2] Japanese Americans felt an affinity with Indigenous Americans who had been placed by the government in a different type of confinement on reservations, and they also felt an alliance with African Americans, fellow "colored" in the "black–white" racial system of the South.

Jerome and Rohwer were unusual among the camps for other reasons as well. The mosquitoes were ubiquitous and reportedly so large that one inmate joked that they could be fried in tempura and made into a meal, and such a wide variety of snake species were present that another set up a display in his barrack of nearly forty different types. Opossum and other indigenous animals added to the mix. Instead of dry heat, bitter cold, and dust, heavy rains soaked the thick clay soil, creating a hot and humid climate on land that was undrainable during the spring months. In fact, some inmates fashioned this clay into functional bowls, plates, and cups. Here, too, detainees made creative and functional use of the natural resources that surrounded them.

Despite the commonalities between Jerome and Rohwer, however, the camp cultures were different in a variety of ways. Jerome was the last camp

That Damned Fence. Heather Hathaway, Oxford University Press. © Oxford University Press 2022.
DOI: 10.1093/oso/9780190098315.003.0009

to open (on October 6, 1942) and thus housed those who had spent the longest period in the horse stalls of the Santa Anita assembly center. This positively affected their perceptions of Jerome, in some instances. Fifteen-year-old Alice Setsuko Takemoto wrote in a letter to her father, an Issei who was arrested by the FBI and was being held at the Lordsburg prison in New Mexico, that the family was reasonably satisfied with the facilities at Jerome.

> It is hotter than California and colder than California. Here it is October but it still is quite warm in the afternoons when Wyoming is having snow. Mother is really glad that we came here. Colorado is a pretty bad place. Gila River is overcrowded with people and not enough living quarters. . . . This is really like a home compared to [the Santa Anita] horse stables.[3]

Jerome also had the lowest crime rate of all the relocation centers. According to a War Relocation Authority (WRA) semiannual report in June 1944, the combined crime rates in all the centers was three times lower than that in American cities of equal population; in its twenty months of existence only thirty-three violations took place.[4] But the single feature that made Jerome different from all other camps was unexpected: trees. The complex issues that arose from this characteristic, ranging from heating shortages to labor strikes to artistic productions, defined the experiences of detainees in Jerome.

The camp's literary journal, the *Denson Magnet*, comments on nearly all these issues. The *Magnet* appears to have been published only once, in April 1943. At twenty-two pages, it was shorter than other camp journals and consisted of seventeen pieces ranging from nonfiction editorials, articles, and "letters from outside," to a few short stories and poems. Contributors included WRA employees such as Chief of Reports Officer John C. Baker and former Tule Lake director Elmer Shirrell, whose articles discussed relocation and the importance of using the camp experience to train for work outside. Most pieces, however, were written by Jerome detainees themselves. According to the opening message from the camp director, Paul A. Taylor, the *Magnet*'s value included its ability to serve "as a tie of better understanding between the administration and the Center population."[5] A look into camp life suggests why this was needed.

Jerome was situated on heavily wooded and wet land that farmers defaulted to the government during the 1930s because it was too difficult to clear and drain. But Director Taylor, having worked for the US Department of Agriculture prior to leading the camp, believed that the area could be not only successfully deforested but also converted into arable land. His goal was to create a camp like Amache, a self-sufficient agricultural enterprise that could fuel and feed the camp population as well as contribute to the war effort by generating crops to be shipped across the nation. A key element of this plan involved heating the buildings with wood instead of coal, thereby rendering unnecessary the costly coal allocations from the WRA that were required by the camps in the intermountain west.[6]

Tree-felling, wood-cutting, and log-hauling is arduous labor, however, particularly in swampland and without proper equipment. Rain-drenched forest floors were impossible to navigate with trucks and tractors, so workers had to drag the lumber out of the woods themselves, sometimes with the assistance of mules, ropes, or sleds. Nearly everyone ended up participating, partly due to a serious fuel shortage during the first winter.[7] Mary Tsukamoto remembered:

> All of a sudden cold weather arrived, and they didn't have enough wood to heat the room. We were on the edge of the Mississippi River, the swamplands of Arkansas. We had to go into the woods to chop wood. All the men stopped everything; school, everything was closed and the young people were told to go out and work. They brought the wood in, and the women helped to saw it.[8]

Richard Itanga's contribution to the *Magnet*, "The Westerners Came Rumbling," also recalled the event:

> The evacuees were not without their worries, however; their biggest came when they faced that critical period in December and January when fuel wood to warm the Project's 2,300 odd apartments was needed immediately. An indefinite holiday was declared and every able-bodied man who could be spared trekked out to the "back yard" and started to fell trees in a feverish race with the weather. Fortunately, the clouds patiently held up their aprons full of water for three weeks during this crisis.[9]

Another inmate, Senbinshi Takaoka, who was known in his hometown of Stockton, California for his calligraphy, watercolor paintings, and freestyle haiku, captured his forced transition from poet to lumberman in *haiku*, a traditional form of Japanese poetry: "Frosty morning / handed a hatchet / today

I became a woodcutter."[10] Another man wrote: "Man carrying hatchet / in field near edge of forest / unable to see anything."[11]

The artist Henry Sugimoto similarly captured his transition from artist to woodsman in several of his paintings. *In Winter of Jerome Camp*, for example, he portrays himself, his wife, and their young daughter hauling wood logs in a wheelbarrow, under a winter sky.[12] Sugimoto was a respected oil painter prior to his incarceration, having trained at the California School (now College) of Arts and Crafts, the California School of Fine Arts (now

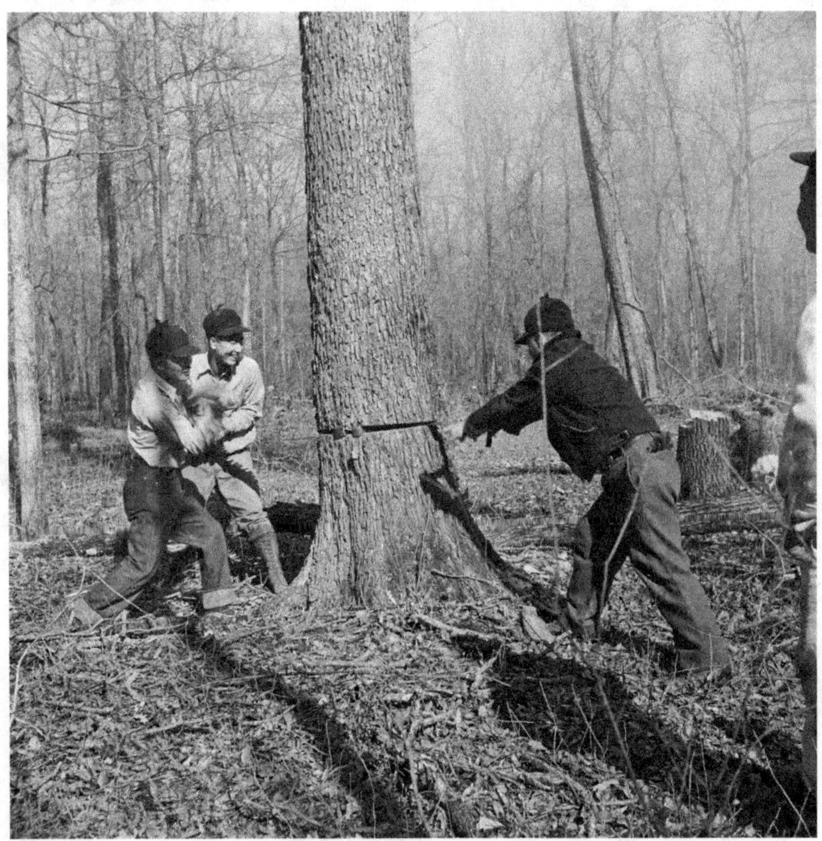

Inmates fell an Arkansas red oak at the Rohwer prison camp in 1943. The Arkansas camps used wood instead of coal to heat the barracks, and inmates were responsible for logging it. Inexperience with the job led to numerous injuries among the workers.

Photo by Tom Parker. Densho, ddr-densho-37-832, courtesy of the National Archives and Records Administration

the San Francisco Art Institute), and the Académie Colarossi in Paris. His work had been exhibited in Paris and throughout California and had been solicited by the Museum of Modern Art in New York. Prior to the war, he focused primarily on landscapes, using techniques influenced by French impressionism.

After being incarcerated, however, Sugimoto's subject shifted to the human form, and elements of the Mexican muralist José Clemente Orozco, another artist whom he admired, began to surface in his paintings. As in *In Winter of Jerome Camp*, Sugimoto focused on telling stories through his paintings.[13] In an interview from the 1980s, Sugimoto remembered:

> In the camp, you know, no good scenery, just barracks, that's all—that's why naturally I take as subjects children, farmer going to farm, you know,

Henry Sugimoto's painting *In Winter of Jerome Camp* depicts a family pushing a wheelbarrow full of wood to their living quarters. All hands, including those of children, were required to chop, collect, and transport this fuel source throughout the Arkansas winters.

Henry Sugimoto Collection, Japanese American National Museum (Gift of Madeleine Sugimoto and Naomi Tagawa, 92.97.90)

> the everyday life. We can go outside; I can paint outside the scenery. I have twenty to twenty-five outside-the-scene pictures. But mostly I concentrated on painting for a record.[14]

Around the Jerome Campfield is one of the pieces Sugimoto painted while in camp that does not involve human subjects, and the monotony conveyed by the bleak barracks and bland, swampy landscape colors suggest why he found the surroundings uninspiring.

By contrast, those paintings that Sugimoto created intending to "record" camp life, such as *In the Winter of Jerome Camp*. Another painting, titled *Am I an American Citizen?*, conveys both a political statement and an image distinctive to the Arkansas camps as it portrays two men wielding axes in the woods. One is seated on a cut log, holding his head in his hands in despair,

Henry Sugimoto's painting *Around the Jerome Campfield* shows the swampland that dominated the camp. The bleak colors of gray and blue convey the desolate and monotone nature of living in the two Arkansas prison camps.

Henry Sugimoto Collection, Japanese American National Museum (Gift of Madeleine Sugimoto and Naomi Tagawa, 92.97.75)

while the other man looks down on him, in a seemingly paternal gesture, offering comfort and consolation. Sugimoto titles this, *Am I an American Citizen?*, reflecting the confusion and alienation experienced by Nisei who found themselves incarcerated in their own land.

The ambition of Jerome administrator Taylor to clear the swamps for cultivation was shared by Rohwer camp director Ray Johnston. Rohwer was located roughly thirty miles north of Jerome, and the two directors pooled their resources, including human laborers, to accomplish their mutual goal. The detained were inexperienced and untrained in forestry, however, and by early 1943 the first death occurred as a result of their logging missions. On January 19, 1943, sixty-year-old Seizo Imada suffered a broken leg, fractured ribs, and severe damage to his hip and spine when a falling tree struck him. His fellow inmate Tom Otani attributed the accident to the strong wind blowing that day and inadequate supervision of the laborers. Imada died from his injuries at the hospital. In yet another tragedy, in October 1943, a trailer carrying woodcutters overturned, injuring all thirty-seven men on board. Six were seriously wounded and sixty-two-year-old Haruji Ego was paralyzed and then died in the hospital.

After the trailer accident and Ego's death, the workers called for a campwide strike. They secretly copied flyers and placed them in the mens' latrines to ensure every worker would be aware of the plan. The flyer caught people's attention with the bold headline, "To Be Or Not To Be—Suckers!! How the WRA Exploits You in the Wood Situation!!" It continued:

> "Chop, Chop," means "hurry up" in Chinese. For us evacuees it means chopping wood and doing that in a hurry before the cold spell hits us. But isn't it a laugh! We chop the wood while the appointed personnel sit on their fannies and use it up.

The flyer noted that "about 1,000 able-bodied men" had left the camp in the past year to resettle or to be shipped to Tule Lake because of their responses to the loyalty questionnaire, and yet the expectations about the amount of wood required to heat the "schools, offices and appointed personnel quarters," which obviously did *not* include the inmates' barracks, remained the same. "Who chops the wood? Most of the workers are old men in their fifties. They strain themselves and go to an early grave. For what? Sixteen dollars a month; fifty cents a day; less than seven cents an hour!"[15]

The flyer further accused Taylor of capitalizing on inmate labor for his own benefit:

> But chopping and hauling wood is half of it! We clear the land so that Taylor and his yes-men . . . can show the Arkansas big shots what a fine job THEY are doing in helping the state of Arkansas. And that state got the nerve to tell us that it doesn't want us; to get the hell out after the war![16]

The latter phrase refers to Arkansas's exclusion of Japanese Americans from settling in the state after the closing of the camps. Governor Homer Adkins had been opposed to establishing relocation centers in Arkansas from the outset and conceded only after Milton Eisenhower, the director of the WRA, guaranteed that all Japanese Americans would be held under armed guard. Adkins also prohibited anyone of Asian descent from remaining in Arkansas after the war.[17] "It's very simple," the flyer continued. "The more pressure the weather and the WRA puts on us to cut wood, the more we cut and the more land is cleared so that Taylor can brag about it to his pull-i-ticians! If this isn't exploitation, what is it?"

The flyer then called for a strike and listed the following as conditions for its cessation. First, the workers demanded that the schools, offices, and quarters of camp administrators and civilian workers be heated with coal, thereby reducing the amount of wood required to be processed by detainees. Second, they insisted that a surplus of coal be maintained so that, if the detained were unable to cut enough wood to heat their own quarters, they would still be able to keep their families warm. Third, they required that power tools rather than hatchets and hand saws be provided for the tasks at hand. Fourth, they petitioned that workers receive adequate compensation for injuries sustained on the job, citing a detainee/carpenter who was given only $12.50 for a broken arm, broken ribs, and lost teeth after falling from a roof while working on one of the appointed personnel's apartments. Fifth, they requested that food of sufficient nutritional and caloric quality be provided to sustain the workers during their arduous labor. Sixth, they demanded a wage increase, noting that "at one time the WRA wage scale was to be the same as that in the armed services. At the present rate, most evacuees are losing their savings" just trying to stay alive in camp. Finally, they insisted on the ouster of Taylor himself, along with any "anti-evacuee elements" who were working as appointed personnel.[18]

The Jerome workers employed a pattern of resistance that was common in the camps: using democracy's ideals to protest democracy's failures. The strikers stated that "we need a fair deal in this center. We are the loyal, but we are loyal to certain principles—justice, fair play, democracy." Taylor's response to any resistance in his camp was to impose increasingly draconian restrictions on inmates. He removed workers from more desirable jobs to work in the woods. He limited movement outside of camp, thereby preventing people from obtaining marriage licenses, attending funerals, or visiting hospitalized relatives in the nearby town.

Taylor's efforts to maintain authority failed, however. By November 1943, the "better understanding between the administration and the Center population" that Taylor allegedly sought in April was unattainable and he resigned his position. For his efforts, though, he was offered a position as the assistant to the director of the Bureau of Budget and Finance in the Department of Agriculture, thereby accomplishing his underlying motive—moving up the government work ladder. Still, Taylor admitted that directing the Jerome center was "the toughest job I have ever undertaken. I feel that the experience gained has been invaluable, but I hope that I have the good judgment never to tackle another job just like it."[19]

Despite the tumult over trees and labor practices at Jerome, the wooded environment, so different from that in all the other camps except Rohwer, did come with some advantages. Several pieces in the *Magnet* that focus on camp life reflect this. "Joe's Diary," penned by an anonymous contributor, describes both negative and positive initial impressions of Jerome. Having arrived there just five days after the camp's official opening to help construct the facilities (volunteers were solicited from all the assembly centers to help build the various camps), the setting stands out most to "Joe":

> Oct. 11, 1942
> Arrived early morning while still dark. First impression of Jerome bad. Everything in upheaval. Construction work still going full blast—lumber piled high and scattered everywhere. Gravel pits, mounds, and barb-wire fence "which a cow could jump over." Fresno induction crew stare curiously with hands in pockets. Lumber jackets, blue jeans, hats. Red arm bands. Morning mist all around.[20]

Upon seeing the barracks, however, Joe notes that the apartments are "large, roomy, light." Though the dimensions of the rooms at Jerome were identical to those in all the camps, here again, given the notorious "living quarters" to which the incarcerated were assigned at the Santa Anita racetrack, the barracks in Arkansas may well have been a marginal improvement.

Joe observes other notable features of Jerome: an October climate " 'just like California,' " soft water that "sure is slippery," "no censorship of mail" (this was not true, however) and according to one administrator, allegedly not one snake-sighting, as unlikely as that was. He also describes an Issei as telling him that the southern countryside reminded her of Japan: "Saw fireflies, heard 'semi' (Cicada) crying. Says there are many insects here in the woods just like in Japan. Her room commands a wonderful view of the forest. Trees surround her barracks, and logs can be seen piled alongside the road."[21]

Indeed, the woods provided a valuable diversion and retreat for Jerome inmates. In his October 31, 1942, entry, "Joe" described his parents' arrival from Santa Anita, noting that "Father [is] extremely enthused about place as we take walk along edge of forest. Mother thinks woods are beautiful." Later he describes the

> beautiful sunny autumn day; leaves on edge of forest changing into all autumnal hues of red, yellow; many people strolling along edge of forest; Issei sawing the moss-covered tree limbs to use for decorative purposes; old men filling a sack with nuts picked from an old, dried up pecan tree, which had been chopped. Leaves dry and crackling.

Rohwer and Jerome were the easternmost camps and located well outside Military Zones 1 and 2, so inmates enjoyed a bit more freedom of movement than in some of the other camps. The woods abutting Jerome proved to have a strong pull. Says "Joe," "sentries had difficulty keeping people off the inner road. People have natural desire to wander into woods. Sammy hunts for acorns with which to make a necklace. Issei cutting twisted and gnarled limbs to make switches, canes. Women taking home leaves of oaks, maples."[22]

In fact, the trees surrounding Jerome served both utilitarian and diversionary purposes. In addition to providing fuel for heat, harvested wood was used to provide necessary materials for the camp. The camp opened a cabinet-making facility and, according to an article in the March 16, 1943 *Denson Tribune*, it was one of the busiest shops in the camp.

> Since the opening of the shop in November, the workers have made approximately 1500 articles vitally needed in the administrative offices, hospital, schools and other departments. . . . Equipment made by the boys for various departments are X-ray stands, stretchers, pharmacist's cabinets, test tube racks, sterilizer shelves and laboratory technician's kits for the hospital; rice pan covers, rice steamers and wooden spatulas or shamojis for the mess halls; sorting tables and letter cases for the Post Office; file cabinets and boxes, tables and drawers for the Administrative offices. . . . Some of the recent orders filled by the shop are 60 book shelves and racks, 4 sand boxes and 200 benches for the Education department; 36 bridge tables, 30 ping pong tables and 144 stools for the Community Activities section.[23]

The same edition of the paper announced that wood would be delivered to each family to construct roofs over their front doors to help allay indoor damage during rain storms and that a model for building them would be provided by the cabinet shop.

Wood also served aesthetic and therapeutic ends at Jerome. In all the camps, local materials were used for arts and crafts. In Tule Lake, for example, residents made beautiful jewelry out of shells remaining in the dry lakebed. In Topaz, carved slate stones found in the area surrounding the camp were transformed into teapots. For Jerome residents, wood carving emerged as a pastime featuring both conventional wood and *kobu*. *Kobu* refers to galls, roots, and other wood growths that can be found at the bases and on the trunks of trees. The cypress swamps near Jerome yielded particularly unusual items. *Kobu* hunting made the long hours cutting wood more bearable as men hunted around for prize pieces to haul back to camp.[24]

Akiko Yamanaka's article in the *Magnet*, "They're Simply Beautiful," playfully comments on the ubiquity of these newly minted "artists" in Jerome. Told from the perspective of a female detainee, it provides instructions about how to thwart the carving impulse among husbands, sons, brothers, and fathers:

> Is there an artistic-minded brute by the name of "man" in your family, who is wildly enthusiastic about making flower vases, ash trays, match

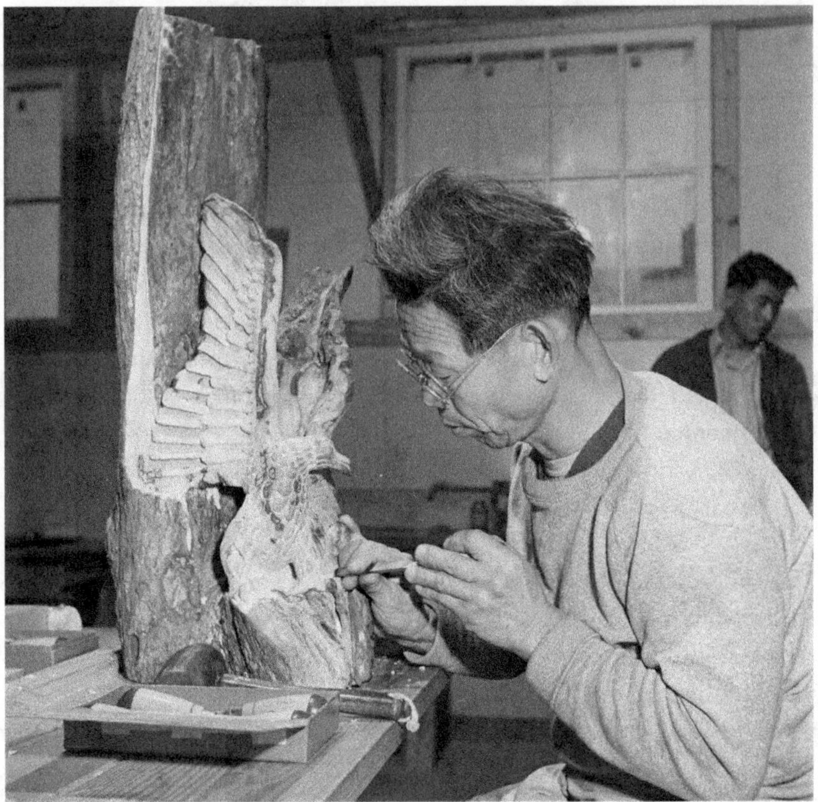

A Japanese American inmate carves a wooden eagle from a local tree stump at the Rohwer prison camp. Wood was not only a valuable natural resource with which to heat the camp, but it also provided a diversion for bored inmates who took up wood carving and furniture making as they awaited their release. The depiction of an eagle seems to be an effort for this man to demonstrate his patriotism under duress.
Densho, ddr-densho-37-551, courtesy of the National Archives and Records Administration

containers, and the like out of stumps, branches, and roots of trees? (Notice that I did not say that all products of these artistic-minded men are decorative, because some of the finished products are similar to poor samples of stove wood.) If you are one of the many patient ladies who is tired of seeing stump after stump of gnarled, decayed pieces of wood in your room, tired of cleaning up the shavings and saw-dust of the same left on the floor, and

> tired of agreeing with him that they're simply beautiful, it's right to for you to go into action.[25]

The author then offers a scheme by which to trick the husband into handing over his latest cache of worm-laden lumber for use in the potbelly stove. Although playful, this article provides another indication of how strongly wood—for better and worse—shaped the lives of those held in the Jerome facility.

All this said, the swamps and woods of Arkansas also brought with them a scourge of environmentally related troubles. Though most of the inmates had previously been inoculated against typhoid fever, diphtheria, smallpox, and whooping cough in the assembly centers—a necessity because of the crowded and unsanitary conditions in which evacuees were forced to live—the mosquitoes at Jerome also required that they take precautions against malaria.[26] Spring floods turned the clay soil into muck, making it very difficult to get from one's barracks to the various administrative buildings, including the hospital, school, and canteen. These trials, too, were documented in the *Magnet*.

A piece titled "We Never Dreamed" by Ikuko Kuratomi focuses solely on the climate and the unique challenges it posed for this easternmost group of inmates: "The weather is one of the most common subjects of casual conversations and a seldom-omitted one of letters. But in Arkansas the climatic conditions vary so much that the weather is a significant topic."[27] Though the tone is light, the spectrum of weather realities Kuratomi describes caused considerable hardship. She first recalls the rain:

> What were you expecting nature's gifts to be in the way of "things" from above? We were told water, and lots of it. Colder, too, than California. When we "unboarded" the train, we didn't meet with water from above, but on bottom. Oh, how muddy the ground was! It was so muddy that we delighted in its unusualness. We laughed as we made, or rather tried to make, our way to the barracks for we could hardly lift our feet from the sticky soil.... Then came the down pour. Having only ordinary shoes, one couldn't possibly go outdoors. Even with galoshes or boots, one would lose them in the mud.[28]

Facing such circumstances in the middle of the night on the way to the latrine was obviously far from funny. Being cooped up during the rainy season in the small apartments, now cluttered with multiple beds, cumbersome homemade furniture, and too many people, tested peoples' patience, compatibility, and mental health.

Kuratomi at once admires the beauty left behind by sleet storms that covered everything with ice and loathes "the unpleasant results of the beautiful sight" which turned the ground "from ice to slush to mud." She also recalls that Jerome detainees often "nearly froze when walking to work," never imagining, from the sunny skies of California, "that we could walk a half mile in temperatures below freezing point."[29] Such seasonal variations, all experienced during only the first five months of living in Arkansas, were shocking to many who came from year-round warmth.

Magnet contributors also commented on the "internal climate," or psychological states, of evacuees. T.D., identified only as a member of the Documents Section staff, contributed this:

A Wish

I'm just a little boy lost in "Japan"
I see soldiers standing by the gate
I see them high up on the guardhouse
They tell me I must stay inside the fence.

I'm just a little boy lost in "Japan"
Where are all my American friends?
Where is Johnny, and Tommy, and Dick?
I want to go home to America.

I'm just a little boy lost in "Japan"
I want to sleep in my own room again.
I want to crawl through the fence
And never, never see "Japan" again.[30]

T.D.'s piece recalls the vignette told in the Topaz magazine, *TREK*, that captured the confusion felt by a young Nisei boy about where he was and why. Both wanted to go home to "America." This is, perhaps, not surprising when we consider that many confined children had grown up in ethnically and racially mixed, or even predominantly white, neighborhoods. Now, they found suddenly being surrounded only by people of Japanese ancestry an unfamiliar experience. A former inmate interviewed by the Commission on Wartime Relocation and Internment of Civilians emphasized this point. Upon arriving at the camp, the inmate states:

> We were greeted by a few volunteers who went to help construct the camp a month before. As I got off the bus late that afternoon, I asked my mother, "What are we doing here with all these Japanese?" She answered, "Shhh, you are one, too." I had to deny this; I learned in school that I was an American.[31]

While the incarcerated adults were aware of their status as "hyphenated Americans," members of minoritized groups in the United States who were, nonetheless, citizens, Nisei children found this hard to comprehend.

The incarcerated painter, Henry Sugimoto, provides a most poignant rendition of this confusion in his painting *When Can We Go Home?* The painting is based on his own daughter's request, after they had arrived at the Fresno Assembly Center, to "go home" since they had already eaten the food they'd packed for what she thought was a picnic.[32] The majority of images Sugimoto painted in Jerome, such as *Family in Jerome Camp*, *Our Washroom, Jerome Camp*, *Susie in Camp Ironing Room*, and *Our Mess Hall*, capture realistically and straightforwardly the daily lives and activities of the detained. But, significantly, in *When Can We Go Home?* he departs in both style and subject. Though still focusing on his wife and daughter, his use of two stylistic techniques, cubism and montage, stand out.

Cubism had emerged as part of the modernist movement in the early twentieth century. Artists moved away from rendering an object from a single, coherent perspective and instead broke it into multiple elements, often viewed from multiple perspectives, in order to create a greater context for the image. In Sugimoto's painting, *When Can We Go Home?*, his daughter's plea is represented by her left finger pointing to architectural images found in California, with her right arm outstretched to her mother. A montage of images from the child's past in Hanford, California, and her present in Jerome, Arkansas, divide the painting in half. Lightning bolts symbolize the storm that the war and incarceration created in the lives of Japanese Americans, and the threatening rattlesnake on the bottom left, licking at the skirt of the girl, suggests the danger that remains for Japanese American

Henry Sugimoto's painting *When Can We Go Home?* depicts a child begging of her mother to return to her prewar life. Sugimoto arranges key symbols around the canvas, including an ax, a rattlesnake, and a guard tower, to indicate the difference between life before and during the incarceration.

Henry Sugimoto Collection, Japanese American National Museum (Gift of Madeleine Sugimoto and Naomi Tagawa, 92.97.3)

confined in the camp. The hatchet on the bottom right, which appears to be leaning against a tractor tread with a squirrel sitting on top, alludes to the woodcutting enterprise in Jerome. Sugimoto's cubist technique embodies the fragmented, confusing, and disjointed life that he and his fellow detainees were being forced to live.

Among those whose lives were most radically disrupted by the incarceration were Nisei who had been finishing high school and planning to go to college prior to evacuation. Alice Setzuko Takemoto recounted to her son the despair she felt over this lost opportunity:

> See, while I was going to Excelsior I was so active. And this would have been my senior year. You looked forward to your senior year, because your senior year was the big year. Your senior year was everything. And what did I come to? Jerome.[33]

Takemoto became one of the many Nisei who were granted leave from the camp to go to college as part of the National Japanese Student Relocation Council (NJSRC).

The sole purpose of NJSRC was to match college-age Nisei to non-West Coast institutions of higher education, but this was no easy task. The haste with which the program was enacted and the absence of a coherent organizational structure forced the NJSRC to work through a wide variety of governmental, philanthropic, religious, and higher education organizations to locate schools, arrange housing, and finance student resettlement. Takemoto chose to attend Oberlin College in Ohio for its music conservatory (she was a highly talented pianist) and because she had heard from friends that a Nisei had been elected as Oberlin's student body president, and her tuition was paid by the Southern Baptist Convention. While her family was supportive of her leaving camp for college, many parents were reluctant to send their children out alone, into a hostile nation at war. The students themselves had to be willing to take a leap of faith concerning their own safety, knowing that they would be highly visible ambassadors for all Japanese Americans.

Most Nisei fully recognized the burdens of this role, as an article from the *Santa Anita Pacemaker* indicated:

> Upon their scholarship, their conduct, their thoughts, their sense of humor, their adaptability, will rest the verdict of the rest of the country as to whether

> Japanese Americans are true Americans. So, upon the students will be the onus of proving to people to whom they are strangers that the first word in "Japanese American" is merely an adjective describing the color of our skin—not the color of our beliefs.[34]

Nearly half of these ambassadors were young women. Whereas Nisei men proved their patriotism by volunteering for the 442nd Army Battalion, Nisei women were enlisted to speak to community groups and local organizations in their college towns to dispel myths about Japanese American disloyalty. Many colleges preferred Japanese American female students over their male counterparts because they believed the women would be a less threatening presence on campus.[35]

These Nisei women, however, still remained the victims of misperception, if not outright discrimination. A Nisei at Wheaton College in Illinois stated that she was always seen as "one of the foreign students. No one could get it through their heads that I wasn't foreign."[36] Takemoto herself did not hold fond memories of the experience, either: "I was shy. It took me a long time to make friends. It was hard for me to make friends. I didn't have much fun in school—I didn't have a social life. It was all hard work."[37] On one hand, gendered stereotypes about Japanese American women as passive opened doors to higher education. On the other, the fear that Japanese American men might be spies indicates the degree to which male Nisei were not fully welcomed into the fold. The governor of Arkansas, in fact, banned enrollment of all Japanese Americans in colleges in the state. Nonetheless, many Nisei sought out the opportunity to continue their schooling, and by the war's end a total of 5,522 Nisei had enrolled in more than 500 colleges and universities in the Midwest and East Coast.[38]

While Nisei women were in school, many Nisei men were serving their country in the military. The first such soldiers forced to navigate the politics of Jim Crow, before the Jerome and Rohwer camps were even built, were the Nisei enlisted men sent to Camp Robinson in Little Rock, Arkansas, shortly following the bombing of Pearl Harbor. Following swiftly thereafter were Nisei volunteers who trained at Camp Shelby near Hattiesburg, Mississippi. Foreshadowing how Jerome and Rohwer prisoners would be received, these soldiers were not welcomed by local communities.

The very presence of Japanese Americans as people who were, from the South's perspective, neither "black" nor "white" caused consternation. If they were considered "white," would that erode the clearly defined segregation of the region's race-based socioeconomic structure? Moreover, treating them as "white" piqued timeworn Southern fears about miscegenation. Members of the Little Rock Chamber of Commerce, upon hearing of the transfer of Nisei soldiers to Camp Robinson, expressed this very concern to Arkansas congressman David D. Terry as they signaled the alarm about the possibility of the " 'co-mingling of Japanese soldiers and Negro women,' " as well as of "white" girls dancing "with these boys without restrictions."[39] If Nisei soldiers were considered "colored," however, might that not encourage African Americans and Asians to unite against the Anglo hegemony? Indeed, so the thinking went, what if Nisei and African American enlisted men created alliances that caused divisions within battalions?

Military and civilian leaders responded in several ways to these fears. First, to calm the nerves of the Little Rock Chamber of Commerce, clear boundaries were established between enlisted soldiers and Japanese American women in social situations. Officials at Camp Robinson and at Camp Shelby, where the 442nd regiment trained, recruited female Nisei inmates from Rohwer and Jerome, rather than local white girls, to attend weekend dances with Nisei soldiers at the bases. The goal was less to promote intraracial relationships than it was to prohibit interracial ones. Second, Nisei servicemen were granted white status by local officials in Arkansas and Mississippi in an attempt to isolate them from African Americans.[40] They were instructed by their commanders to use "white-only" facilities at water fountains, restaurants, and restrooms. The Hattiesburg, Mississippi, City Council, in fact, formally approved that Japanese Americans "use the facilities reserved for whites."[41] The irony was palpable: although Nisei were not white enough for their families to live freely during the war, Japanese American soldiers in the South were also not black enough to be Jim Crowed. Clearly politics, as opposed to skin color or ancestry, was the force driving these decisions.

This rigid racial hierarchy was new to the enlisted men coming from the West Coast. Francis Mas Fukuhara recalled that he and his peers were surprised by the racial segregation they encountered in southern states when traveling from Camp Douglas in Utah to Camp Blanding in Florida:

> That was kind of an eye-opener for me because . . . it was the first time I ran into real segregation. . . . In spite of all the badgering that we had in [the state

> of] Washington, . . . we never saw "black" and "white" drinking fountains and toilets. This really left us in a little bit of a quandary because we didn't know whether we were white or black! . . . We had a lot of difficult learning experiences.[42]

Among these experiences were Nisei soldiers' education about and then resistance to segregation on the troop bus that picked up soldiers from their segregated barracks in Camp Blanding. Fukuhara recalls:

> When we got down to Camp Blanding, . . . the camp was separated. They had the white camp and then the blacks were separated in another impoundment . . . and you couldn't go in there. But the same bus picked everybody up, . . . through the camp. And we'd sit where there are seats so if there were seats in the back, we'd go sit in the back and geez, you know, we used to catch all kinds of flack. . . . The bus driver wouldn't move until we got out of the back seats . . . and up front where we belonged. Cripes, I don't know if the white guys thought we belonged up front, but that's the way it went.

Fukuhara recounted multiple times when servicemen got into "pitched battles" with bus drivers "because somebody tried to kick them out of an open seat in the back and make them stand in the front."[43] When a white bus driver physically kicked an African American GI off the bus, his Nisei brother-in-arms attacked the driver. When another driver pushed an elderly African American woman to the ground, a Nisei soldier again responded with force. Arvarh Strickland, an African American resident of Hattiesburg, stated that "black Hattiesburg was rife with rumors" about Nisei who "did not readily accept their classification as 'white.' . . . My community especially enjoyed the reports of conflicts between men of the 442nd Regiment and white bus drivers and policemen."[44]

At the same time, however, some Nisei embraced their "conferred whiteness." The soldier and former Japanese American Citizens League leader, Mike Masaoka, explained:

> [T]hat meant using the white latrines, sitting in the front of streetcars and buses when we went to town, eating in the restaurants instead of being handed food out in the back. While we were uncomfortable with a double

> standard and sympathetic with the blacks, we as a matter of principle were not going to accept inferior status.[45]

Fellow soldier Fukuhara acknowledges the conflicts this situation posed. When asked about his classification as simultaneously "nonwhite" and "white," Fukuhara insightfully notes that, on the contrary, it was not that he and his peers were white but rather that they were nonblack and "so we learned how to behave as non-blacks."[46] Countless examples of the confusion this caused for the incarcerated can be found in memoirs, interviews, and reflections.

White soldiers did not necessarily adhere to the system of segregation, either. In a 1943 piece on relocation contributed to the *Magnet*, Eddie Shimano stated:

> on the train from Jerome to St. Louis, three soldiers (white—but forgive them; they couldn't help that) asked me to join them in nibbling out of a common quart bottle and we spent the night singing "As Long as You're Not in Love with Anyone Else, Why Don't You Fall in Love with Me?" to every pretty girl who passed down the aisle. . . . We had fun.[47]

Shimano himself was not a soldier; rather, he was an experienced newspaperman and writer who was traveling to New York to begin work as an assistant to the editor of *Common Ground*, the journal published by the Common Council for American Unity, a group that worked on behalf of immigrants and other oppressed groups. In his letters back to Jerome and printed in the *Magnet*, he described encountering little discrimination after a month living in the city, providing detainees with a little vicarious pleasure.

Shimano took great joy in riding the subway and enjoying the freedom the city offered, so much so that he had already worn out his shoes. He relished living once again "in the mainstream of American life." By contrast, he described the camps as "stagnant pools, becoming fetid and slimy, left by the backwash of the flood following December 7, 1941. The flood is subsiding; the main current sweeps on, fresh and strong and steady. The sinkholes remain, growing more stagnant daily, breeding fever and noxious germs.[48] A few months later, in the summer of 1943, Shimano detailed the type of "noxious germs" developing in the centers in an article in *Common Ground* titled "Blueprint for a Slum," which was part of a feature titled "Democracy Begins at Home—II."[49]

Common Ground had intermittently been publishing articles on the incarceration, and this edition included a cluster of such pieces: "Get The Evacuees Out!," by M. Margaret Anderson; "Relocating a People," by Robert W. Frase; "Student Relocation," by Robert W. O'Brien; "St. Paul Lends a Hand," by Alice L. Sickels; and Shimano's "Blueprint for a Slum." The first four address various aspects of the relocation experience, but Shimano's focuses on the conditions of camp life and the dangers they posed to the future of democracy. Here he rails at the "United States government" for having "built, in the past year, ten huge slum areas and call[ing] them relocation centers." In these slums, he states, "it is an uphill fight to maintain a balance, a perspective, and a faith, in the nightmare of demoralization and despair that is a relocation center." [50] He knows this based on his firsthand experience, having been released from Jerome just months earlier.

Shimano delineates many characteristics of the centers that other writers also lamented, ranging from the absence of privacy to the "spiritual crack-up" that manifests itself in "adolescent delinquency." He is one of the few, however, to allude to the ways in which relocation center "slum-life" is, fundamentally, racializing inmates in ways common to the experiences of African Americans in the United States:

> No evacuee, regardless of competence or experience, is allowed to head a department or division, a policy which not only frustrates any desire on his part to work at his highest skill, but makes him lethargic and allows his skills to deteriorate. In addition, this system makes him so dependent on the "white superior" that a two-faced subservience becomes synonymous with survival.[51]

Later, Shimano's description of cooperatives—the collective barbershops and small businesses that emerged in the camps since "no private enterprises are allowed"—alludes to the system of debt peonage that recalls the Reconstruction era immediately following the Civil War.

At that time in American history, recently liberated African Americans could farm, but the only way to do so was to rent land from a white property owner and to pay him out of the crops one raised. This led to a system of perpetual overcharging that effectively re-enslaved the laborer to the landowner. Shimano explains that the leaders of the co-ops in the camps "are not allowed to erect their own buildings, but must pay the government a rental of 45 cents per square foot. They must also pay their help for doing work which, after all, seems to be the responsibility of the WRA. It is discouraging to evacuees on salaries of $16 a month to be required to help WRA show a profit on community enterprises."[52]

Most disturbingly, though, Shimano points to the ways in which incarceration is festering a "racial hyper-sensitivity" among detainees themselves that further challenges the foundations of democracy. Lines between the Japanese "self" and the Caucasian "other" were seen as definitive, of course, but also emerging among Japanese Americans were antipathies toward other groups. Shimano expresses concern that a "growing tide of anti-Semitism" is emerging among evacuees, partly in reaction to the discrimination to which they were subject.

> The recent statement of Lieut. Gen. John L. DeWitt, "A Jap's a Jap. It doesn't matter whether he's an American citizen or not," serve only as added proof that military necessity was a convenient, if true, excuse for an anti-Japanese pogrom. Faced with a growing bitterness, a drab, dreary future in the centers, denied participation in the war effort, wanting to assert his status, the evacuee in his involution and need of a scapegoat has turned to Jew-baiting. Unhampered by the fact that there are no individual Jews in the centers, the race-baiters indulge in long-range sniping at the WRA as a Jewish-dominated government organization.[53]

Shimano explains that, following "the same familiar pattern of anti-Semitism spread by native fascists before the war," inmates labeled Eisenhower, Myer, and Roosevelt as Jewish names. He continues:

> Negroes, Mexicans, Filipinos, Hindus, and even white trash are disparaged. Especially baited are Koreans—far more so than the Chinese, who, strangely enough, are disliked only for being such "smooth, slick propagandists" while "Korean" becomes synonymous with "informer" or "stooge." Italians in America also are sometime sneered at as inferior because the Attorney General labeled them as "friendly aliens" and "harmless"—not forcing them to be evacuated.[54]

Then, as now, failures of justice beget further failures of justice in ways that fundamentally endanger the very principles on which the nation was founded.

No one in Jerome escaped the noxious toxin of racism, though some people attempted to defy it. Camp administrators tried to establish boundaries between African Americans who worked in the camps and Japanese American held there. The anonymous author of the *Magnet* article "Joe's Diary" recorded that

> every morning 3,000 construction workers, black and white, converge upon the center. Hence, MP's are posted around the now occupied blocks of this section of the Center . . . so workers will not interfere with the residents, and so the residents will not go into the construction area.[55]

In the end, however, because of the physical proximity of Jerome to nearby towns, as well as the administrative structures that had been established to allow the camp to function effectively, there was no reasonable way to keep the three "racial" groups successfully segregated from one another. Jerome inmates were regularly given "passes"—eerily evoking those distributed to enslaved people who had to travel beyond the confines of antebellum plantations—to leave the camps for school outings, intercamp sports events, and even shopping trips. These outings revealed to the incarcerated the extent to which their African American peers were equally excluded from full membership in their nation.

Grace Sugita Hawley, originally from Hawai'i, recalled a shopping trip she and her mother took into a nearby town while they were detained:

> We also didn't know where to go in the bus because it said "Colored in the Rear," they always have a sign, "Colored in the Rear." And [we looked at] the bus driver, "we don't know what to do," and he looked at us and he says us, "you stay in front." Oh, so we found out we're not colored so we stay in the front! So we get to the station and the restrooms are "colored" and "white." So we decided we'll go the "white" section since the bus driver told us not to go in the back. But that's when we first learned about segregation; we never had that here [in Hawaii]. It's kind of sad, you know, we had to learn all those things because we were in the South.[56]

During the war, Japanese Americans were used as pawns to preserve the racially segregated hierarchy on which Southern culture was based. By accepting their designation as "white" they, often unintentionally as Hawley describes, played a role in supporting the same system of racial segregation that was at the root of their own oppression. Nisei soldiers during the war, however, formed allegiances with other nonwhite groups, and upon the war's end, many Japanese Americans continued to work on cross-racial alliances. Charles Kikuchi, Yuri Kochiyama, Larry Tajiri, and Mary Oyama, among others, all went on to become leaders in the postwar civil rights movement, in fact.[57] Just as alliances developed between Japanese American and Indigenous Peoples at the camps in Arizona and Colorado, so, too, did a mutual experience of oppression establish links between Nisei and African Americas in the Jim Crow South.

9
Humiliation and Hope in Rohwer's *The Pen*

A drawing of the Rohwer camp mascot, Li'l Daniel, appeared on the cover of *The Pen*, the literary magazine published at the Rohwer prison camp. Camp mascots were regularly used in the camp newspapers and literary magazines to critique the incarceration.

The Pen, *cover page, Rohwer prison camp, Rohwer, Arkansas. Densho, ddr-densho-167-42, courtesy of the Kuroishi Family Collection*

Lil Dan'l, the Rohwer camp mascot, was a fitting image to grace the November 1943 cover of the single volume of Rohwer Relocation Center's literary magazine, *The Pen*, because he embodied the main theme of the edition: namely,

That Damned Fence. Heather Hathaway, Oxford University Press. © Oxford University Press 2022.
DOI: 10.1093/oso/9780190098315.003.0010

who and what defined an "American." Lil Dan'l was created by the incarcerated artist, George Akimoto, and was one of a handful of cartoon mascots featured in camp newspapers. These included Jankee at Topaz, Denny at Denson/Jerome, and Lil Neebo (Nisei boy) at Amache.[1] The adventures of Lil Dan'l ran as a comic in the *Outpost*, Rohwer's newspaper, and the character was also featured in a mimeographed booklet, *Lil Dan'l: One Year in a Relocation Center*. The cover image for *The Pen* is Akimoto's most detailed portrayed of Lil Dan'l, however, and it is rich with symbolism.

Akimoto depicts Lil Dan'l as partly Japanese, signaled by the round glasses used to stereotype Asians during the period, and footwear that resembles geta (elevated Japanese sandals, which were worn in many camps to keep feet above the muck and mud).[2] He also portrays Lil Dan'l as partly American, indicated by a coonskin cap and his name evoking Daniel Boone, the frontiersman, pioneer and American folk hero who expanded settlement into the interior of the United States in the late eighteenth century. In the Lil Dan'l booklet telling of his "year in a relocation center," Akimoto jokingly revealed, in fact, that, "although he has kept his last name a deep secret, we are led to believe that his full name is *Lil Dan'l Boon* [*sic*]."[3] Akimoto adds one more dimension to his portrayal of Lil Dan'l and that is as a knight. This he suggests by Dan'l's suit of armor and the knight's helmet he holds in his hand. Importantly, however, Lil Dan'l wields not a jousting lance but rather a fountain pen, next to which runs the slogan, "mightier than the sword."

This fusion of identities, designed to represent the writers of *The Pen,* served not only as a clever representation of creators of the magazine but also of the competing forces faced by detainees in Rohwer. Because they were people guarded by armed soldiers, physical resistance necessarily had to take a back seat to less violent but potentially equally confrontational verbal forms of protest. To use words in this way, as weapons to fight injustice, was noble, in a knightly fashion, as Lil Dan'l's armor and quill indicated. It was also distinctly American. The opening piece of *The Pen*, "Foreword: A Transition," reminded Rohwer residents that the "Pen is mightier than the Sword." The allusion to this phrase in the title of the journal suggested a keen understanding of the Constitutional significance of both freedoms of the press and of protest among the magazine staff.[4] Whether known to the "Foreword's" author or not, that phrase is inscribed in the Thomas Jefferson Building of the Library of Congress as a reminder that words are often more effective than violence in righting a wrong.

As significantly, the author of the "Foreword" also invoked the words of another great American agitator, Abraham Lincoln, in his Gettysburg Address. The author described the first year in Rohwer:

> To the outside world, our transition has not even been felt. To the nation, the effect has touched only a few, but to us, the past year has been one of sorrow, of insecurity, of fear, of deliberation and finally, of renewed hope. As Lincoln said, "The world will little note nor long remember what we did here," but in the minds of the evacuees, the year in Rohwer and at other centers will be retained as the turning point of our lives.[5]

Akimoto's rendition of Lil Dan'l as a frontiersman also evoked Lincoln, who was commonly associated with the frontier during his presidency because of his birth in a log cabin in Illinois.[6]

This portrayal of Lil Dan'l as a pioneer, combined with allusions to Japanese stereotypes, highlighted the absurdity of characterizations of the incarceration as akin to early American settlers conquering the wilderness. Akimoto seemed to have been taking aim at War Relocation Authority (WRA) director Milton S. Eisenhower's characterization of detainees in the 1942 propaganda film *The Japanese Relocation*. There, Eisenhower described the prison camps as "new pioneer communities [on] land that was raw, untamed but filled with opportunity."[7] Rohwer inmates were fully aware of the land's ruggedness, since they were forced, alongside those at Jerome, to clear the trees and cultivate it.

They were also acutely conscious that this alleged frontier was a space of loss and misfortune, not of opportunity. Japanese Americans were designated as "white" in the binary racial system of the American South. This put them in the position of unintentionally being complicit in the subjugation of African Americans while they, themselves, were also subjugated. This left a dual scar on the lives of many confined in Rohwer, as pieces in *The Pen* predict. The first scar marked the injury of incarceration itself and the second marked the wound of inadvertent participation in race prejudice.

Led by this complex image of Lil Dan'l, *The Pen* proceeded to address some of the most pressing concerns in November 1943, including the urgent push toward "resettlement." On the minds of many Rohwer detainees was the question of how one resumed being an "American" in communities where white residents had decided that the detained were definitely not that.

By now the government had realized the risks and consequences of the incarceration, including the development of a demoralized generation of Issei who, the government feared, might grow dependent on federal support. In response, officials began to advocate fiercely for resettlement. Relocation Program Division administrator E. B. Moulton's contribution to *The Pen* acknowledged this:

> there is a growing realization that resettlement opportunities must be provided for family groups, and as soon as suitable employment for family heads come in, the impetus for resettlement should increase. The WRA offices are trying their best, and our office is looking forward to that time.[8]

Moulton emphasized the resettlement of "family groups" because in the early stages of the program, the majority who left the camp were single Nisei who departed to attend college or who obtained indefinite leave thanks to securing full-time employment elsewhere.

Issei were the most reluctant to leave, for obvious reasons. Sansei Delphine Hirasuna explained,

> When they came out [of the camps], their jobs were gone, their property was gone. People were being told, "we're going to close the camps and you [can] leave, and we're going to give you twenty-five dollars and train fare home." But where is home?[9]

The Issei had already been through a number of challenges. First, they successfully acculturated to a new country upon their immigration to the United States. Many developed successful business and careers in America. Suddenly, with the bombing of Pearl Harbor, Issei were ripped from the lives they established and forced into prison camps. Demoralization and hopelessness soon followed. Now, having limited employment prospects given their advanced ages, the Issei were forced to make yet another radical life move. This was understandably daunting.

The WRA did its best to mask the plight of all of the incarcerated, but its propaganda most certainly mischaracterized the Issei. They were, it claimed, "not prisoners, they are not internees. They are merely dislocated people; the unwounded casualties of war."[10] *The Pen* contributor John Aki challenged this misrepresentation in his piece, "Effects of Evacuation," which explored the psychological toll that the incarceration had taken on Japanese Americans. Aki sent his article from Tule Lake: *The Pen* welcomed contributions from writers incarcerated elsewhere. "Effects of Evacuation" was primarily concerned about those who "were reluctant to leave the protection of the barbed wire fence. . . . What had happened," he asked, "to this group of industrious people to make them stagnant and also fearful of a normal life on the outside?"[11] He proposed several explanations.

First, he argued that evacuation and incarceration bred in people "resentment toward the American public and government for the loss of property and home." Aki explained that the spark of resentment grew into a flame of rage because the

> evacuation had taken place on a racial basis, the Japanese alone having been forced to move. It came as a culmination of years of discrimination and segregation directed against Orientals on the Pacific Coast, and for many, it added just more load on the burden of humility they had borne for years unconsciously or consciously.[12]

Second, he noted that the denial of freedom and conditions of dependency sapped the motivation of detainees:

> The evacuees were dependent upon the administration for practically all of their major needs—food, shelter, clothing allowance, medical care—a helplessness which did not increase their desire to maintain self-respect and independence.

These conditions, Aki claimed, "resulted in sporadic outbursts of indignation, of sullenness, of uncooperativeness on the part of the evacuees, which the level-headed could do very little to avert."[13]

Finally, he observed, fear dominated the imprisoned:

> [They] feared they would be discriminated against, humiliated and their lives endangered. They feared that they would be without adequate protection against want, physical violence. They feared that they were too old to make a living, to support their family, to get a job.[14]

Evacuation and incarceration, Aki believed, stole not merely the physical possessions, homes, and livelihoods of the Issei; it also stole the "spirit which had made them brave an ocean journey" to become Americans.[15]

The entire experience broke some people, including Zenichi Imamoto. Alice Setsuko Takemoto described her father as being forever changed by the experience of incarceration:

> It ruined him. It did. The whole thing was rough on him.
>
> [*Thinks.*] See, before the war, as the principal of a Japanese school, he was the leader of the community. *The* leader. People came to him for advice. And he had a very strong feeling of responsibility for those people. He had civic pride. He always went to PTA meetings—he was the only Asian who did. He was straight as an arrow. . . .
>
> But after the war, after relocation, he was cleaning a house. He had a record [he was arrested by the FBI and held for a time at Camp Lordsburg], and the only job he could get was as a domestic. Mother had more status than him—she was a cook. Just think what that would do to you. He was fifty-four. . . . Think about what would happen to you if you had to leave everything you've been building up to. When he left camp his total worth was thirty dollars. That's what his personal belongings were worth, all that he owned. Thirty dollars. Mother's was eleven.[16]

Employment prospects for the Issei were bleak, indeed. The majority of people who remained at Rohwer until its closing on November 30, 1945, not surprisingly, were single Issei or multigenerational family groups.

It was incumbent on the Nisei, then, to determine how best to forge paths for success through resettlement, both for themselves and their elders. The JERS employee, Tom (Tomatsu) Shibutani, who would later become a prominent sociologist, addressed this question in his contribution (also sent from Tule Lake) to *The Pen*, "Ideologies of the Nisei: A Crucial Test Case."[17] In this piece, Shibutani hypothesized about what he believed to be the origin of "race antagonism" and suggested how those who were relocating might best confront it. Though both "scientists and less profound thinkers often have attributed the entire matter to economic competition," Shibutani wrote, "it seems that the crucial factor is the fact that the nisei [*sic*] or the Negro or any other colored individual can be identified and placed in a separate category in the mind of the dominant group." By focusing on skin color rather than class, Shibutani echoed the most renowned scholar of the era who was wrestling with these issues, Robert Park, one of the leaders of the Chicago School of sociology.[18]

As early as 1914, de facto Jim Crow segregation had proved able to undercut legislative efforts toward equality for African Americans in the United States. Park argued that people of Japanese ancestry, whom he included under the umbrella term "Oriental" which was commonly used at the time, could also never be fully assimilated because of phenotypical differences from the dominant group:

> The chief obstacle to the assimilation of the Negro and the Oriental are not mental but physical traits. It is not because the Negro and the Japanese are so differently constituted that they do not assimilate. If they were given an opportunity the Japanese are quite as capable as the Italians, the Armenians, or the Slavs of acquiring our culture, and sharing our national ideals. The trouble is not with the Japanese mind but with the Japanese skin. The Jap is not the right color.

Though the term "Jap" is as offensive to modern ears as "Oriental," Park's use of it here seems a deliberate effort to mock American attitudes toward racialized groups, given that he uses the term "Japanese" in the remainder of the passage. Park continues:

> The fact that the Japanese bears in his features a distinctive racial hallmark, that he wears, so to speak, a racial uniform, classifies him. He cannot become a mere individual, indistinguishable in the cosmopolitan mass of the population, as is true, for example, of the Irish and, to a lesser extent, of some of the other immigrant races. The Japanese, like the Negro, is condemned to remain among us an abstraction, a symbol, and a symbol not merely of his own race, but of the Orient and of that vague, ill-defined menace we sometimes refer to as the "yellow peril." This not only determines, to a very large extent, the attitude of the white world toward the yellow man, but it determines the attitude of the yellow man to the white. It puts between the races the invisible but very real gulf of self-consciousness.[19]

By concurring with Park's analysis of the role that skin color plays in the social hierarchy, Shibutani—writing in 1943—suggested that not much had changed since 1914. Shibutani, however, presented what he believed to be the only solution to overcome it: namely, ridding the world of racial prejudice. He believed the Nisei bore the brunt of this responsibility.

Shibutani first condemned the "hardships and heartbreaks" foisted on the Nisei, initially through expulsion and incarceration and then through resistance from white communities during resettlement.

> There now seem to be in formation a concerted effort on the part of certain so-called "patriotic" groups to drive all nisei [*sic*] back to the centers for the duration—with a possible objective of deportation after the war. And yet, there seems to be no antagonism against Germans and Italians—not even the aliens. Why, we might ask, are we treated like this?[20]

Shibutani observed that some social scientists had attributed racism to economic competition, but he disagreed, arguing that "people of the same race compete with one another without similar conflicts." Rather, to Shibutani, discrimination was caused by phenotypical differences. The Nisei were phenotypically marked by physical features as different from whites and so were categorized as "other" in the minds of dominant group members. One's "racial uniform," as Park described it, governed social status. Shibutani explained that the Nisei's tendency to self-segregate in the face of discrimination further contributed to the problem, causing the Nisei to "have been erroneously identified with one of the most dangerous enemies that this nation has ever had." The result was the entrenchment of what Shibutani called "racialism," an element of the "fascist ideology" or "fascist disease" that had infected the world and caused war.[21]

The solution to this problem lay in the hands of the Nisei themselves, according to Shibutani. He demanded that the first step was to contest the "reactionary press" and those "in the United States posing as super-patriots . . . fanning the flame of hatred" to such an extent that the nation may "split," making "impossible" a "concerted effort toward final victory." To do this, Shibutani believed, the Nisei needed to eliminate their own racial prejudices.

> It seems that the only salvation for the nisei [*sic*] or for anyone in a racial minority is to throw off the narrow interest in local and personal problems and to join in the larger battle for a better world. . . . By being prejudiced

> against the Negroes, Jews, Chinese and Filipinos the Nisei are contributing to their own self-destruction.[22]

Only through affirming democratic ideals, Shibutani insisted, would Japanese Americans flourish.

Fictional stories in *The Pen* made similarly political points about how to rid America of racism. Ichiro Hori, for example, explored the issue through a consideration of the psychological consequences of evacuation on children. In "A Young Evacuee," Hori depicted a boy, in trouble for misbehaving in school, who attributed his own naughtiness to the emotional turmoil he was experiencing because of the war. His father had been arrested by the FBI, his brother had been drafted into the military, and the rest of his family had been imprisoned in a concentration camp. Hori used this frame to call into question the very issue addressed in Shibutani's article: namely the idea that racism could be eliminated if all oppressed groups in the United States recognized their similarities and worked together to forge a true democracy.

Hori names the teacher in the story Miss Johnston, which seems likely to be an intentional allusion to Rohwer camp director Ray Johnston. This suggests, of course, that Hori's article is aimed at him. In it, Hori casts the boy as describing for his teacher another soldier whom his brother met on the train on his way to Rohwer. "His name was Manuel Alfonso, a Mexican, from Texas," the boy stated. "Manuel, too, was on his way home to bid goodbye to his parents." Soon, the soldiers are joined by another named James Wong, a Chinese American. The boy explained that, despite their coming from three different ancestral groups, all found their families suffering similarly:

> My brother knew Wong in California; they used to work at the same wholesale produce market. These three soldiers, all going to bid goodbye to relatives or friends, compared notes. Manuel said his parents lived in Texas, but they were destitute. His father had five children to support and he was working on a sugar beet ranch in the state of Michigan, but now had returned to Texas, after a season's work. Wong's parents were dead but his friends lived in New Orleans, and they too were desperately in need. They agreed that they all faced the same economical situation of being limited in their occupational fields. After much discussion, they promised that after

> the war in Europe was over, they will all come back to this country to fight for a real democracy at home.[23]

Through this boy's story, Hori made a plea similar to Shibutani's: he called for a panethnic effort to overcome the despotism that existed both abroad *and* at home.

Like Shibutani, Hori included whites in this effort. When the soldier in the story encourages the boy to "carry on this real fight against ignorance, intolerance, and prejudice at home after the war," the boy responded, "With the help of my Caucasian friends and the help of all real Americans, we shall carry on this second fight for a real democracy here."[24] Hori's didacticism is not particularly artful, but the message is clear: whites, including camp director Johnston, must join forces with oppressed racialized groups in the United States to overcome prejudice.

The Pen's preoccupation with what or who constituted an American—and how skin color and ancestry affected that—was a concern of all incarcerees. Jerome detainee, Marielle Tsukamoto, put this quite simply:

> My mother and father were born here. They were American citizens. I was born here. I'm an American citizen. My grandfather came to the United States in 1889, but we are not accepted because . . . ? Why aren't we accepted as Americans? Is an American a white person?[25]

Another contribution to *The Pen*, "Random Whirligig" by Mitsu Yasuda who was held in Minidoka, also explored the role of whites in fighting the oppression of minoritized groups in the United States through letters exchanged between the incarcerated and their white friends.

"Random Whirligig" originally ran in the first anniversary issue of the *Minidoka Irrigator*, on September 25, 1943, and was reprinted in *The Pen*. In it, Yasuda spoke of how the correspondence from her free peers had evolved over the course of the war.

> Letters didn't mean too much in the pre-war days of happy and mad school days. But since evacuation, and the bewildering days of assembly centers, those messages, kind and encouraging, played not a little part in keeping the fast-dwindling light of faith flickering in our hearts.

Yasuda traced the shift from "gay missives, filled with chatter about the people we knew and loved, written to make us forget the injustice done" to more poignant letters that lamented their peers' absences: "The school has been a trifle dead since so many livewires left with evacuation," wrote one white friend. "No spirit, nor more of that happy cosmopolitanism."

As the war progressed, Yasuda explained, students came to recognize its disrupting force on free and imprisoned alike.

> But with the advancement of the war, nearly all of the friends either joined the army or went out for defense work. . . . The missives were no longer from "one fourth-estater" zany to another. They were from fighting men ready to die for their country, to an evacuee who with thousands left a major portion of her life to submit to a military ruling.[26]

Like Hori, Yasuda suggested that the white soldiers were in step with their incarcerated peers and that, in the end, white military men and women were the people most likely to join Japanese Americans in fighting for liberation for all. Yasuda described soldiers as most acutely aware of the problem. Writes one to a Japanese American schoolmate:

> It may seem kind of thin coming from a guy who's still got just about all the freedom he's ever had, but anyway I'm still going to enter the old plea, "Don't give up hope! You may never hear any of them express it audibly but you people over there have a lot of friends over here who have not forgotten what swell comrades you've been and they all realize the position you're in.[27]

Another enlisted man wrote: "You may call me a dreamer, but when I get into this fight, I will, and I don't think I will stand alone, be fighting for your rights, as much as anyone's." Still another, according to Yasuda, promised that "we won't stop fighting, when the war's over. We will lay down our arms, but we won't sign the truce until everybody's free." Yasuda concluded that to increase "chances of really lasting peace," it would be wisest for the truce to be "written by the soldiers themselves."[28]

This harmonious theme does not characterize all contributions to *The Pen*, however. In another story by Ichiro Hori, "Hard to Choose," the author again used fiction as a screen through which to air other political concerns related to life after the war, focusing in particular on race, gender, and loyalty. He tells the story of twin sisters, Kimiko and Miyo, as they try to choose between two suitors.

One of the two potential mates, Tom Tanaka, is a Nisei who decides to expatriate to Japan following his release from camp. He explains that discrimination in employment prior to the war, combined with the race-based evacuation that excluded "German aliens and Italian aliens" who were deemed "white," tested his trust in his native country. This behavior, in addition to "the race riots in Detroit" and "the trouble with Mexicans in L.A.," leads Tom to think, "Maybe we're not wanted here, at least they treat us so."[29]

Tom's suspicions were backed up by evidence beyond the incarceration of Japanese Americans. His mention of Detroit refers to the 1943 race riots that grew out of a history of discrimination in the city, which, ironically, prided itself on being the "Arsenal of Democracy." The 1943 riot was catalyzed by the building of housing for African Americans in an area that was largely inhabited by whites. When African American residents arrived to move in, they were greeted by a mob of more than 1,000 white people, a burning cross, and virulent racism. This event led to multiple other clashes between the groups for months to come.

The L.A. issues to which Tom refers similarly involved conflicts between African Americans, Latinos, and Filipinos versus white Navy sailors who were stationed in the area. These were called the Zoot Suit riots because victims were targeted partly based on their clothing. Ostensibly, the "zoot suits" favored by ethnic Americans were perceived as requiring a great deal of fabric at a time when cloth, like so many other things, was rationed in support of the war effort. In this instance, the "racial uniform"—skin color—that Robert Park identified as a cause of discrimination was augmented by another type of "uniform" that doubly targeted nonwhite Americans.

The final blow to Tom's confidence in his nation was delivered by the WRA when it refused him permission to leave camp and resettle in the Midwest. Kimiko is shocked by the news: "'Refused? How could they? You're an American citizen, and you have never been to Japan.' She was dumbfounded." But Tom replies that apparently "the government questions my sincerity, my loyalty and my patriotism." He explains that, given this rejection, he feels as though he has no choice but to choose Japan as "his future home." Though a "strange land" to him, Tom states, "at least there [I] won't be treated like [an] unwanted citizen." He asks Kimi to marry and expatriate with him: "Japan needs us. I think we can contribute more to society by working in the Orient. Win or lose, the Orient is changing. It's progressing."[30]

Hori sets up the second suitor, Hiro Miyake, a Kibei (an American-born Japanese who lived for a time in Japan, typically for educational purposes), as a foil to Tom's cynicism. Kimiko assumes, given Hiro's experience in Japan, that he, too, intends to expatriate. But Hiro had decided to stay in the United States. Though he was frustrated by the likelihood that anti-Japanese racism would prevent him, a college graduate, from getting the sorts of jobs he'd studied for, Hiro echoes Shibutani's beliefs:

> I'll admit that I can't possibly see that this country will treat us better after the war, but we must fight for our rights, we must fight for real democracy here. It's up to us, who have been privileged with a good education to dedicate our lives so that our children will have a better life.

Kimi asks Hiro to elaborate and he replies that "there are many Americans who realize that real democracy does not exist here in its perfect form." Hiro believes, however, that they, too, are willing to fight for the ideal that "liberty and justice for all" will become a reality. "They are anxious to see that better relations are developed among all men, especially among those in this country," explains Hiro. "We are emerging as a leader of democracy in the world, and first prerequisite for that is to establish one here."[31] He, too, proposes to Kimi.

In the end, Hori does not indicate which suitor's arguments swayed Kimiko most. Instead, he poses the question directly to his readers: "Who do you think Kimi chose?," forcing us to determine where we stand.[32] Hori's story illuminated competing visions among Nisei men, but it was also helpful in understanding the complexities surrounding gender and patriotism. He constructed the central action as Kimiko's decision about which man to marry because Hori imagined her future to be determined by her suitor's. In trying to choose a partner, Kimi tells her sister, "I don't care where my husband lives, do you?" Her sister replies, "I'll go anywhere he goes."[33] This exchange makes clear a 1940s heterosexual gender stereotype. While the men in the story weighed their own political perspectives when making decisions about their futures, the sisters' political views and plans were bound by those of their male partners or parents.

In reality, however, following family was only one option for Nisei women during and after the war. The government's push toward resettlement, combined with the support of the National Japanese American Student Relocation Council, led some Nisei women to embark on educations and careers they had not considered before the war. Nursing, for example, proved both enticing and welcoming: by July 1944, more than three hundred female Nisei had enrolled in more than a hundred nursing programs in twenty-four states. Prior to the war, most Issei and Nisei women's employment was limited to domestic positions, but the clerical work many had undertaken in camp administrative offices provided young women, especially, with skills and experience that placed them in contention for a variety of jobs that the wartime labor shortage created. By 1950, in fact, nearly 50% of working Japanese American women held non-domestic-service jobs.[34]

This does not prove correct, however, the WRA propaganda claiming that work in the camp was intended to prepare detainees for postwar professional success. Only a limited number of young women, and only those in prized clerical, educational, or healthcare positions while incarcerated were able to parlay their camp employment into steady jobs upon release. Even among those who did, the entire incarceration experience took a psychological, financial, physical, and emotional toll. Cherry Tanaka's contribution to *The Pen* from the Minidoka camp, "Feminidoka," makes this clear.

"Feminidoka" was a regular column in the Minidoka newspaper and it often addressed stereotypically feminine issues such as fashion, helpful hints for homemaking, or youth activities. Similar domestically focused articles ran in most camp newspapers. The piece by Tanaka that was reprinted in *The Pen*, however, was unusual in that she reflects on her first year of the incarceration rather critically.

Tanaka acknowledges at the outset that she

> cannot write the banal sentimentalities usually associated with a-year-has-gone-by column. In a sudden perverse and pessimistic mood, with each reminiscence the focus of my mind seems but to center on the disagreeableness along with the pleasantness.[35]

The disagreeable things she recalls include a "dirty, wearying, and comfortless" train ride to the camp, only to be greeted, upon disembarking, with a "lungful of eroded dust" and the "stench of the outhouses, the inexpediencies of washing, the cramped one-room quarters." Of barracks life, she remembers the erosion of privacy, "the unavoidable throwing together of remote strangers, so that one wants to cry out against the infringement of personal freedom," and the need to suppress the "secret inferno" of rage that these circumstances engendered. She recalls the desecration of holidays, which involved sharing the supposedly celebratory meal across the table from "strangers . . . while the fourth member of the family washes dishes back in the kitchen." Diversions such as weekly movies proved not to be: they were viewed "through a thimble's space between obstructing heads after hour long waits in the numbing and freezing wind." Attending church was no better because of the cold, and navigating the "gumbo mud, fighting the suction with each step and tug . . . step and tug" was only made worse by a having to do it in the middle of the night to go to the latrine. Finally, Tanaka notes with pain how, when "taking an evening stroll," she "finds the obstruction of barbed wires—symbolic in meaning" of the undeniably "grim reality" of incarceration. She urges her readers never again to take "the glory of freedom, the pricelessness of one's rights" for granted.[36]

The contribution to *The Pen* that perhaps best summarized the writers' collective queries about how being "American" was defined in this wartorn context is a poem titled "We Are But Refugees." It picks up the themes addressed by all these writers: Shibutani's warning that perpetuation of "the color line" would lead to the breakdown of democracy; Aki's concerns about the long-term psychological effects of eviction and incarceration among the detained; Yasuda's belief that unity would prevail, in the end; and Hori's and Tanaka's recognition that the entire experience had permanently altered detainees' outlooks on the past and the future.

The first two stanzas importantly define the Nisei, in particular, as refugees in their own homeland.

We are but refugees,
in the land of the free,
We're not from overseas,
this is our own country.

We were born and bred here,
our parents, Japanese.
Yet, within our nation dear,
we are still refugees.

The use of the term "refugees" is particularly important because a refugee flees a country to escape persecution. Japanese Americans, however, experienced the opposite. They were metaphorically forced out of their own country and into persecution.

The poem then challenges America to honor the rights of its very own citizens: "Must we seek another land, / where as free men, we can stand!" Echoing Aki's concerns about the loss of spirit among those who have been detained, the poem speaks of a loss of "faith" that might dangerously alter the community's willingness to seek unity:

> Tomorrow may be a little late
> for, time may change our hearts.
> Today we want to know our fate,
> before our faith departs.

Recalling both Shibutani's recognition that racial prejudice was the primary cause of the incarceration and that preservation of it would lead to democracy's demise, the author of "Refugees" implores:

> Don't let color line be drawn;
> for, evil will be the spawn,
> And victory for democracy
> will lead to an autocracy.

Finally, the author pledges, as did so many other authors in *The Pen*, that Japanese Americans, despite the wrongs inflicted upon them, would continue to fight for the justices that true freedom entails, if only given the chance.

> Without a single thought of hate,
> a hundred thousand strong, we wait,
> Waiting for the call to sound
> saying—freedom has won its round.[37]

Despite the humiliation of being incarcerated, Japanese Americans and Nisei in particular, retained the hope that the democratic principles on which the nation was founded would govern when the war ended.

As a Fourth of July pageant photo from one of the Arkansas camps reflected, however, racism was so endemic in the United States that it proved seemingly impossible to escape, even for those who were victims of it. In this play, which was intended to both demonstrate and engender patriotism, a girl in blackface and another in a kimono were relegated to the back of the stage. Those waving US flags or playing Uncle Sam, the Statue of Liberty, and a representation of wartime "Victory" stood in the foreground.[38] The ideology of white supremacy that ruled in the Jim Crow South left its scars on all involved. Whether the Japanese Americans imprisoned in Arkansas adopted conferred "whiteness," out of ignorance, convenience, or as a matter of survival, or they internalized the loathing directed at them, no one escaped this atrocity unharmed.

Notes

That Damned Fence

1. My colleague, Frank Abe, and I have been unable to definitively determine the author of this poem. It circulated widely among several, if not all, of the camps and has been variously attributed to Min Yasui, also know as the "Mad Mongolian," and to Jim Yoshihara, who was said to be an inmate in Minidoka. Multiple copies of the poem exist in family and personal document collections that are available through the Densho Digital Repository. As a typed original, the poem was likely repeatedly transcribed for distribution, resulting in differences that appear to be errors. A misspelling of the final word, "defense," as "defence," for example, could be a mistake or, as Abe has suggested, an intentional play on the word "fence." Regardless of the poem's provenance, it was well known among incarcerees.

Introduction

1. Toyo Suyemoto, *I Call to Remembrance: Toyo Suyemoto's Years of Internment*, ed. Susan B. Richardson (New Brunswick: Rutgers University Press, 2007), 10.
2. Both Amache and Jerome were referred to differently by inmates and the government. Amache was officially called the Grenada Relocation Center but its postal address was Amache, Colorado, so inhabitants of the camp referred to it as such. Jerome was officially named the Jerome Relocation Center but its proximity to the town of Denson, Arkansas, caused a similar semantic slippage that occurred in the Colorado facility: some called it Denson, as is reflected in the title of its literary magazine, the "Denson Magnet," while others referred to it as Jerome.
3. In 1936, President Franklin Delano Roosevelt proposed to the Chief of Naval Operations "that every Japanese citizen or non-citizen on the Island of Oahu who meets these Japanese ships or has any connection with their officers or men should be secretly but definitely identified and his or her name be placed on a special list of those who would be the first to be placed in a concentration camp in the event of trouble." Cited in Peter Irons, *Justice at War: The Story of the Japanese American Internment Cases* (New York: Oxford University Press, 1983), 20. In 1944, Roosevelt continued to use the term. "In most of the cases . . . I am now talking about Japanese people from Japan who are citizens . . . Japanese Americans. I am not talking about the Japanese themselves. A good deal of progress has been made in scattering them throughout the country, and that is going on almost every day. I have forgotten what

the figures are. There are about roughly a hundred—a hundred thousand Japanese-origin citizens in this country. And it is felt by a great many lawyers that under the Constitution they can't be kept locked up in concentration camps." Cited by Greg Robinson, *By Order of the President: FDR and the Internment of Japanese Americans* (Cambridge, MA: Harvard University Press, 2001), 2.

4. The wartime usurpation of Japanese American–owned fisheries, farms, and businesses was the end result of long-standing efforts by the Native Sons and Daughters of the Golden West, the California State Grange, and the California Federation of Labor to minimize their dominance in these industries. In 1942–1943, John Regan, secretary of the Native Sons of the Golden West, in alliance with the American Legion, sued Cameron King, the Registrar of voters in San Francisco, for keeping 2,600 Japanese Americans on the voting roster following the bombing of Pearl Harbor. His goal was to deny Japanese Americans the right to land ownership and to do so, he had to overturn the 1898 decision, rendered in the case of *U.S. v. Wong Kim Ark*, which recognized that the rights of citizenship apply to all people born in the United States. *Regan v. King* failed, however, in part due to the explicit anti-Chinese racism of U. S. Webb, the attorney arguing the case for Regan. See Charlotte Brooks, *Alien Neighbors, Foreign Friends: Asian Americans, Housing, and the Transformation of Urban California* (Chicago: University of Chicago Press, 2009), 148–149. For a full-length study of anti-Japanese movements before the war, see Roger Daniels, *The Politics of Prejudice: The Anti-Japanese Movement in California and the Struggle for Japanese Exclusion* (Berkeley: University of California Press, 1962). For an analysis of *Regan v. King*, see Greg Robinson, "When Birthright Citizenship Was Last 'Reconsidered': *Regan v. King* and Asian Americans Part IV," " *The Faculty Lounge* (blog), August 9, 2010 (http://www.thefacultylounge.org/2010/08/page/3/). See also Eckard Toy, "Whose Frontier? The Survey of Race Relations on the Pacific Coast in the 1920s," *Oregon Historical Quarterly* 107, no. 1 (2006): 36–63, for a compelling analysis of how anti-Japanese sentiments coalesced around the "Survey of Race Relations on the Pacific Coast," a study intended to improve cross-cultural understanding that was conducted with the assistance of the famous sociologist Robert Park, who founded the Chicago School of sociology. The Chicago School initially specialized in urban sociology and race relations and, after the war, became known for the "symbolic interactionist" approach that analyzed human behavior as a product of social and environmental factors over biological. This approach would come to influence greatly the thinking of the internees Tamotsu Shibutani and Charles Kikuchi, both of whom attended the University of Chicago after release from captivity. For more on Shibutani's methodologies, see Karen Inouye, "Japanese American Wartime Experience: Tamotsu Shibutani and Methodological Innovation, 1935–1978," *Journal of the History of the Behavioral Sciences* (2012): 318–338.

5. For a brief explanation of the use of terms and its political consequences, see encyclopedia.densho.org/terminology/. For a comprehensive, five-part historical overview and analysis, see Roger Daniels, "Words Do Matter: A Note on Inappropriate Terminology and the Incarceration of the Japanese Americans," February 2, 2008, *Discover Nikkei* (http://www.discovernikkei.org/en/journal/2008/2/1/words-do-matter/). I have tried to vary the terms I use to describe the event for purposes of less

repetitive prose, but my personal view is clear: The experience was unquestionably a violation of both civil and human rights and one of the greatest injustices of the twentieth century. No euphemisms can or should be used to deny that.

6. *Personal Justice Denied: Report of the Commission on Wartime Relocation and Internment of Civilians* (Seattle: University of Washington, 1997), xxviii.
7. The British writer George Orwell, whose actual name was Eric Arthur Blair (1903–1950), was the author of the antitotalitarian and dystopic novels, *Animal Farm* (1945) and *1984* (1949), both of which criticized governmental authoritarianism.
8. Jerome was the first camp to close on June 30, 1944. The majority closed in the fall of 1945: Granada/Amache on October 15, 1945; Minidoka on October 28, 1945; Topaz on October 31, 1945; Heart Mountain on November 10, 1945; Gila River on November 16, 1945; Manzanar on November 21, 1945; Poston on November 28, 1945; and Rohwer on November 30, 1945. The Tule Lake camp was the last to close, on March 30, 1946.
9. Okubo's memoir, though seen in later years as revelatory of the internment experience, was not necessarily an unvarnished account of her time in Tanforan and Topaz. For analysis of this, see Caroline Chung Simpson, *An Absent Presence: Japanese Americans in Postwar American Culture, 1945–1960* (Durham: Duke University Press, 2002), 12–42. See also Deborah Gesensway and Mindy Roseman, "Miné Okubo," in *Beyond Words: Images from America's Concentration Camps* (Ithaca: Cornell University Press, 1987), 66–74. For a comprehensive discussion of Okubo's art and career, see Greg Robinson and Elena Tajima-Creef, eds., *Miné Okubo: Following Her Own Road* (Seattle: University of Washington Press, 2008).
10. Peter Suzuki, "Introduction," in *Treadmill: A Documentary Novel*, by Hiroshi Nakamura (Oakville, Ontario, Canada: Mosaic Press, 1996).
11. See Hiroshi Kashiwagi, *Swimming in the American: A Memoir and Selected Writings* (San Mateo, CA: Asian American Curriculum Project, 2005), for more discussion of this. The play is printed in Kashiwagi, *Shoe Box Plays* (San Mateo: Asian American Curriculum Project, Inc., 2008), 67–101. See also Brian Niiya, "Laughter and False Teeth (play)," *Densho Encyclopedia*, October 5, 2020 (https://encyclopedia.densho.org/Laughter%20and%20False%20Teeth%20(play)/, accessed June 29, 2019).
12. The first comprehensive study of Okada and his life was recently published. See Frank Abe, Greg Robinson, and Floyd Cheung, eds., *John Okada: The Life and Rediscovered Work of the Author of "No-No Boy,"* (Seattle: University of Washington Press, 2018). The redress movement that emerged in the 1960s and 1970s stimulated the recovery of literature about the incarceration. A variety of cultural and political factors converged during these decades to stimulate a resurgence of civil rights activism among African Americans through the Black Power movement, Indigenous Americans through the American Indian movement (AIM), and Mexican Americans through the Chicano movement. Japanese Americans joined the fight as they sought legal restitution of the civil rights denied them, recognition of and apology for the injustice of incarceration, and monetary compensation. Their work resulted in the Civil Liberties Act of 1988, which acknowledged directly that racial prejudice, wartime hysteria, and political failure created the tragedy. All survivors were "compensated" with $20,000 payments.

13. Shortly after the war a number of works about the injustices of internment were produced by African American and white authors. For a comprehensive overview of these, see Greg Robinson, "Writing the Internment," in *The Cambridge Companion to Asian American Literature*, ed. Crystal Parikh and Daniel Y. Kim (Cambridge, UK: Cambridge University Press, 2015), 45–58. For an overview of Japanese American writing more generally, see Stan Yogi, "Japanese American Literature," in *An Interethnic Companion to Asian American Literature*, ed. King-Kok Cheung (Cambridge, UK: Cambridge University Press, 1997), 125–154.
14. See Yuji Ichioka, ed., *Views from Within: The Japanese American Evacuation and Resettlement Study* (Los Angeles: Asian American Studies Center, University of California-Los Angeles, 1989), for an assessment of JERS. For a study of the prominent sociologist Charles Kikuchi, a JERS community analyst, see Matthew Briones, *Jim and Jap Crow: A Cultural History of 1940s Interracial America* (Princeton: Princeton University Press, 2012). For a study of Thomas Shibutani, another internee who went on to excel in the field of sociology, see Karen Inouye, *The Long Afterlife of Nikkei Wartime Incarceration* (Stanford: Stanford University Press, 2016).
15. See, for just a few examples, Greg Robinson, *By Order of the President: FDR and the Internment of Japanese Americans* (Cambridge, MA: Harvard University Press, 2001); Robert Dallek, *Franklin D. Roosevelt and American Foreign Policy, 1932–1945* (New York: Oxford University Press, 1979); Roger Daniels, *Concentration Camps USA: Japanese Americans and World War II* (New York: Holt, Rinehart, 1971); Michi Nishiura Weglyn, *Years of Infamy* (1976; reprint, Seattle: University of Washington Press, 1996); Brian Masaru Hayashi, *Democratizing the Enemy: The Japanese American Internment* (Princeton: Princeton University Press, 2008).
16. See Eileen H. Tamura, *In Defense of Justice: Joseph Kurihara and the Japanese American Struggle for Equality* (Urbana: University of Illinois Press, 2013); Naomi Paik, *Rightlessness: Testimony and Redress in U.S. Prison Camps since World War II* (Chapel Hill: University of North Carolina Press, 2016); Lorraine K. Bannai, *Enduring Conviction: Fred Korematsu and His Quest for Justice* (Seattle: University of Washington Press, 2015); Gordon K. Hirabayashi et al. *A Principled Stand: The Story of Hirabayashi v. United States* (Seattle: University of Washington Press, 2013); Cherstin M. Lyon, *Prisons and Patriots: Japanese American Wartime Citizenship, Civil Disobedience, and Historical Memory* (Philadelphia, PA: Temple University Press, 2012).
17. See Takeya Mizuno, "Censorship in a Different Name: Press 'Supervision' in Wartime Japanese American Camps 1942–1943," *Journalism and Mass Communication Quarterly* 88, no. 1 (2011): 121–141; Mizuno, "Government Suppression of the Japanese Language in World War II Assembly Camps," *Journalism and Mass Communication Quarterly* 80, no. 4 (2003): 849–865; Lauren Kessler, "Fettered Freedoms: The Journalism of World War II Japanese Internment Camps." *Journalism History* 15, no. 2 (1988): 70–79; Louis Fiset, "Censored! U.S. Censors and Internment Camp Mail in World War II," in *Guilt by Association: Essays on Japanese Settlement, Internment, and Relocation in the Rocky Mountain West*, ed. Mike Mackey (Powell, WY: Western History Publications, 2001), 69–100.

18. See Robert Sadamu Shimabukuro, *Born in Seattle: The Campaign for Japanese American Redress* (Seattle: University of Washington Press, 2001); John Tateishi, *Redress: The Inside Story of the Successful Campaign for Japanese American Reparations* (Berkeley: Heyday, 2020); Roger Daniels, Sandra C. Taylor, and Harry H. L. Kitano, eds., *Japanese Americans: From Relocation to Redress* (Seattle: University of Washington Press, 1991); Nikkei for Civil Rights and Redress, *NCRR: The Grassroots Struggle for Japanese American Redress and Reparations* (Los Angeles: UCLA Asian American Studies Center Press, 2018).
19. See Jane E. Dusselier, *Artifacts of Loss: Crafting Survival in Japanese American Concentration Camps* (New Brunswick: Rutgers University Press, 2008) and Delphine Hirasuna and Kit Hinrichs, *The Art of Gaman: Arts and Crafts from the Japanese American Internment Camps, 1942–1946* (Berkeley: Ten Speed Press, 2005).
20. See Connie Y. Chiang, *Nature Behind Barbed Wire: An Environmental History of the Japanese American Incarceration* (New York: Oxford University Press, 2018).
21. See Jasmine Alinder, *Moving Images: Photography and the Japanese American Incarceration* (Urbana: University of Illinois Press, 2009); Dorothea Lange, et al. *Impounded: Dorothea Lange and the Censored Images of Japanese American Internment* (New York: W.W. Norton, 2006); Lane Ryo Hirabayashi, Kenichiro Shimada, and Hikaru Iwasaki, *Japanese American Resettlement through the Lens: Hikaru Carl Iwasaki and the WRA's Photographic Section, 1943–1945* (Boulder: University Press of Colorado, 2009).
22. For color photos of the incarceration in Heart Mountain, Wyoming, see Bill T. Manbo and Eric L. Muller, *Colors of Confinement: Rare Kodachrome Photographs of Japanese American Incarceration in World War II* (Chapel Hill: University of North Carolina Press, in association with the Center for Documentary Studies at Duke University, 2012).
23. On education, see Allan W. Austin, *From Concentration Camp to Campus: Japanese American Students and World War II* (Urbana: University of Illinois Press, 2004). On healthcare, see Louis Fiset, "Public Health in World War II Assembly Centers for Japanese Americans," *Bulletin of the History of Medicine* 73, no. 4 (1999): 565–584, Gwenn M. Jensen, "System Failure: Health-Care Deficiencies in the World War II Japanese American Detention Centers," *Bulletin of the History of Medicine* 73, no. 4 (1999): 602–628, Susan Lynn Smith, "Women Health Workers and the Color Line in the Japanese American 'Relocation Centers' of World War II," *Bulletin of the History of Medicine* 73, no. 4 (1999): 585–601; Naomi Hirahara and Gwenn M. Jensen, *Silent Scars of Healing Hands: Oral Histories of Japanese American Doctors in World War II Detention Camps* (Fullerton: Center for Oral and Public History, California State University, 2004). On individual camp histories, see Robert Harvey, *Amache: The Story of Japanese Internment in Colorado during World War II* (Dallas, TX: Taylor: Distributed by National Book Network, 2003); Harry N. Scheiber and Jane L. Scheiber, *Bayonets in Paradise: Martial Law in Hawai'i during World War II* (Honolulu: University of Hawai'i Press, 2016); Sandra C. Taylor, *Jewel of the Desert: Japanese American Internment at Topaz* (Berkeley: University of California Press, 1993); Priscilla Wegars, *Imprisoned in Paradise: Japanese Internee*

Road Workers at the World War II Kooskia Internment Camp (Moscow, ID: Asian American Comparative Collection, University of Idaho, 2010), John Howard, *Concentration Camps on the Homefront: Japanese Americans in the House of Jim Crow*, (Chicago: University of Chicago Press, 2008), for a few representative examples.

24. For rhetorical analysis of how diary entries, note-taking, manifestos, and multiple drafts of single documents were used as political tools of engagement by Japanese Americans, both during the war and since, see Mira Shimabukuro, *Relocating Authority: Japanese Americans Writing to Redress Mass Incarceration* (Boulder: University Press of Colorado, 2015).

Chapter 1

1. As quoted by Stan Yogi, "Japanese American Literature," in *An Interethnic Companion to Asian American Literature*, ed. King-Kok Cheung (New York: Cambridge University Press, 1997), 130. See Yogi's section titled "Establishing an Identity: Prewar Nisei Writing" in the larger essay on Japanese American Literature for a more thorough discussion of the idea that Nisei would bridge Japanese and American cultures.
2. Hisaye Yamamoto, "Introduction," in *The Chauvinist and Other Stories*, by Toshio Mori (Los Angeles: Asian American Studies Center, University of California, Los Angeles, 1979), 6. This feeling persisted after the war as well. Yamamoto noted that Kenneth Yasuda, also known as Shōson, dedicated his collection of Japanese poems and original haiku, *A Pepper-Pod*, to "Bashō and Buson . . . in a hope that a bridge may be built between East and West" (New York: Knopf, 1947), vi.
3. Toyo Suyemoto, *I Call to Remembrance: Toyo Suyemoto's Years of Internment*, ed. Susan B. Richardson (New Brunswick, NJ: Rutgers University Press, 2007), 29.
4. Suyemoto, *I Call to Remembrance*, 29.
5. Suyemoto, *I Call to Remembrance*, xviii.
6. Suyemoto, *I Call to Remembrance*, 32.
7. See Susan M. Schweik, *A Gulf So Deeply Cut: American Women Poets and the Second World War* (Madison: University of Wisconsin Press, 1991), for a discussion of Suyemoto's position in the lineage of American women's poetry. For an exploration of how her work is similar to Emily Dickinson's, see Lillian Faderman and Barbara Bradshaw, *Speaking for Ourselves* (Glenview, IL: Scott, Foresman, 1969), 223.
8. Isshin H. Yamasaki, ed., *American Bungaku*, (Tokyo: Keigan Sha Publisher, 1938), 64–65.
9. Suyemoto, *I Call to Remembrance*, xxii.
10. Suyemoto, *I Call to Remembrance*, xxvii.
11. Suyemoto, "Writing of Poetry," *Amerasia* 10, no. 1: 73–79, as cited by Susan Richardson in Suyemoto, *I Call to Remembrance*, 27.
12. Stan Yogi, "Japanese American Literature," in *An Interethnic Companion to Asian American Literature*, ed. King-Kok Cheung (New York: Cambridge University Press, 1997), 128.

13. Suyemoto adopted her husband's surname, Kawakami, upon their marriage but returned to her birth name after their divorce. Some of her poetry is published under the name Toyo Kawakami.
14. Suyemoto, *I Call to Remembrance*, 11–12.
15. Suyemoto, *I Call to Remembrance*, 13–15.
16. Suyemoto, *I Call to Remembrance*, 14.
17. *Personal Justice Denied: Report of the Commission on Wartime Relocation and Internment of Civilians* (Washington, DC: United States Government Printing Office, 1992), 103.
18. Suyemoto, *I Call to Remembrance*, 14.
19. Suyemoto, *I Call to Remembrance*, 20.
20. Suyemoto, *I Call to Remembrance*, 17.
21. Suyemoto, *I Call to Remembrance*, 24.
22. Suyemoto, *I Call to Remembrance*, 37.
23. Suyemoto, *I Call to Remembrance*, 37.
24. Suyemoto, *I Call to Remembrance*, 38.
25. Suyemoto, *I Call to Remembrance*, 39–40.
26. Suyemoto, *I Call to Remembrance*, 39–40.
27. Louis Fiset, "Public Health in World War II Assembly Centers for Japanese Americans," *Bulletin of the History of Medicine* 73 no. 4 (1999): 573. For an analysis of the actual conditions in camp in comparison to the War Relocation Authority (WRA) report, see Gwenn M. Jensen, "System Failure: Health-Care Deficiencies in the World War II Japanese American Detention Centers," *Bulletin of the History of Medicine* 73 no. 4 (1999): 602–628. For interviews of physicians and nurses who served in the camps, see Naomi Hirahara and Gwenn M. Jensen, *Silent Scars of Healing Hands: Oral Histories of Japanese American Doctors in World War II Detention Camps*, A Project of the Japanese American Medical in conjunction with the Japanese American National Museum and UCLA Asian American Studies Center, (Los Angeles, CA, 2004).
28. Suyemoto, *I Call to Remembrance*, 55–56.
29. Comparatively little work has been done on healthcare in the camps. The primary researchers include Louis Fiset, Susan Smith, Susan McKay, and Gwenn Jensen. Fiset's work has been foundational in documenting the "what" with facts and figures. A dentist himself, he documents the experience from the perspective of a healthcare professional, weighing the care provided against the circumstances and, in general, considers it to have been adequate. Citing the widespread inoculation programs, pre- and postnatal care, and dentistry provided to the incarcerated, Fiset concludes that the US Public Health Services, augmented by the Japanese American health workers maintained, for the most part, incarcerees' health at a nominal level. See Fiset, "Public Health in World War II Assembly Centers for Japanese Americans." Smith's work focuses on nursing and midwifery in the camps. She argues that the shortage of RNs in the camps opened doors for rudimentary nursing assistant training for many Nisei, and also allowed a limited number of African American nurses to work during the war. At the same time, however, Smith also acknowledges that labor shortages of trained medical professionals compromised healthcare to inmates. Physicians

and nurses in the hospitals and clinics were recruited from the inmate population itself, but paid far less than the white workers. Nurse Velma Kessel, for example, was paid $80/month, her Japanese American coworkers were paid $16–$19. See Susan Lynn Smith, "Women Health Workers and the Color Line in the Japanese American 'Relocation Centers' of World War II," *Bulletin of the History of Medicine* 73 no. 4 (1999): 585–601. Susan McKay's work concentrates explicitly on maternal care provided to thirty-six women at Heart Mountain. See McKay, *The Courage Our Stories Tell: The Daily Loves and Maternal Child Health Care of Japanese American at Heart Mountain* (Powell, WY: Western History Publications, 2002). Gwenn Jensen's work, written from the perspective of a medical anthropologist, provides valuable documentary evidence of the considerable "system failures" that stymied the provision of adequate healthcare, including "poor planning and design, adverse environmental conditions, the contamination of food and water, overcrowding, inadequate staffing, and racism." See Jensen, "System Failure."

30. Gwenn M. Jensen, "Dysentery, Dust, and Determination: Health Care in the World War II Japanese American Detention Camps," *Discover Nikkei*, June 21, 2008 (http://www.discovernikkei.org/en/journal/2008/6/21/enduring-communities/).
31. Jensen, "System Failure," 610.
32. Jensen, "System Failure," 611.
33. Suyemoto, *I Call to Remembrance*, 57–58.
34. Suyemoto, *I Call to Remembrance*, 58.
35. Suyemoto, *I Call to Remembrance*, 59.
36. Suyemoto, *I Call to Remembrance*, 60.
37. Suyemoto, *I Call to Remembrance*, 55.
38. Suyemoto, *I Call to Remembrance*, 68–69.
39. Shoko Suzuki, "In Search of the Lost *Oikos*: Japan after the Earthquake of 11 March 2011," in *Hazardous Future: Disaster, Representation and the Assessment of Risk*, ed. I. C. Gil and C. Wulf (Boston: De Gruyter 2015), 109–123. The Chinese American humanistic geographer Yi-Fu Tuan initiated the study of topophilia in his 1974 work, *Topophilia: A Study of Environmental Perception, Attitudes, and Values* (Englewood Cliffs, NJ: Prentice-Hall 1974) and went on to explore it in depth throughout his career. Humanistic geology examines the relationship between humanity and geographic concepts such as space, place, home, mobility, landscape, region, nature, and human-made environments in order to understand the dynamic relationship between how the human experience defines and is simultaneously defined by physical geographical locations and landforms.
40. Suzuki, "In Search of the Lost *Oikos*," 110.
41. Suyemoto, *I Call to Remembrance*, 74–75.
42. Suyemoto, *I Call to Remembrance*, 75.
43. For an excellent and thorough analysis of Suyemoto's attitudes toward landscape, see John Streamas, "Toyo Suyemoto, Ansel Adams, and the Landscape of Justice," in *Recovered Legacies: Authority and Identity in Early Asian American Literature*, ed. Keith Lawrence and Floyd Cheung (Philadelphia, PA: Temple University Press, 2005), 141–157.

44. Suyemoto, *I Call to Remembrance*, 77–78.
45. Suyemoto, *I Call to Remembrance*, 75.
46. Suyemoto, *I Call to Remembrance*, 85.
47. For a rare and important rhetorical study of this, see Mira Shimabukuro, *Relocating Authority: Japanese Americans Writing to Redress Mass Incarceration*, (Boulder: University Press of Colorado, 2015).
48. For studies of this, see J. W. Pennebaker, "Writing about Emotional Experiences as a Therapeutic Process," *Psychological Science* 8(1997): 162–166; B. A. van der Kolk, A. C. McFarlane, and L. Weisaeth, eds., *Traumatic Stress: The Effects of Overwhelming Experience on Mind, Body, and Society* (New York: Guilford, 2007). For an outstanding documentary exploration of the healing power of the arts more generally on victims of the incarceration, see Satsuki Ina et al., *Children of the Camps: [Videorecording]: A Documentary and Educational Project*. (San Francisco, CA: National Asian American Telecommunications Association [distributor], 1999).
49. Karen A. Baikie and Kay Wilhelm, "Emotional and Physical Health Benefits of Expressive Writing," *Advances in Psychiatric Treatment* 11, no. 5 (2005): 338–346.
50. Suyemoto, *I Call to Remembrance*, 194.
51. Suyemoto, *I Call to Remembrance*, 188. The National Japanese American Student Relocation Council was founded to coordinate the enrollment of incarcerated Nisei of college age into universities in the Midwest and the East Coast. For two book-length studies of this, see Allan W. Austin, *From Concentration Camp to Campus: Japanese American Students and World War II* (Urbana: University of Illinois Press, 2004) and Thomas James, *Exile Within: The Schooling of Japanese Americans, 1942–1945* (Cambridge, MA, and London: Harvard University Press, 1987).
52. Suyemoto, *I Call to Remembrance*, 195.

Chapter 2

1. As quoted by Frank Chin, *Born in the USA: A Story of Japanese America, 1889–1947* (Lanham, MD: Rowman & Littlefield, 2002), 128. Larry Tajiri was an influential Nisei editor and columnist for a variety of Japanese American newspapers. Prior to the war he worked for the *Kashu Mainichi* in Los Angeles, the San Francisco *Nichi Bei Shimbun*, and the Japanese *Asahi Shimbun* newspaper. The latter closed after the bombing of Pearl Harbor, and Tajiri returned to San Francisco and became active in resisting the incarceration. In 1942, he and his wife Guyo (also a journalist) were offered the editorship of the *Pacific Citizen*, the Japanese American Citizens League (JACL) paper run out of Salt Lake City, Utah, and they accepted, thus avoiding incarceration. Tajiri toured a number of the camps as well as the Camp Shelby military training ground for Nisei soldiers in Mississippi in early 1943 and contributed an article titled "Relocation" to *TREK* for the June 1943 edition. This article was largely straightforward in its encouragement of inmates to embrace relocation. It assured them of friendly audiences and warm receptions from people in the Midwest and the eastern United States: "Today, this morning, this afternoon, this evening, young

Japanese Americans are arriving in bus and railroad stations throughout America, leaving the dust of relocation centers behind and returning to the broad boulevards, the movie palaces and the skyscrapers of America" on the "Sunshine Special" (*TREK*, June 1943: 7). For a full study of Larry and Guyo Tajiri, see Greg Robinson, *Pacific Citizens: Larry and Guyo Tajiri and Japanese American Journalism in the World War II Era* (Urbana: University of Illinois Press, 2012).

2. Isshin H. Yamasaki, ed., *America Bungaku* (Tokyo: Keigan Sha,1938), ii.
3. Omura, himself, was not incarcerated; rather, he chose to move out of the exclusion zone to Colorado to continue his activist journalism. For more details on Omura's life and activism, see James Matsumoto Omura, *Nisei Naysayer: The Memoir of Militant Japanese American Journalist, Jimmie Omura*, ed. Arthur A. Hansen (Stanford, CA: Stanford University Press, 2018).
4. Chin, *Born in the USA: A Story of Japanese America, 1889–1947*, 180.
5. Chin, *Born in the USA: A Story of Japanese America, 1889–1947*, 184.
6. For other examples from the Harlem Renaissance, see Claude McKay's "Baptism," "If We Must Die," and "America"; Langston Hughes' "I, Too"; or Georgia Douglas Johnson's "Common Dust."
7. Countee Cullen (1903–1946) was an African American poet of the Harlem Renaissance who, not unlike Toyo Suyemoto, favored traditional poetic forms through which to express rather unconventional messages. Claude McKay, another Harlem Renaissance writer, was perhaps the most obvious proponent of this unusual juxtaposition. For more on the paradoxical relationship between McKay's form and content, see Heather Hathaway, *Caribbean Waves: Relocating Claude McKay and Paule Marshall* (Bloomington: Indiana University Press, 1999).
8. Richard Wright, in his autobiography, *Black Boy*, describes marveling at H. L. Mencken's ability to use "words as a weapon" and determined that he would do so as well. Wright, *Black Boy* (Cleveland, OH: World Publishing Co., [1937] 1947), 218..
9. The camp newspapers, which primarily contained factual reporting of events in the camps, were also used as propaganda to demonstrate to outsiders that the incarcerated were being well treated under not simply sufficient but enriching conditions.
10. Takeya Mizuno, "Censorship in a Different Name: Press 'Supervision' in Wartime Japanese American Camps 1942–1943," *Journalism and Mass Communication Quarterly* 88, no. 1 (Spring 2011): 121.
11. Mizuno, "Censorship in a Different Name," 124, citing original.
12. Mizuno, "Censorship in a Different Name," 128.
13. As cited by Mizuno, "Censorship in a Different Name," 126.
14. Lauren Kessler, "Fettered Freedoms: The Journalism of World War II Japanese Internment Camps," *Journalism History* 15, no. 2 (1988): 72, citing the "War Relocation Administrative Manual," Chapter 20, Part 10, paragraph 8, final revision February 8, 1945.
15. Mizuno, "Censorship in a Different Name," 129. For a discussion of how Japanese language materials were taken from inmates, see Mizuno, "Government Oppression of the Japanese Language in World War II Assembly Camps," *J&MC Quarterly* 8, no. 4 (2003): 849–865.
16. Kessler, "Fettered Freedoms," 75–76.

17. Kessler, "Fettered Freedoms," 75.
18. Toyo Suyemoto, *I Call to Remembrance: Toyo Suyemoto's Years of Internment*, ed. Susan B. Richardson (New Brunswick, NJ: Rutgers University Press, 2007), 136.
19. Taro Katayama, "Haru," in *Ayumi: A Japanese American Anthology*, ed. Janice Mirikitani (San Francisco, CA: Japanese American Anthology Committee, 1980), 120.
20. David Yoo, *Growing Up Nisei: Race, Generation and Culture among Japanese Americans of California, 1924–1949* (Urbana: University of Illinois Press, 2000), 99, 205.
21. Yoo, *Growing Up Nisei*, 99
22. Suyemoto, *I Call to Remembrance*, 187.
23. The blurb about Frank Beckwith in *TREK* suggests he was respected by the inmates. It reads: "Frank Beckwith, publisher of the Millard County Chronicle, has lived in Delta for almost 30 years and probably knows more about this region than any other man around. Between issues of his paper, he has roamed this territory, collecting fossils and Indian lore. The Smithsonian Institute gave a fossil Merostome the name of *Beckwithia type* in his honor. Many visitors to Delta from Topaz have seen his collection of minerals, arrowheads, and other Indian artifacts. His articles, which he often composes on the linotype, have appeared in many national and regional publications." *TREK*, December 1942, Topaz concentration camp, Utah, ddr-densho-142-425. Densho, Courtesy of the Library of Congress, 20.
24. *TREK*, December 1942, 2.
25. *TREK*, December 1942, 3.
26. *TREK*, December 1942, 3.
27. Suyemoto, *I Call to Remembrance*, 88–89.
28. This is called epideictic oratory and refers to a ceremonial speech issuing both praise and blame, as defined by Aristotle in his classic work, *Rhetoric.*
29. *TREK*, December 1942, 7, 6.
30. The planting of "Victory Gardens" containing vegetables for a family's consumption were encouraged during World Wars I and II to allow the government to divert food supplies to the war effort.
31. *TREK*, December 1942, 8.
32. *TREK*, December 1942, 6.
33. Susan Schweik, *A Gulf So Deeply Cut: American Women Poets and the Second World War* (Madison: University of Wisconsin Press, 1991), 188, and John Streamas, "Toyo Suyemoto, Ansel Adams, and The Landscape of Justice" in *Recovered Legacies: Authority and Identity in Early Asian American Literature*, eds. Keith Lawrence and Floyd Cheung (Philadelphia, PA: Temple University Press, 2005), 141–157.
34. Susan B. Richardson, Introduction to Suyemoto, *I Call To Remembrance*, xx.
35. Suyemoto dedicates her memoir to Kay: "This day, my son, is the fifteenth anniversary date since you were hospitalized in a coma from which you never awakened. Much has happened in the intervening years, the good and the bad, rewarding and disappointing, the joyous and the sad, woven into a texture of living that was denied to you. I only wish that I could share, as we once did, these moments to remember.

The task that I now have before me is the story of the internment years, which began before you were able to comprehend what loss of freedom and rights meant. Because your health and the length of your life were affected by your early years in an internment camp, the story must be told—for those who will wonder what happened to the Japanese Americans on the West Coast after Pearl Harbor. July 25, 1971." Suyemoto, *I Call to Remembrance*, 4.

36. A number of excellent studies on resettlement exist. See Greg Robinson, *After Camp: Portraits in Midcentury Japanese American Life and Politics* (Berkeley: University of California Press, 2012); Brian Komei Dempster, ed., *Making Home from War: Stories of Japanese American Exile and Resettlement* (Berkeley, CA: Heydey Books, 2010); and Lane Ryo Hirabayahi and Kenichiro Shimada, *Japanese American Resettlement through the Lens: Hikaru Carl Iwasaki and the WRA's Photographic Section, 1943–1945* (Boulder: University of Colorado Press, 2009).
37. *TREK*, February 1943, Topaz concentration camp, Utah, ddr-densho-142-426, Densho, Courtesy of the Library of Congress, 2–3.
38. *TREK*, February 1943, 5.
39. *TREK*, February 1943, 10.
40. Ultimately, no reparations were made to incarcerated Japanese Americans until the passing of the Civil Liberties Act of 1988. Through this, approximately 82,000 surviving detainees were issued checks for $20,000 and a letter of apology from then-president George H. W. Bush. For a thorough discussion of the Evacuation Claims Act, see Greg Robinson, *A Tragedy of Democracy: Japanese Confinement in North America* (New York: Columbia University Press, 2009), chap. 6.
41. *TREK*, December 1942, 28.
42. *TREK*, December 1942, 28.
43. *TREK*, December 1942, 28–29.
44. *TREK*, December 1942, 28–29.
45. *TREK*, February 1943, 41.
46. *TREK*, February 1943, 40, 41.
47. *TREK*, June 1943, Topaz concentration camp, Utah, ddr-densho-142-427, Densho, Courtesy of the Library of Congress, 40.
48. *TREK*, June 1943, 41.
49. Laura Card has analyzed the writing of "Schraubi" and assessed it to have been authored by Yamada. Card, "'TREK' Magazine, 1942–1943: A Critical Rhetorical Analysis," Phd diss, (University of Utah, 2005).
50. Hisaye Yamamoto, "Introduction," in *The Chauvinist*, by Toshio Mori (Los Angeles: Asian American Studies Center, 1981), 9. Much less is known about Yamada's background and activities after the war. Stan Yogi describes him as a "budding writer and Berkeley student" prior to the war, but few other references to him exist, including in the most comprehensive resource on the incarceration, the *Densho Project*. See Stan Yogi, "Japanese American Literature," in *An Interethnic Companion to Asian American Literature*, ed. King-Kok Cheung (New York: Cambridge University Press, 1997), 132. In an interview of Yamamoto and Wakako Yamauchi with King-Kok Cheung, Yamauchi notes, however, that after Yamada's move from Topaz to Poston by March of 1943, "he didn't write when he came to Poston. He was deep in

his sociological surveys" by then, suggesting that he may have begun working for the Japanese [American] Evacuee Relocation Survey (JERS) at that point. See King-Kok Cheung, *Words Matter: Conversations with Asian American Writers* (Leiden; Boston: Brill, 2000), 360. Interestingly, Yamamoto's writing also waned during her incarceration. She published just one story, "Death Rides the Rails to Poston," on January 9, 1943, in the camp newspaper, the *Chronicle*, with the intention that it grow into a serialized mystery. This never materialized. "Death Rides the Rails to Poston" has since been republished in the 2001 edition of her short story collection, *Seventeen Syllables* (New Brunswick, NJ: Rutgers University Press, 2001), 131–141.

51. Congressional Record, 78th Cong., 1st sess., A408. For more on Rankin, see John Howard, *Concentration Camps on the Home Front: Japanese Americans in the House of Jim Crow* (Chicago, IL: Chicago University Press, 2008), chap. 2.
52. *TREK*, February 1943, 42.
53. Eleanor Roosevelt, draft of *Collier's* article reprinted as "To Undo a Mistake Is Always Harder Than Not to Create One Originally," in *Confinement and Ethnicity: An Overview of World War II Japanese American Relocation Sites*, ed. Jeffery F. Burton et al. (Seattle: University of Washington Press, 2002), 21–22.
54. *TREK*, December 1942, 16.
55. *TREK*, December 1942, 13.
56. *TREK*, December 1942, 15.
57. For a thorough discussion of the relationship between US government organizations and the Japanese American community between 1880 and 1945, see Brian Masaru Hayashi, *Democratizing the Enemy: The Japanese American Internment* (Princeton, NJ: Princeton University Press, 2004).
58. *TREK*, December 1942, 13.
59. High-profile beatings in both Poston and Manzanar actually triggered strikes and riots in the two camps, instigated by the FBI's attempts to arrest the perpetrators. The businessman and JACL leader, Fred Tayama, for example, was attacked on December 5, 1942, in Manzanar. Though six masked people carried out the assault, only Henry Ueno was jailed. Ueno's arrest led to demonstrations and a subsequent crackdown by the military police in which two inmates were shot and killed. The artist Henry Sugimoto characterizes the beating of another alleged "inu," John Yamazaki, an Issei reverend and JACL member in Jerome, who was assaulted for translating, at the request of camp administrators, the loyalty questionnaire into Japanese. See Sugimoto's 1943 painting, "Reverend Yamazaki was Beaten in Camp Jerome."
60. *TREK*, December 1942, 15.

Chapter 3

1. Russell Leong, "An Interview with Toshio Mori," *Amerasia Journal* 7, no. 1 (1980): 89–108, reprinted in Steven Y. Mori, ed., *Unfinished Message: Selected Works of Toshio Mori* (Berkeley, CA: Heyday Books, 2000), 228.

2. Mori in Leong, "Interview," 94–95. "The Brothers," which was included in *Yokohama, California* upon its publication in 1949, is different from another of Mori's works with a similar title, "The Brothers Murata." "The Brothers" is a short story written prior to the war and tells a tale of two children. "The Brothers Murata" was written in 1944 and is a novella set in Topaz and addresses the vexing issue of whether or not to enlist in the army.
3. Frank Chin, *Born in the USA: A Story of Japanese America, 1889–1947* (Lanham, MD: Rowman & Littlefield, 2002), 128. Here, James Omura describes his and Larry Tajiri's "ambitions to write The Great Nisei Novel."
4. Peter Horikoshi, "Interview with Toshio Mori," in *Counterpoint: Perspectives on Asian America*, ed. Emma Gee et al. (Los Angeles: Asian American Studies Center, University of California, 1976), 474.
5. Leong, "Interview," 224.
6. Hisaye Yamamoto, "Introduction," in *The Chauvinist and Other Stories*, by Toshio Mori (Los Angeles: Asian American Studies Center, University of California, 1979), 8. Yamamoto emphasizes this point because, she believes, some Nisei and Sansei writers have unfairly judged Saroyan for what they deem to be his condescending tone in the Introduction that he contributed to the first edition of *Yokohama, California*. She disagreed with this view and believed that Saroyan was an important influence on Mori.
7. William Saroyan, "Introduction to the Original Edition," in *Yokohama, California*, by Toshio Mori (Caldwell, ID: Caxton Printers, 1949), 1.
8. Lawson Fusao Inada, "Standing on Seventh Street: An Introduction to the 1985 Edition," in *Yokohama, California*, by Toshio Mori (Seattle: University of Washington Press, [1949] 1985), xviii.
9. Inada, "Standing on Seventh Street," xix.
10. Inada, "Standing on Seventh Street," xx.
11. Inada, "Standing on Seventh Street," v.
12. Yamamoto, "Introduction," 1.
13. Yamamoto, "Introduction," 4.
14. The phrase, "just like everybody else," refers to the prejudice of then California Attorney General and future Chief Justice of the Supreme Court, Earl Warren, who reasoned that it would disrupt "national unity" and be a "crime" to confine German and Italian nationals because "they were just like everybody else." That is to say, they were white while Japanese Americans were not. For a valuable discussion of this, see Stephen C. Fox, "General John DeWitt and the Proposed Internment of German and Italian Aliens during World War II," *Pacific Historical Review* 57: 4 (Nov. 1988): 407–438.
15. Mori, *Yokohama, California*, 23.
16. Mori, *Yokohama, California*, 24–25.
17. Mori, "Foreword," in *Unfinished Message*, x.
18. Mori, *Yokohama, California*, 91.
19. Mori, *Yokohama, California*, 94–95.
20. Mori, *Yokohama, California*, 91.
21. Mori, *Yokohama, California*, 71.

22. Mori, *Yokohama, California*, 71.
23. Mori, *Yokohama, California*, 72–73.
24. Mori, *Yokohama, California*, 73.
25. Mori, *Yokohama, California*, 76.
26. Yamamoto, "Introduction," 6. This feeling persisted after the war as well. Yamamoto noted that Kenneth Yasuda, also known as Shōson, dedicated his collection of Japanese poems and original haiku, *A Pepper-Pod*, to "Bashō and Buson . . . in a hope that a bridge may be built between East and West" (New York: Knopf, 1947), vi.
27. Mori, *Yokohama, California*, 155.
28. Mori, *Yokohama, California*, 155–156.
29. Mori, *Yokohama, California*, 152.
30. Mori, *Yokohama, California*, 158–159.
31. Mori, *Yokohama, California*, 159.
32. Mori, *Yokohama, California*, 160.
33. Mori, *Yokohama, California*), 160–161.
34. Horikoshi, "Interview with Toshio Mori," 476.
35. See Werner Sollors, "Introduction," in *The Life Stories of {Undistinguished} Americans, as Told by Themselves*, ed. Hamilton Holt (New York: Routledge, 1990).
36. *TREK*, February 1943, 13.
37. *TREK*, February 1943, 13.
38. *TREK*, February 1943, 14.
39. *TREK*, February 1943, 15.
40. *TREK*, February 1943, 16.
41. *TREK*, February 1943, 14.
42. *TREK*, February 1943, 15.
43. *TREK*, June 1943, Topaz concentration camp, Utah, ddr-densho-142-427, Densho, Courtesy of the Library of Congress, 16.
44. *TREK*, June 1943, 13.
45. *TREK*, June 1943, 13.
46. *TREK*, June 1943, 13.
47. Mori retells this story from his own personal first-person perspective in "The Long Journey and the Short Ride," contained in *The Chauvinist and Other Stories.*
48. *All Aboard*, Spring 1944, Topaz concentration camp, Utah, ddr-densho-282-1 Densho, Courtesy of the War Relocation Authority Documents Collection, 50, 53).
49. *All Aboard*, 51.
50. *TREK*, December 1942, Topaz concentration camp, Utah, ddr-densho-142-425 Densho, Courtesy of the Library of Congress, 24.
51. *TREK*, December 1942, 23–24.
52. *TREK*, December 1942, 24.
53. *TREK*, December 1942, 24.
54. Mori, "1, 2, 3, 4, Who Are We For?," *The Chauvinist and Other Stories*, 119.
55. *TREK*, December 1942, 24.
56. Walt Whitman, "Song of Myself," 15, in *Leaves of Grass* (1892). https://www.poetryfoundation.org/poems/45477/song-of-myself-1892-version.

57. *TREK*, December 1942, 24.
58. *TREK*, December 1942, 24, 25. The phrase, "it's morning in America," was used by the 1984 Ronald Reagan presidential campaign in a television ad to signal optimism and renewal.
59. *TREK*, December 1942, 25.
60. Yamamoto, "Introduction," 5.
61. Mori, "Foreword," in *Unfinished Message*, ix.
62. Inada, "Standing on Seventh Street," xx–xxi.
63. Mori, *Yokohama, California*, 128.
64. Mori, *Yokohama, California*, 130.
65. Mori, *Yokohama, California*, 131.
66. Mori, *Yokohama, California*, 132.
67. Mori, *Yokohama, California*, 132.
68. For more information about this, see James C. McNaughton, "Japanese Americans and the U.S. Army," *Army History* 59 (Summer–Fall 2003).
69. Mori, *Yokohama, California*, 133–134.
70. Mori, *Yokohama, California*, 134.
71. Mori, *Yokohama, California*, 135.
72. See King-Kok Cheung, *Articulate Silences: Hisaye Yamamoto, Maxine Hong Kingston, and Joy Kogawa* (Ithaca, NY: Cornell University Press, 1993), for a study of silence in Asian American women's literature. Mori's literary strategies fit well within Cheung's frame.
73. Mori, "Foreword," in *Unfinished Message*, ix.

Chapter 4

1. Luis-Martín Lozano and Juan Rafael Coronel Rivera, *Diego Rivera: The Complete Murals, Photographs by Rafael Doniz and Francisco Kochen*, ed. Benedikt Taschen (Los Angeles: Taschen, 2008), 384. For a fuller discussion of leftist artists in San Francisco during the period, see Anthony W. Lee, *Painting on the Left: Diego Rivera, Radical Politics, and San Francisco's Public Murals* (Berkeley: University of California Press, 1999), especially pages 184–203. For information about Rivera's role in the exposition specifically, and for beautiful large-scale reproductions of all of his murals, see Lozano and Coronel Rivera, *Diego Rivera*, especially chap. 10, "The Fight against Fascism."
2. Lozano and Coronel Rivera, *Diego Rivera*, 383.
3. For a full list of Rivera's assistants, see https://riveramural.org/diegosassistants/.
4. https://riveramural.org/overview/.
5. For a discussion of this conflict, see Pete Hamill, *Diego Rivera* (New York: Harry N. Abrams, 1999), 162–168. See also Lozano and Coronel Rivera, 348–349. For a discussion of Rivera's leftist politics in the years leading up to the reigns of Hitler and Mussolini, see Elsie Casler, "Pan American Unity, Diego Rivera's Dramatic Interlude

with Trotsky" (PDF), *Ex Post Facto: Journal of the History Students at San Francisco State University* (2001).

6. Lozano and Coronel Rivera, *Diego Rivera*, 384. For a more thorough analysis of Rivera's theoretical political leanings, see Jeffrey Belnap, "Diego Rivera's Greater America Pan-American Patronage, Indigenism, and H.P.," *Cultural Critique*, no. 63 (2006): 61–98.
7. As cited by Elena Tajima Creef, "Following Her Own Road: The Achievement of Miné Okubo," in *Miné Okubo: Following Her Own Road*, eds. Greg Robinson and Elena Tajima Creef (Seattle: University of Washington Press, 2008), 6. Rivera, in 1940, was actually on his fourth marriage: he and his famous wife, artist Frieda Kahlo, had divorced in 1939 only to remarry in 1940.
8. For a glimpse of Okubo at work on the mural, see the silent video depicting artists at work on "The Living New Deal" website: https://livingnewdeal.org/tag/golden-gate-international-exposition/. The link to the film is: https://diva.sfsu.edu/collections/sfbatv/bundles/187038. Okubo appears briefly at 2:31 into the film. The description of the film is this: "Silent, color footage from the Golden Gate International Exposition on Treasure Island in San Francisco (1939/40), produced by Orville C. Goldner. Features scenes from the Art in Action exhibition, including coverage of Diego Rivera and Miné Okubo working on the Pan American Unity Mural and of various artists demonstrating: sculpture; mosaics; printing; doll making; weaving; pottery and axe carving. Movette Film Transfer of San Francisco remastered this 16mm negative film print in March 2018 in 2K resolution (2048x1556 pixels), using a Lasergraphics film scanner. Opening graphic designed by Carrie Hawks."
9. Miné Okubo, *Citizen 13660* (Seattle: University of Washington Press, 1983, 1946), 10.
10. https://www.topazmuseum.org/topaz-history/topaz-art-school; Chiura Obata, *Topaz Moon: Art of the Internment*, ed. Kimi Kodani Hill, intro. Timothy Anglin Burgard, fwd. Ruth Asawa (Berkeley, CA: Heyday Books, 2000); Deborah Gesensway and Mindy Roseman, *Beyond Words: Images from America's Concentration Camps* (Ithaca, NY: Cornell University Press, 1987). Jane Beckwith, lifelong champion of preserving the history of the Topaz camp and president of the Topaz Museum Board, curated an exhibit of the Topaz artists for the Springville, Utah, art museum in 2010.
11. Obata, *Topaz Moon*, 35–37.
12. Obata, *Topaz Moon*, 41.
13. Obata, *Topaz Moon*, 35.
14. Obata, *Topaz Moon*, 19.
15. Christine Hong, "Illustrating the Postwar Peace: Miné Okubo, the 'Citizen-Subject' of Japan, and 'Fortune' Magazine," *American Quarterly* 64, no. 1 (March 2015): 105–140. Hong argues that Okubo's work became part of a larger postwar United States effort to establish a "*pax Americana* that would reconfigure the Asia-Pacific region as a US security zone upon Japan's military defeat" (106). She explains the complex logic by which Okubo's work was co-opted by the WRA to rehabilitate democracy both at home and abroad. "To no small degree," Hong asserts, "the 'democratic' rehabilitation of the Japanese 'enemy' in the Pacific was perceived as hinging on the successful Americanization of the alienized Japanese American—all within the militarized

contours of a US-sponsored 'peace'" (111). Greg Robinson offers an important analysis of the public reception of Okubo's memoir, set within the context of the postwar period, as well as a historical tracing of how her comments about and exhibition of her work, and her attitude toward her creation changed over time. He both resists the notion that it was a subversively resistant text and recognizes the constraints placed upon Okubo by the circumstances of her time. Greg Robinson, "Birth of a Citizen: Miné Okubo and the Politics of Symbolism," in Robinson and Creef, *Miné Okubo*, 159–176.

16. Heather Fryer, "Miné Okubo's War: *Citizen 13660*'s Attack on Government Propaganda," in Robinson and Creef, *Miné Okubo*, 94. Fryer provides a compelling analysis of the range of reviews of the work that appeared in 1946, drawing attention to "three general trends": one saw it as "objective reporting"; another variously identified certain aspects of the text as either "Japanese" or "American," according to prevailing stereotypes of the era; and a third "erased the federal government's role as the agent of Okubo's oppression" (92–94). Robinson and Creef's collection provides the most interdisciplinary analysis of *Citizen 13660* and is an excellent introductory resource for readers.
17. Dorothy Fuccinelli, "Review of the Art Association's Annual Exhibition of Drawings and Prints," *California Art and Architecture* 60, no. 3 (April 1943): 12, as cited by Greg Robinson, "Birth of a Citizen: Miné Okubo and the Politics of Symbolism," in Robinson and Creef, *Miné Okubo*, 173.
18. Robinson, "Birth of a Citizen," 163. Hong, "Illustrating the Postwar Peace," 105–140, explores this issue at length. *Fortune* magazine, however, was not without its biases: Okubo commented on the oddity of her being asked to illustrate the article with images of Japan, given that she was neither Japanese nor had been to Japan herself.
19. Robinson, "Birth of a Citizen," 159–176, offers an analysis of the role Okubo played in promoting the idea that Japanese Americans were "model" citizens ready for resettlement.
20. Hana Wirth-Nesher, "Between Mother Tongue and Native Language: Multilingualism in Henry Roth's 'Call It Sleep,'" *Prooftexts* 10, no. 2 (1990): 297.
21. Vivian Fumiko Chin analyzes the juxtaposition of Okubo's drawings and captions at length in Chin, "Gestures of Noncompliance: Resisting, Inventing, and Enduring in *Citizen 13660*," in Robinson and Creef, *Miné Okubo*, 67–81.
22. Okubo, *Citizen 13660*, 18.
23. Obata, *Topaz Moon*, 20.
24. Okubo, *Citizen 13660*, 31.
25. *TREK*, December 1942, 28-29.
26. Okubo, *Citizen 13660*, 89.
27. "The Learned," though not depicting an actual meal, resembles the other two and Okubo's *TREK* cover in layout. While "Our Bread" extols peasant life and the fruit of the land, and "Wall Street Banquet, 1928" skewers capitalists, the satirical "The Learned" is no less harsh on intellectuals as it portrays an elderly wise man with a funnel on his head, surrounded by lackeys listening to his every word.

28. Lee, *Painting on the Left: Diego Rivera, Radical Politics, and San Francisco's Public Murals*, 200. Lee also notes the similarity between Okubo's work and "Wall Street Banquet, 1928."
29. Okubo, *Citizen 13660*, 89.

Chapter 5

1. I thank Greg Robinson, Professor of History at l'Université du Québec à Montréal, for generously sharing with me his copy of the *Pulse*. It is also now available in digital format: *Pulse*, Amache/Granada concentration camp, Amache, Colorado, War Relocation Authority, Colorado College Special Collections, MS 0221, FD4. Colorado Springs, CO (https://coloradocollege.edu).
2. Yamato Ichihashi and Gordon H. Chang, *Morning Glory, Evening Shadow: Yamato Ichihashi and His Internment Writings, 1942–1945* (Stanford, CA: Stanford University Press, 1997), 97, 98.
3. Ichihashi and Chang, *Morning Glory, Evening Shadow*, 98.
4. Robert Harvey, *Amache: The Story of Japanese Internment in Colorado during World War II* (Dallas, TX: Taylor, 2003), 41.
5. Ichihashi and Chang, *Morning Glory, Evening Shadow*, 100.
6. Ichihashi and Chang, *Morning Glory, Evening Shadow*, 100, 102.
7. Gordon. H. Chang, editor of Ichihashi's diary, translates "mutsuki" as "diapers," but I have been unable to confirm the accuracy of this translation. Lily Yuriko Nakai Havey pointed out to me that the word for diaper is "omutsu." Perhaps Ichihashi was using a dialect or slang term in this instance.
8. Ichihashi and Chang, *Morning Glory, Evening Shadow*, 102–103.
9. Harvey, *Amache*, 42.
10. Lily Yuriko Nakai Havey, *Gasa Gasa Girl Goes to Camp: A Nisei Youth behind a World War II Fence* (Salt Lake City: University of Utah Press, 2014), 11.
11. Havey, *Gasa Gasa Girl*, 5–6.
12. Havey, *Gasa Gasa Girl*, 9.
13. Havey, *Gasa Gasa Girl*, 9.
14. Havey, *Gasa Gasa Girl*, 11–13.
15. Harvey, *Amache*, 42.
16. Harvey, *Amache*, 42, 45–46.
17. Harvey, *Amache*, 45.
18. Ichihashi and Chang, *Morning Glory, Evening Shadow*, 260–261.
19. Ichihashi and Chang, *Morning Glory, Evening Shadow*, 260.
20. Brian Niiya "Salt Lake City Governors' Meeting," *Densho Encyclopedia* (https://encyclopedia.densho.org/Salt%20Lake%20City%20governors'%20meeting).
21. Ichihashi and Chang, *Morning Glory, Evening Shadow*, 265–266.
22. Ichihashi and Chang, *Morning Glory, Evening Shadow*, 266.
23. Ichihashi and Chang, *Morning Glory, Evening Shadow*, 266–267.

24. "Granada Pioneer," vol. 1, number 18, December 24, 1942. Joseph H McClelland collection, Auraria Library Digital Collection, (http://digital.auraria.edu/AA00005572/00017?search=McClelland).
25. Ichihashi and Chang, *Morning Glory, Evening Shadow*, 266–267.
26. Harvey, *Amache*, 207.
27. *Pulse*, Amache/Granada concentration camp, Amache, Colorado, War Relocation Authority, Colorado College Special Collections, MS 0221, FD4. Colorado Springs, CO (https://coloradocollege.edu).
28. John Embree, Report on Granada, January 30–February 1, 1943, War Relocation Authority Community Analysis Section, 1. Bancroft Library, University of California Berkeley, as cited by Bonnie Clark, "Amache (Granada)," *Densho Encyclopedia* (https://encyclopedia.densho.org/Amache%20(Granada)/).
29. Granada *Pioneer*, July 14, 1943, ddr-densho-147-83, Courtesy Library of Congress, 2.
30. For a full history of farmers from this community, see Valerie J. Matsumoto, *Farming the Home Place: A Japanese Community in California, 1919–1982* (Ithaca, NY: Cornell University Press, 1993).
31. https://www.nps.gov/parkhistory/online_books/5views/5views4h103.htm.
32. For a discussion of this, see Greg Robinson, *A Tragedy of Democracy: Japanese Confinement in North America* (New York: Columbia University Press, 2009), chap. 6.
33. https://www.nps.gov/parkhistory/online_books/5views/5views4h103.htm.
34. Harvey, *Amache*, 61.
35. Harvey, *Amache*, 124.
36. Jeffery F. Burton et al. *Confinement and Ethnicity: An Overview of World War II Japanese American Relocation Sites* (Seattle: University of Washington Press, [1999] 2002), 44.
37. Harvey, *Amache*, 124.
38. But farming was not Amache's only notable business enterprise: it also ran a substantial silk-screening shop that produced camp documents ranging from commencement programs and annuals to WAC posters, Red Cross booklets, Blue Star Mothers' (those with children serving in the military) stationery and calendars. The December 24, 1943, Christmas Edition of the Granada *Pioneer* celebrated "the 14 by 20-inch calendar" printed in "20 bright colors" that required the dedication of workers putting in "night hours" to produce. It was given as a Christmas gift to everyone in the camp from "Santa Claus," whose army of elves, the silk-screen staff, hand-delivered to each office and family group. The majority of materials produced by the shop, however, were for the US Navy. More than 250,000 recruitment and informational posters were printed at Amache. "We used to make posters for the navy and the army—'Come Join the Army'—signs like that. . . . I wasn't an artist, but I helped make the posters. The artists would draw something and [we would] cut the film and use the screens to make the print. I think it was about the first of its kind. It was very new at the time. . . . We had all our friends working together, it was kind of fun. We used to make our own Christmas cards and things like that," remembered Tae Namura (Harvey, *Amache*, 124). This work on behalf of the war effort was acknowledged far

beyond the barbed-wire boundaries of the camp; the April 22, 1944, edition of the Granada *Pioneer* noted that the shop was highlighted in a full-page spread in the April 1944 edition of the national advertising magazine *Signs of the Times*, and credited with demonstrating the "remarkable achievement of the war training program." Not surprisingly, as with the farm, the irony of detainees creating recruitment materials for the government that had incarcerated them was not addressed. Clark, "Amache (Granada)."

39. *Pulse*, 11.
40. Harvey, *Amache*, 130–131.
41. Havey, *Gasa Gasa Girl*, 96–97.
42. *Havey, Gasa Gasa Girl*, 96.
43. Havey, *Gasa Gasa Girl*, 97.
44. Havey, *Gasa Gasa Girl*, 99.
45. *Pulse*, 16.
46. Havey, *Gasa Gasa Girl*, 179.
47. Havey, *Gasa Gasa Girl*, 180.
48. Havey, *Gasa Gasa Girl*, 179–180.
49. Havey, *Gasa Gasa Girl*, 121–123.
50. Ichihashi and Chang, *Morning Glory, Evening Shadow*, 266.
51. Toshiko Aiboshi, Interview with Richard Potashin, Culver City, California, January 20, 2011, *Densho Digital Archive*, courtesy of the Manzanar National Historic Site Collection (http://ddr.densho.org/interviews/ddr-manz-1-112-1/).
52. Harvey, *Amache*, 130, 131.
53. I thank the Oxford Press reviewer for alerting me to Abe's writing career. For a brief biography of Abe, see Kazuo Yamane, "Introduction to Yoshio Abe's *The Man of Dual Nationality*," *Journal of Ethnic Studies* 12, no. 4 (1985): 87.
54. *Pulse*, 1. The punctuation and layout of Abe's "Imperfect Prairie" is accurately represented here. Abe did not use conventional grammatical patterns in this poem.
55. Yamane, "Introduction," 88–99.
56. Yamane, "Introduction," 87.
57. Michael Jin, "A Transnational Generation: Japanese Americans in the Pacific before World War II," *Ritsumeikan Language and Culture Studies* 21, no. 4 (2010): 185.
58. Yoshio Abe, "The Man of Dual Nationality," *Journal of Ethnic Studies* 12, no. 4 (1985): 90.
59. For a lengthy discussion of this range of attitudes about Kibei, see Jin, "A Transnational Generation," 185–196.
60. The terms by which Indigenous People in the United States refer to themselves has varied over time, by tribe, and even by individual. Most groups prefer to be identified by their tribal affiliation. When discussed as a larger entity, multiple terms have been used, including "Indigenous American," "Native American," and "American Indian." The National Museum of the American Indian, a division of the Smithsonian, advises that Indigenous Peoples be asked what term they prefer. In my study, I have used tribal names whenever possible. See https://americanindian.si.edu/nk360/informational/impact-words-tips.

61. *Pulse*, 15.
62. Cynthia Kadohata fictionally recreates the complex relationship between Japanese American detainees and American Indians in her depiction of the friendship between a young girl, Sumiko, and a young Mohave boy in the 2006 novel *Weedflower.* Cynthia Kadohata, *Weedflower* (New York: Atheneum Books for Young Readers, 2006).
63. Havey, *Gasa Gasa Girl*, 58.
64. Havey, *Gasa Gasa Girl*, 58.
65. Havey, *Gasa Gasa Girl*, 58.
66. Lawson Fusao Inada, *Legends from Camp: Poems* (Minneapolis, MN: Coffee House Press, 1992), iii, iv.
67. Lawson Fusao Inada, *Drawing the Line* (Minneapolis, MN: Coffee House, 1997), 110–111.

Chapter 6

1. Barbara Takei, "Tule Lake," *Densho Encyclopedia*, April 10, 2018 (https://encyclopedia.densho.org/Tule%20Lake).
2. Mark Clark, "'The Deadly Enemies That They Are': Local Reaction to the Tule Lake Internment Camp," *Journal of the Shaw Historical Library* 19 (2005): 46–47.
3. Gary Y. Okihiro, "Tule Lake under Martial Law: A Study in Japanese Resistance," *Journal of Ethnic Studies* 5, no. 3 (Fall 1977): 73.
4. This history is examined by Okihiro, "Tule Lake under Martial Law," 71–85.
5. *Tulean Dispatch Magazine*, August 1942, 1, Tulean Dispatch Magazine collection, Densho, Courtesy of the Library of Congress.
6. *Tulean Dispatch Magazine*, October 1942, 1.
7. *Tulean Dispatch Magazine*, October 1942, 1.
8. *Tulean Dispatch Magazine*, November 1942, 22.
9. *Tulean Dispatch Magazine*, November 1942, 23.
10. *Tulean Dispatch Magazine*, December 1942, 4.
11. *Tulean Dispatch Magazine*, December 1942, 4.
12. *Tulean Dispatch Magazine*, December 1942, 6, 5.
13. *Tulean Dispatch Magazine*, December 1942, 6.
14. This area is now part of the Lava Beds National Monument.
15. For a full-length study of the Modoc war, see Boyd Cothran, *Remembering the Modoc War: Redemptive Violence and the Making of American Innocence* (Chapel Hill: University of North Carolina Press, 2014).
16. *Tulean Dispatch*, "Farewell Issue," September 1943, 5, 18.
17. See Hiroshi Nakamura, *Treadmill: A Documentary Novel* (Oakville, Ontario, Canada: Mosaic Press, 1996), 78–79, 88–89, for references to this fear.
18. *Tulean Dispatch Magazine*, December 1942, 15; *Tulean Dispatch Magazine*, December 1942, 23.
19. *Tulean Dispatch Magazine*, December 1942, 23.

20. Shelley Cannady describes Tule Lake as an inherently "racialized landscape created by the expulsion of its original inhabitants, the Modoc people. It had been physically transformed by the US Bureau of Reclamation's Klamath project that drained and channelized much of the area's extensive shallow lake/wetland system for agriculture and homesteading, and opened it up to (white only) homesteaders." Cannady, "Tule Lake Today: Internment and Its Legacies," *Boom: A Journal of California* 3, no. 1 (Spring 2013), 20. For a poetic exploration of Captain Jack and the Modoc warriors, as well as their imagined affinity with internees, see Lawson Fusao Inada, "At the Stronghold," in *Legends from Camp: Poems by Lawson Fusao Inada* (Minneapolis: Coffee House Press, 1993), 101–113. See also Cynthia Kadohata's novel, *Weedflower* (New York: Simon and Schuster: 2006), for a fictional portrayal of a friendship between an incarcerated Japanese American girl and an Indigenous boy on a reservation. Finally, see Cynthia Wu, "A Comparative Analysis of Indigenous Displacement and the World War II Japanese American Internment," *Amerasia Journal* 42, no. 1 (2016): 1–15, for a valuable explanation of how the carceral histories of Indigenous and Japanese Americans in the United States are both similar but also significantly different.
21. *Tulean Dispatch*, "Farewell Issue," September 1943, 6.
22. See Brian Masaru Hayashi, *Democratizing the Enemy: The Japanese American Internment* (Princeton, NJ: Princeton University Press, 2004); Eric Muller, *American Inquisition: The Hunt for Japanese American Disloyalty in World War II* (Chapel Hill: University of North Carolina Press, 2007); and Cherstin Lyon, *Prisons and Patriots: Japanese American Wartime Citizenship, Civil Disobedience, and Historical Memory* (Philadelphia, PA: Temple University Press, 2011), which valuably casts the citizenship debates within the context of the daily life of one resister, Joe Norikane, one of the "Tucsonians," a group of Nisei draft resisters who chose this name for themselves based on their incarceration in the Tucson Federal Prison Camp.
23. Paul Howard Takemoto, *Nisei Memories: My Parents Talk about the War Years* (Seattle: University of Washington Press, 2006), 171.
24. *Tulean Dispatch Magazine*, April 1943, 1, 6.
25. *Tulean Dispatch Magazine*, April 1943, 1, 6.
26. *Tulean Dispatch Magazine*, April 1943, 21.
27. *Tulean Dispatch Magazine*, March 1943, 7.
28. *Tulean Dispatch Magazine*, March 1943, 8.
29. *Tulean Dispatch Magazine*, March 1943, 9, 27.
30. *Tulean Dispatch Magazine*, February 1943, 23.
31. See Muller, *American Inquisition: The Hunt for Japanese American Disloyalty in World War II*, for a full exploration of the issue. See also Emiko Omori's acclaimed documentary, *Rabbit in the Moon* (Hohokus, NJ: New Day Films, 1999), for a discussion of how responses to these questions were considered "evidence" of national affiliation and loyalty. For the most thorough analysis of draft resisters, see Frank Abe's award winning *Conscience and the Constitution* (San Francisco, CA: ITVS, 2000).
32. For a photo image of an original "Loyalty Questionnaire," see "The So-Called Loyalty Questionnaire," ddr-densho-72–4, Densho, Courtesy of the Ikeda Family Collection.

33. In this case the US Supreme Court determined that Takao Ozawa, an Issei who had resided in the United States for two decades, was not eligible for naturalization and citizenship. At stake was how Japanese Americans in the United States were to be defined according to the racial classifications of the time. The Naturalization Act of 1906 allowed only "free whites" and those of "African descent" naturalization. Japanese were deemed neither of these. https://supreme.justia.com/cases/federal/us/260/178/.
34. Dillon S. Myer, *Uprooted Americans: The Japanese Americans and the War Relocation Authority during World War II* (Tucson: University of Arizona Press, 1971), 72.
35. The Sole Survivor Policy, enacted by the Department of Defense and intended to protect members of a family from the draft or from combat duty if the family has already lost members in military service, was not put in effect until 1948.
36. See Matthew Briones, *Jim and Jap Crow: A Cultural History of 1940s Interracial America* (Princeton, NJ: Princeton University Press, 2013), for an extended analysis of the multiple systems of segregation pitting minoritized groups against one another during the period.
37. *Tulean Dispatch*, May 27, 1943, 2.
38. *Tulean Dispatch*, May 27, 1943, 2.
39. *Tulean Dispatch Magazine*, July 1943, 5.
40. *Tulean Dispatch Magazine*, July 1943, 3.
41. *Tulean Dispatch Magazine*, July 1943, 6.
42. *Tulean Dispatch*, "Farewell Issue," September 1943, 1.

Chapter 7

1. Frank Abe, "Introduction," *John Okada: The Life and Rediscovered Work of the Author of No-No Boy*, ed. Frank Abe, Greg Robinson, and Floyd Cheung (Seattle: University of Washington Press, 2018), 5.
2. Hiroshi Kashiwagi's play *The Betrayed* was written after the war and offers a poignant depiction of a couple who split up during the war because of the loyalty test and then reunited forty years later, only to question what their lives would have been like if they had been able to stay together. See Hiroshi Kashiwagi, *The Betrayed*, in *Shoe Box Plays* (San Mateo, CA: Asian American Curriculum Project, 2008).
3. Toshio Mori, *The Brothers Murata: A Novel*, in *Unfinished Message: Selected Works of Toshio Mori*, ed. Steven Y. Mori, intro. Lawson Fusao Inada (Santa Clara, CA: Heyday Books, 2000), 141.
4. Mori, *The Brothers Murata*, 156.
5. Mori, *The Brothers Murata*, 166.
6. Mori, *The Brothers Murata*, 166.
7. Mori, *The Brothers Murata*, 167.
8. Mori, *The Brothers Murata*, 168.
9. Mori, *The Brothers Murata*, 184.
10. Mori, *The Brothers Murata*, 198.
11. Mori, *The Brothers Murata*, 171.

12. Mori, *The Brothers Murata*, 199–200.
13. Mori, *The Brothers Murata*, 201.
14. Mori, *The Brothers Murata*, 204.
15. Mori, *The Brothers Murata*, 205.
16. Mori, *The Brothers Murata*, 186.
17. Mori, *The Brothers Murata*, 205.
18. Mary Sato Nakamura and Isami Nakamura, "Hiroshi Nakamura, 1915–1973," (1995), in *Treadmill: A Documentary Novel*, by Hiroshi Nakamura (Oakville, Ontario, Canada: Mosaic Press, 1996), i–iii.
19. Peter T. Suzuki, "Introduction," in *Treadmill: A Documentary Novel*, by Hiroshi Nakamura (Oakville, Ontario, Canada: Mosaic Press, 1996), v.
20. Peter T. Suzuki, "*Treadmill*: The Premier Novel of the Wartime Camps for Japanese Americans," *Asian Profile* 20, no. 2 (April 1992): 175–176.
21. Nakamura, *Treadmill*, 57.
22. Nakamura, *Treadmill*, 57.
23. Nakamura, *Treadmill*, 57.
24. Nakamura, *Treadmill*, 59.
25. Nakamura, *Treadmill*, 122–123.
26. See Karon Kehoe, *City in the Sun* (New York: Dodd, Mead, 1946). For a thoughtful discussion of homoeroticism in *City in the Sun*, see Greg Robinson, "The Great Unknown and the Unknown Great: Queer Non-Nikkei Figures in Japanese American History (Part V)," *Nichi Bei: A Mixed Plate of Japanese American News and Culture*, October 2, 2014 (https://www.nichibei.org/2014/10/the-great-unknown-and-the-unknown-great-queer-non-nikkei-figures-in-japanese-american-history-part-v).
27. Nakamura, *Treadmill*, 142–143.
28. For a compelling article written in an unusual epistolary format that explores, from a sociological perspective, the origins and nature of Buraku discrimination, see Kokichiro Miura, "Walking on the Edge: Towards a Sociography of Discrimination against the Buraku: Lectures on Discrimination in Letter Format," *International Journal of Japanese Sociology* 23 (March 2014): 1, 46–62. For a full-length history of the Burakamin in Japan, see Jeffrey Paul Bayliss, *On the Margins of Empire: Buraku and Korean Identity in Prewar and Wartime Japan* (Cambridge, MA: Harvard University Asia Center, 2013).
29. For a discussion of present-day discrimination against etta, see Mike Sunda, "Japan's Hidden Caste of Untouchables," BBC News, October 23, 2015 (https://www.bbc.com/news/world-asia-34615972).
30. Nakamura, *Treadmill*, 144–145.
31. Nakamura, *Treadmill*, 144.
32. Nakamura, *Treadmill*, 144.
33. Nakamura, *Treadmill*, 145.
34. Nakamura, *Treadmill*, 150.
35. Nakamura, *Treadmill*, 153.
36. Nakamura, *Treadmill*, 79.
37. Nakamura, *Treadmill*, 79. The Hualapai tribe was sent to the Colorado River Indian Reservation as part of the eradication of Indigenous Peoples conducted throughout

the United States in the mid- and late nineteenth century. Each year the tribe commemorates this through a road race from their ancestral lands to the reservation. Reported *ParkerLive*, on April 20, 2016: "In 1874, several years after the United States waged a campaign of ethnic cleansing against Indigenous groups in the region, the military rounded up hundreds of Pai's and forcibly relocated them to the Colorado River Indian Reservation in Parker, Arizona. Children, the elderly, and the sick died on the two-week march, but more died of disease and starvation during their year-long internment in the place referred to as La Paz at the sweltering northern tip of the Sonoran Desert. Nearly one year later, in 1875, the surviving band members escaped imprisonment and returned home to northwestern Arizona. The annual La Paz Run memorializes these experiences by allowing Hualapai's to retrace the steps of their ancestors from the point of internment northward to the Hualapai Reservation" (http://www.parkerliveonline.com/2016/04/20/hualapai-tribe-trail-of-tears/).

38. Nakamura, *Treadmill*, 89.
39. "Rudy Tokiwa Talks about Extreme Weather Conditions at Poston," *Densho Encyclopedia*, July 2, 2012 (https://encyclopedia.densho.org/sources/en-denshovh-trudy-02-0017-1/).
40. Nakamura, *Treadmill*, 66.
41. Nakamura, *Treadmill*, 66–67.
42. Nakamura, *Treadmill*, 68.
43. Nakamura, *Treadmill*, 69.
44. Nakamura, *Treadmill*, 79.
45. Hisaye Yamamoto, "The Legend of Miss Sasagawara," *Kenyon Review* 12, no. 1 (Winter 1950): 101..
46. Yamamoto, "The Legend," 101.
47. Yamamoto, "The Legend," 102.
48. Yamamoto, "The Legend," 107.
49. Yamamoto, "The Legend," 107.
50. Yamamoto, "The Legend," 113.
51. Yamamoto, "The Legend," 113.
52. Yamamoto, "The Legend," 112.
53. Yamamoto, "The Legend," 114.
54. Yamamoto, "The Legend," 114.
55. Yamamoto, "The Legend," 114.
56. "Ted Nagata Talks about the Psychological Toll the Incarceration Experience Took on His Mother," *Densho Encyclopedia*, March 31, 2016 (https://encyclopedia.densho.org/sources/en-denshovh-nted-01-0008-1/).
57. Nakamura, *Treadmill*, 128. *Hakujin* means white person.
58. Nakamura, *Treadmill*, 135.
59. Nakamura, *Treadmill*, 135.
60. Nakamura, *Treadmill*, 191.
61. Nakamura, *Treadmill*, 191–192.
62. Nakamura, *Treadmill*, 217.
63. Nakamura, *Treadmill*, 204–205.

Chapter 8

1. Daisuke Kitigawa, as cited by Emily Roxworthy, "Nisei Girls' Kabuki in Wartime Arkansas: Cultural Segregation and Cross-Dressing at Rohwer and Jerome," *Women and Performance: A Journal of Feminist Theory* 20, no. 2 (July 2010): 186.
2. Larry Tajiri, ddr-densho-338-430, Courtesy of the Tajiri Estate, Densho (https://ddr.densho.org/ddr-densho-338-430/). For a full-length study of the Tajiri's and *The Pacific Citizen*, see Greg Robinson, *Pacific Citizens: Larry and Guyo Tajiri and Japanese American Journalism in the World War II Era* (Urbana: University of Illinois Press, 2012).
3. Paul Howard Takemoto, *Nisei Memories: My Parents Talk about the War Years* (Seattle: University of Washington Press, 2006), 125.
4. Russell Bearden, "Life inside Arkansas's Japanese-American Relocation Centers," *Arkansas Historical Quarterly* 48, no. 2 (Summer 1989): 180.
5. *Denson Magnet*, Documents Section, Jerome Relocation Center, Denson, Arkansas, 1, Japanese American Evacuation and Resettlement Records, BANC MSS 67/14 c, The Bancroft Library, University of California, Berkeley.
6. John Howard, *Concentration Camps on the Homefront: Japanese American in the House of Jim Crow* (Chicago, IL: University of Chicago Press, 2008), 183–184.
7. Howard, *Concentration Camps on the Homefront*, 180.
8. John Tateishi, *And Justice for All: An Oral History of the Japanese American Detention Camp* (Seattle: University of Washington Press, 1984), 14.
9. *Denson Magnet*, 13.
10. Howard, *Concentration Camps on the Homefront*, 180.
11. Violet Kazue de Cristoforo, *May Sky: There Is Always Tomorrow* (Los Angeles, CA: Sun and Moon Press, 1997), 121.
12. For a lengthy discussion of Sugimoto's wartime and postwar paintings and career, see Edward Tang, *From Confinement to Containment: Japanese/American Arts during the Early Cold War* (Philadelphia, PA: Temple University Press, 2019).
13. Kristine Kim, *Henry Sugimoto: Painting an American Experience* (Berkeley, CA: Heyday, 2000), 35, 39.
14. Deborah Gesensway and Mindy Roseman, *Beyond Words: Images from America's Concentration Camps* (Ithaca, NY: Cornell University Press, 1987), 37.
15. Howard, *Concentration Camps on the Homefront*, 191.
16. Howard, *Concentration Camps on the Homefront*, 191.
17. Brian Niiya, "Jerome," *Densho Encyclopedia*, January 16, 2018 (https://encyclopedia.densho.org/Jerome/).
18. Howard, *Concentration Camps on the Homefront*, 191–192.
19. Howard, *Concentration Camps on the Homefront*, 185, 195.
20. *Denson Magnet*, 4.
21. *Denson Magnet*, 4–5.
22. *Denson Magnet*, 9.
23. *Denson Tribune*, March 16, 1943, ddr-densho-144-46, Densho, Courtesy of the Library of Congress, 3.

24. For a beautiful collection of a variety of aesthetic projects produced in the camps, see Delphine Hirasuna, *The Art of Gaman: Arts and Crafts from the Japanese American Internment Camps, 1942–1946* (Berkeley, CA: Ten Speed Press, 2005). Kobu from Jerome is featured on page 44. For an analysis of arts and crafts from the camps, see Jane Dusselier, *Artifacts of Loss: Crafting Survival in Japanese American Concentration Camps* (New Brunswick, NJ: Rutgers University Press, 2008). For an overview of gardening among prisoners in a variety of situations, see Kenneth Helphand, *Defiant Gardens: Making Gardens in Wartime* (San Antonio, TX: Trinity University Press, 2006). See also Connie Y. Chiang, *Nature behind Barbed Wire: An Environmental History of the Japanese American Incarceration* (New York: Oxford University Press, 2018).
25. *Denson Magnet*, 22.
26. Louis Fiset, "Public Health in World War II Assembly Centers for Japanese Americans," *Bulletin of the History of Medicine* 73 (1999): 565–584.
27. *Denson Magnet*, 21.
28. *Denson Magnet*, 21.
29. *Denson Magnet*, 21.
30. *Denson Magnet*, 9.
31. Gordon Nakagawa, "'What Are We Doing Here with All These Japanese?' Subject-Constitution and Strategies of Discursive Closure Represented in Stories of Japanese American Internment," *Communications Quarterly* 38, no. 4 (Fall 1990): 338.
32. Gesensway and Roseman, *Beyond Words*, 34.
33. Takemoto, *Nisei Memories*, 139, 174, 170.
34. For a complete history of this aspect of the incarceration, see Allan Austin, *From Concentration Camp to Campus: Japanese American Students and World War II* (Urbana: University of Illinois Press, 2004).
35. Leslie A. Ito, "Japanese American Women and the Student Relocation Movement, 1942–1945," *Frontiers: A Journal of Women's Studies* 21, no. 3 (2000): 3–4.
36. Allan Austin, "National Japanese Student Relocation Council," *Densho Encyclopedia*, April 16, 2014 (https://encyclopedia.densho.org/National%20Japanese%20American%20Student%20Relocation%20Council/). Austin attributes this quotation to Leslie Ito's article, but I have been unable to locate it there.
37. Takemoto, *Nisei Memories*, 185.
38. Ito, "Japanese American Women and the Student Relocation Movement, 1942–1945," 2.
39. Jason Morgan Ward, "'No Jap Crow': Japanese Americans Encounter the World War II South," *Journal of Southern History* 73, no. 1 (February 2007): 78.
40. Ward, "'No Jap Crow,'" 76; Howard, *Concentration Camps on the Homefront*, 128–129.
41. Howard, *Concentration Camps on the Homefront*, 129.
42. Francis Mas Fukuhara, Segment 16, September 25, 1997, Seattle, Washington. Digital Archives, Densho, Densho ID:denshovh-ffrancis-01-0016.
43. Fukuhara, Segment 16.

44. Howard, *Concentration Camps on the Homefront*, 128.
45. Mike Masaoka, *They Call Me Moses Masaoka: An American Saga* (New York: William Morrow, 1987), 143; as cited by Howard, *Concentration Camps on the Homefront*, 129.
46. Fukuhara, Segment 16.
47. *Denson Magnet*, 9.
48. *Denson Magnet*, 8.
49. I am indebted to an anonymous Oxford press reviewer for directing me to this article.
50. Eddie Shimano, "Blueprint for a Slum," *Common Ground* (Summer 1943): 78–85, 79. The article can be accessed here: https://www.unz.com/print/CommonGround-1943q2-00078/.
51. Shimano, "Blueprint for a Slum," 80.
52. Shimano, "Blueprint for a Slum," 80.
53. Shimano, "Blueprint for a Slum," 83.
54. Shimano, "Blueprint for a Slum," 84.
55. *Denson Magnet*, 5.
56. Grace Sugita Hawley interview, segment 11 (2009), Digital Archives, Densho (http://encyclopedia.densho.org/sources/en-denshovh-hgrace-01-0011-1/).
57. See Matthew M. Briones, *Jim and Jap Crow: A Cultural History of 1940s Interracial America* (Princeton, NJ: Princeton University Press, 2012).

Chapter 9

1. Akimoto went on to be a major producer of film poster art. After his release from Rohwer, Akimoto illustrated broadsides for films such as *The Wild Party* (1975) starring Raquel Welch; *The Hindenburg*, also released in 1975 and starring George C. Scott and Anne Bancroft; *Crime and Passion* (1976), starring Omar Sharif and Karen Black; numerous Blaxploitation films such as *Black Caesar* (1973), for which James Brown wrote the musical score, and *Hell up in Harlem* (1973), both starring Fred Williamson, as well as *Slaughter's Big Rip-Off* (1973), starring Jim Brown; and numerous science fiction films including *Silent Running* (1972) with Bruce Dern and a 1976 version of Edgar Rice Burroughs's *At the Earth's Core*.
2. For a classic example of the racist stereotypes used to depict Japanese and Japanese Americans during the war, see *Tokio Jokio*, the 1943 Warner Brothers short animated film written by Don Christensen and directed by Norm McCabe.
3. John Howard, in *Concentration Camps on the Homefront: Japanese Americans in the House of Jim Crow* (2008) makes a case for "Lil Dan'l" being a pro-US nationalist figure, though I contend that this image challenges that notion. For a full magazine edition of "Lil Dan'l's" adventures, see George Akimoto, *Lil Dan'l: One Year in a Relocation Center* (Mcgeehee, AR: Rohwer *Outpost*, 1943).

4. *The Pen*, 1. The specific phrase, "the pen is mightier than the sword," was coined by the English playwright Edward Bulwer-Lyton in 1839 for his play *Richelieu: or, The Conspiracy*:

    True, This!—Beneath the rule of men entirely great The pen is mightier than the sword. Behold The arch-enchanters wand!—itself is nothing!—But taking sorcery from the master-hand To paralyse the Cæsars, and to strike The loud earth breathless!—Take away the sword—States can be saved without it!

5. *The Pen*, 1. This is a modification of Lincoln's actual words, which were: "The world will little note, nor long remember what we say here, but it can never forget what they did here."
6. Avard T. Fairbanks, American sculptor, created his famous statue, "Lincoln the Frontiersman" in 1942, further solidifying the president's image in the eyes of the American public.
7. "The Japanese Relocation," War Relocation Authority film (https://www.youtube.com/watch?v=ja5o5deardA). See also Allan Austin, "OWI/WRA documentaries,." *Densho Encyclopedia*, April 16, 2014 (https://encyclopedia.densho.org/OWI/WRA%20documentaries/).
8. *The Pen*, 25.
9. Delphine Hirasuna in *Relocation, Arkansas*, 2017. Dirs. Vivienne Schiffer and Johanna Demetrakas (http://www.relocationarkansas.com/).
10. *Relocation, Arkansas*.
11. *The Pen*, 45.
12. *The Pen*, 45.
13. *The Pen*, 45–46.
14. *The Pen*, 46.
15. *The Pen*, 48.
16. Paul Howard Takemoto, *Nisei Memories: My Parents Talk about the War Years* (Seattle: University of Washington Press, 2006), 159.
17. Shibutani was among of a group of Nisei intellectuals in the social sciences who had attended or were attending Berkeley at the outset of the war and who, along with Charles Kikuchi and S. Frank Miyamoto, pursued advanced degrees in sociology and social work after the war. While incarcerated, they worked as "community analysts" for the study, recording daily events and attitudes in the camps. For an excellent study of his life and work, see Karen Inouye, *The Long Afterlife of Nikkei Wartime Incarceration* (Stanford, CA: Stanford University Press, 2016).
18. The "Chicago school" of sociology was based at the University of Chicago and focused, in the 1920s and 1930s, on urban and immigrant sociology.
19. Robert E. Park, "Racial Assimilation in Secondary Groups with Particular Reference to the Negro," *American Journal of Sociology* 19, no. 5 (March 1914): 611.
20. *The Pen*, 41.
21. *The Pen*, 41–42.
22. *The Pen*, 44.
23. *The Pen*, 53.
24. *The Pen*, 53.

25. *Relocation, Arkansas.*
26. *The Pen*, 65. The "Fourth Estate" typically refers to the press, or any group that significantly influences society without being officially part of the political system. Here, I assume the letter writers worked together on a school newspaper.
27. *The Pen*, 65–66.
28. *The Pen*, 65–66.
29. *The Pen*, 56. See https://detroithistorical.org/learn/encyclopedia-of-detroit/race-riot-1943.
30. *The Pen*, 56.
31. *The Pen*, 57.
32. *The Pen*, 57.
33. *The Pen*, 56.
34. Valerie Matsumoto, "Japanese American Women during World War II," *Frontiers: A Journal of Women's Studies* 8, no. 1 (1984): 11, *passim.*
35. *The Pen*, 58.
36. *The Pen*, 58.
37. *The Pen*, 47. The layout of this poem in the original is not reproduced here.
38. Cited by Emily Roxworthy, "Nisei Girls' Kabuki in Wartime Arkansas: Cultural Segregation and Cross-Dressing at Rohwer and Jerome," *Women and Performance: A Journal of Feminist Theory* 20, no. 2 (July 2010): 191.

Further Reading

In the introduction to this book, I outline the general categories of academic scholarship on the incarceration and identify some premier studies in each area. The notes to the chapters and the Works Cited reference numerous additional resources. As these demonstrate, extensive research exists on the incarceration, despite the historical lack of awareness or surprising inattention to the event among the general public. But I am pleased to see the subject increasingly taught in elementary and secondary schools; represented in fiction, documentaries, drama, and even feature films; focused on by museums of history, culture, and art; and commonly acknowledged as a historical tragedy that has left a legacy of community trauma.

To further understanding of the complexities of the incarceration, I offer here a variety of other resources through which to explore the subject. Any static list of this type is bound to become outdated as soon as it is put into print, however, so consider this a noncomprehensive point of departure, with apologies and humility to those whose works I neglect.

Densho

The most accurate and valuable comprehensive resource can be found at Densho.org. This is a grass-roots, live, educational website that is continually updated and enriched. Its Digital Archives contain primary sources from the period ranging from newspapers to photographs to letters to governmental documents. Most richly, the archives hold hundreds of oral interviews of those who were incarcerated that provide personal reflections and insights about the experience and its impact on the lives of those involved.

The Densho Encyclopedia contains thousands of entries, written by experts in the field, about all aspects of the event. Most entries are accompanied by bibliographic notes that point to further studies about the specific topic. The Densho Learning Center offers lesson plans and curricula that focus on civil liberties in relation to discriminated groups in the United States, as well as podcasts and blogs of interest to students of all ages.

Camp Historic Sites

A second important resource is the national historic sites of the camps themselves. Most are run jointly by local site committees and the National Park Service, and each is in a different state of development. Shortly after World War II, the sites went to ruin as the nation and the prisoners themselves sought to move on from the tragedy. But with the redress movement in the 1970s, the importance of preserving the artifacts and history of the incarceration became apparent and organizations were developed at each camp to begin this process. Today, annual pilgrimages (both virtual and in person) to the various camps provide an experiential engagement with the past that is unsurpassable. For a documentary overview of each site, see *Discoveries . . . American National Parks: Japanese American Incarceration, 1942–1945*. Bennett-Watt HD Productions, 2013. 56 minutes.

Museums and Libraries

Museums, large and small, also focus on the incarceration. The Smithsonian Institute's National Museum of American History has sponsored exhibits throughout the years, based on its rich archive. The Japanese American National Museum in Los Angeles is perhaps the premier resource for issues pertaining to Japanese American culture and history in general. Calisphere, run by the University of California system and numerous municipal libraries, maintains the Japanese American Relocation Digital Archive (JARDA). The Bancroft Library of the University of California at Berkeley also houses a large collection of primary sources in its Japanese American Evacuation and Resettlement Digital Archive. These materials can be accessed both through Calisphere and the Online Archive of California (OAC). Finally, many university libraries in the states in which the camps were located also hold materials of interest to scholars and students alike.

Documentary Films

Documentaries about the incarceration can be divided roughly into three categories: government propaganda produced during the war itself; films that focus on individual people or specific camps; and films that interrogate the lasting impact of the event in American culture. A simple internet search will identify many, and Densho attempts to keep an updated list (https://encyclopedia.densho.org/Documentary_films/videos_on_incarceration/). The Watase Media Arts Center of the Japanese American National Museum produces films about Japanese American history and culture, not exclusive to the incarceration, while the thirteen volumes of *Speak Out for Justice*, produced by Visual Communications and Nikkei for Civil Rights and Redress, uniquely capture the full testimony of survivors who spoke, in 1981, to the Los Angeles hearings of the Commission on Wartime Relocation and Internment of Civilians (CWRIC), a nine-member congressional panel tasked with reviewing the facts and circumstances surrounding Executive Order 9066. These hearings, and others like them across the country, eventually led to the Civil Liberties Act of 1988 that granted reparations to the victims of the incarceration.

Though my viewing history is not comprehensive, four documentaries have made a lasting impact on me, personally, and are available for streaming. They are *Conscience and the Constitution,* directed by Frank Abe, which focuses on the Heart Mountain draft resisters; *Children of the Camps*, directed by Ina Satsuki, which depicts the healing journeys of six Nisei incarceration survivors (https://www.pbs.org/childofcamp/index.html); *Rabbit in the Moon*, directed by Emiko Omori, which examines intergenerational effects of the incarceration (https://www.pbs.org/pov/watch/rabbitinthemoon/); and *Relocation, Arkansas*, directed by Vivienne Schiffer, which reveals the lasting impact that the prejudices of the Jim Crow South had on those who were detained (http://www.relocationarkansas.com/). (Schiffer has also written a novel about the incarceration, *Camp Nine* [2011]).

Memoirs

In addition to *Citizen 13660* (1946) by Miné Okubo and *I Call to Remembrance* (2007) by Toyo Suyemoto, which are discussed in this study, memoirs of the incarceration have been produced since shortly after the camps closed. Initially, a small number of Issei memoirs were published in Japanese, the most prominent of which are Yasutaro Soga's *Tessaku Seikatsu* (1948), which was translated into English by Kihei Hirai under the title *Life behind Barbed Wire: The World War II Internment Memoirs of a Hawaii Issei* and published in 2008, and Sasabune Sasaki's *Yokuryujo Seikatsuki* [*Life in Camp*] (1950), which recorded the author's experience as an "enemy alien" in the Fort Missoula Department of Justice Detention Center. Noboru Shirai's *Tule Lake: An Issei Memoir* was also written in Japanese and published in 1981; in 2001, the English version appeared.

Postwar works in English include Monica Sone's *Nisei Daughter* (1953) which, like Okubo's memoir, was influenced by the immediate postwar context in which is it was written and reflects a somewhat sanitized view of the experience. The foreword to the 1979 reissued edition, however, tempers this tone. Similarly, Yoshiko Uchida's *Desert Exile* was written in the 1960s but not published until 1982. Among the more popular memoirs is Jeanne Wakatsuki Houston's and James Houston's *Farewell to Manzanar* (1973), which was made into a TV movie in 1976 and taught widely in schools during the "multicultural" movements of the 1980s.

The 1993 memoir *Adios to Tears*, by Seiichi Higashide, brings a different perspective to the incarceration as it tells of the experience of a Japanese Peruvian who was held, along with many other Japanese immigrants living in South and Central America during the period, in the Crystal City facility in Texas. More recently, Mary Matsuda Gruenewald, in *Looking Like the Enemy* (2005), recounts her family's detention in multiple camps: Tule Lake, Heart Mountain, and Minidoka. Hiroshi Kashiwagi's *Swimming in the American: A Memoir and Selected Writings* (2005) and *Starting from Loomis and Other Stories* (2013) combines memorial vignettes with creative pieces, including his play *The Betrayed*, which focuses on the incarceration from two historical moments, 1943 and 1983.

More recently, as the generation of Nisei who were incarcerated pass on, memoir has merged into coauthorship, as younger writers assist elders in recording their life stories. In 2012, Kimi Cunningham Grant published a biography/memoir of her grandmother's experience in Heart Mountain, *Silver Like Dust: One Family's Story of America's Japanese Internment*. Most recently, Jeanette S. Arakawa published her partially fictionalized memoir *The Little Exile* (2017). In 2019, Norman Mineta paired with Andrea Warren to tell his story in *Enemy Child: The Story of Norman Mineta, a Boy Imprisoned in a Japanese American Internment Camp during World War II*. Though directed toward a young adult audience, this volume, richly illustrated with Mineta family photographs, may also be of interest to adults who have admired Mineta's long political career. In 2020, Judy Kawamoto added a new dimension to our understanding of the impact of the incarceration on all Japanese Americans, including those who were not detained, in her memoir, *Forced Out: A Nikkei Woman's Search for a Home in America*. Shortly after the bombing of Pearl Harbor, Kawamoto's family took advantage of the short-lived opportunity to move inland voluntarily, thereby escaping incarceration, though the psychological effects on Kawamoto were no less significant than on her imprisoned peers.

Fiction, Poetry, and Drama

An ideal place to begin to explore fiction, poetry, and drama about the incarceration is *Ayumi: A Japanese American Anthology* (1980), edited by the poet and activist Janice Mirikitani and published by the Japanese American Anthology Committee. Authors are divided by generation—Issei, Nisei, Sansei, and Yonsei—and, taken as a whole, this anthology provides a comprehensive overview of Japanese American writers in the United States. It includes graphics by celebrated Japanese American artists as well and as such, should be a staple in every library or personal collection. I also look forward to the forthcoming collection tentatively titled *The Penguin Book of the Literature of the Japanese American Incarceration*, edited by Frank Abe and Floyd Cheung, as part of the Penguin Classics collection. This collection will focus solely on literature directly pertaining to the incarceration and will undoubtedly become a cornerstone for future teaching and research in this area.

Fiction, poetry, and drama by Japanese Americans about the incarceration is plentiful, and numerous authors write in multiple genres, so I'll limit my list to individuals rather than book titles. Early fiction writers not discussed at length in this study include the authors Joy Kogawa, John Okada, Yoshiko Uchida, and Hisaye Yamamato, while post-redress works have been produced by the Sansei and Yonsei writers David Ikeda, Cynthia Kadohata, Stanley Kanzaki, Sanae Kawaguchi (whose novel, like Julie Kawamoto's memoir, is also about "voluntary" relocation), Edward Miyakawa, Perry Miyake, Jan Morrill, David Mura, Gene Oishi, Julie Otsuka, Nina Revoyr, Rahna Reiko Rizzuto, Julie Shikeguni, and Karen Tei Yamashita. Among my personal favorites are Otsuka's *When the Emperor Was Divine* (2003), Rizzuto's *Why She Left Us* (1999), and Mura's *Famous Suicides of the Japanese Empire* (2008).

Poetry evokes the incarceration in ways different from fiction. In addition to Toyo Suyemoto, early poets include Violet Kazue de Cristoforo (formerly Kazue Matsuda), Lawson Fusao Inada, Lonny Kaneko, Janice Mirikitani, James Masao Mitsui, Chiye Mori, Taisanboku Mori, Mary Oyama, Muin Ozaki, Keiho Soga, Sojin Takei, and Mitsuye Yamada, all of whom reflect on their experience in the camps. More recently, Brian Komei Dempster, Garrett Hongo, and Claire Kageyama-Ramakrishnan continue to explore the injustice and its aftermath in their poetry.

Dramatic works that focus on the incarceration are rarer. Wakako Yamauchi is considered a premier playwright of the incarceration, having written numerous works that are now collected, alongside pieces of fiction and memoir, in *Songs My Mother Taught Me* (1994). Hiroshi Kashiwagi published *Shoe Box Plays* in 2008, a collection of works written between 1949 and 1993, which includes his most well-known plays, *Laughter and False Teeth* and *The Betrayed* (expanded from his one act play written in 1978 titled *A Question of Loyalty*). Ken Narasaki adapted John Okada's 1957 novel *No-No Boy* into a play in 2010. Philip Kan Gotanda has produced work from the 1970s to the present, and I find his play *After the War Blues* (2014) particularly compelling in its exploration of the polyethnic communities into which Japanese Americans were asked to assimilate following the incarceration. The musical *Allegiance* (2012), by Jay Kuo, Lorenzo Thione, and Marc Acito, is perhaps the most recently well-known dramatic rendition of the experience because of its run on Broadway from October 2015 to February 2016. Though based on the experiences of the actor George Takei, who was incarcerated as a child at Rohwer and Tule Lake, the musical is largely a fictionalized account of the incarceration. (Takei himself has also written an autobiography, *To the Stars: The Autobiography of George Takei* (1994) and *The Called Us the Enemy* (2019), a graphic memoir of his experiences in camp as a child).

A significant subset of work about the incarceration has been written for children or young adults. Most recently, two graphic novels directed toward children have focused on wartime resistance to the incarceration. Stan Yogi and Laura Atkins worked with the illustrator Yutaka Houlette to create *Fred Korematsu Speaks Up* (2017), which highlights Korematsu's legal fight against his imprisonment. In 2021, Frank Abe and Tamiko Nimura, along with illustrators Ross Ishikawa and Matt Sasaki, published *We Hereby Refuse: Japanese American Resistance to Wartime Incarceration.* It, too, teaches young people about the value of resistance to oppression through its retelling of the stories of Jim Akutsu, who refused to be drafted into the military while incarcerated; Hiroshi Kashiwagi, who resisted pressure to sign the loyalty oath; and Mitsuye Endo, whose lawsuit against the government led to the release of inmates and allowed for their return to the West Coast. I find these works inspirational as they engage a new generation of learners with the history of the incarceration and encourage ongoing fights against discrimination and oppression.

Works Cited

Abe, Frank, dir. *Conscience and the Constitution*. 2000; San Francisco, CA: ITVS.

Abe, Frank, Tamiko Nimura, Ross Ishikawa and Matt Sasaki. *We Hereby Refuse: Japanese American Resistance to Wartime Incarceration*. Seattle: Chin Music Press, 2021.

Abe, Frank, Greg Robinson, Floyd Cheung, and John Okada. *John Okada: The Life and Rediscovered Work of the Author of "No-No Boy."* Seattle: University of Washington Press, 2018.

Aiboshi, Toshiko. Interview by Richard Potashin. January 20, 2011. http://ddr.densho.org/interviews/ddr-manz-1-112-1/. Manzanar Historical Site Collection. Densho, 2011.

Alinder, Jasmine. *Moving Images: Photography and the Japanese American Incarceration*. Urbana: University of Illinois Press, 2009.

All Aboard (Topaz). *Central Utah Relocation Center.* Courtesy of the Library of Congress. Densho, (Spring) 1944. https://ddr.densho.org/ddr-densho-142-428/.

America Bungaku. Edited by Isshin H. Yamasaki. Tokyo, Japan: Keigan Sha, 1938.

Austin, Allan. *From Concentration Camp to Campus: Japanese American Students and World War II*. Urbana: University of Illinois Press, 2004.

Austin, Allan. "National Japanese American Student Relocation Council." *Densho Encyclopedia*. Last modified October 8, 2020. https://encyclopedia.densho.org/National%20Japanese%20American%20Student%20Relocation%20Council.

Austin, Allan. "OWI/WRA documentaries." *Densho Encyclopedia*. Last modified April 16, 2014. https://encyclopedia.densho.org/OWI/WRA%20documentaries.

Baikie, Karen A., and Kay Wilhelm. "Emotional and Physical Health Benefits of Expressive Writing." *Advances in Psychiatric Treatment* 11, no. 5 (August 2005): 338–346. https://www.cambridge.org/core/journals/advances-in-psychiatric-treatment/article/emotional-and-physical-health-benefits-of-expressive-writing/ED2976A61F5DE56B46F07A1CE9EA9F9F.

Bannai, Lorraine K. *Enduring Conviction: Fred Korematsu and His Quest for Justice*. Seattle: University of Washington Press, 2015.

Bayliss, Jeffrey Paul. *On the Margins of Empire: Buraku and Korean Identity in Prewar and Wartime Japan*. Cambridge, MA: Harvard University Asia Center, 2013.

Bearden, Russell. "Life Inside Arkansas's Japanese-American Relocation Centers." *Arkansas Historical Quarterly* 48, no. 2 (Summer 1989): 169–196.

Briones, Matthew M., and Charles Kikuchi. *Jim and Jap Crow: A Cultural History of 1940s Interracial America*. Princeton, NJ: Princeton University Press, 2012.

Brooks, Charlotte. *Alien Neighbors, Foreign Friends: Asian Americans, Housing and the Transformation of Urban California*. Illustrated ed. Chicago: University of Chicago Press, 2012.

Burton, Jeffery F., Eleanor Roosevelt, and Irene J. Cohen. *Confinement and Ethnicity: An Overview of World War II Japanese American Relocation Sites*. Seattle: University of Washington Press, 2002.

Cannady, Shelley. "Tule Lake Today: Internment and Its Legacies." *Boom: A Journal of California* 3, no. 1 (Spring 2013): 17–33.

Card, Laura. "'TREK' Magazine, 1942–1943: A Critical Rhetorical Analysis." PhD dissertation, (University of Utah, 2005).

Cheung, King-Kok. *Articulate Silences: Hisaye Yamamoto, Maxine Hong Kingston, Joy Kogawa*. Reading Women Writing. Ithaca, NY: Cornell University Press, 1993.

Cheung, King-Kok. *An Interethnic Companion to Asian American Literature*. New York: Cambridge University Press, 1997.

Cheung, King-Kok. *Words Matter: Conversations with Asian American Writers*. Honolulu: University of Hawaii Press, 2000.

Chiang, Connie Y. *Nature behind Barbed Wire: An Environmental History of the Japanese American Incarceration*. New York: Oxford University Press, 2018.

Chin, Frank. *Born in the USA: A Story of Japanese America, 1889–1947*. Lanham, MD: Rowman & Littlefield, 2002.

Chin, Vivian Fumiko. "Gestures of Noncompliance: Resisting, Inventing, and Enduring in *Citizen 13660*." In *Miné Okubo: Following Her Own Road*, edited by Greg Robinson and Elena Tajimi Creef, 67–81. Seattle: University of Washington Press, 2008.

Clark, Bonnie. "Amache (Granada)." *Densho Encyclopedia*. Last modified June 22, 2020. https://encyclopedia.densho.org/Amache_(Granada)/.

Clark, Mark. "'The Deadly Enemies That They Are': Local Reaction to the Tule Lake Internment Camp." *Journal of the Shaw Historical Library* 19 (2005): 46–47.

Conscience and the Constitution. Directed by Frank Abe. San Francisco, CA: Independent Television Service, 2000.

Cothran, Boyd. *Remembering the Modoc War: Redemptive Violence and the Making of American Innocence*. Chapel Hill: University of North Carolina Press, 2014.

Counterpoint: Perspectives on Asian America. Edited by Emma Gee. Los Angeles: Asian American Studies Center, University of California, 1979.

Creef, Elena Tajima. "Following Her Own Road: The Achievement of Miné Okubo." In *Miné Okubo: Following Her Own Road*, edited by Greg Robinson and Elena Tajima Creef, 3–10. Seattle: University of Washington Press, 2008.

Dallek, Robert. *Franklin D. Roosevelt and American Foreign Policy, 1932–1945*. New York: Oxford University Press, 1979.

Daniels, Roger. *Concentration Camps USA: Japanese Americans and World War II*. New York: Holt, Rinehart and Winston, 1971.

Daniels, Roger. *The Politics of Prejudice: The Anti-Japanese Movement in California and the Struggle for Japanese Exclusion*. Gloucester, MA: Peter Smith, 1966.

Daniels, Roger. "'Words Do Matter': A Note on Inappropriate Terminology and the Incarceration of the Japanese Americans." *Discover Nikkei*, February 2, 2008. Japanese American National Museum. http://www.discovernikkei.org/en/journal/2008/2/1/words-do-matter/.

Daniels, Roger, Sandra C. Taylor, Harry H. L. Kitano, and Leonard J. Arrington. *Japanese Americans, from Relocation to Redress*. Rev. ed. Seattle: University of Washington Press, 1991.

De Cristoforo, Violet Kazue. *May Sky: There Is Always Tomorrow, An Anthology of Japanese American Concentration Camp Kaiko Haiku*. Los Angeles: Sun & Moon Press, 1997.

Dempster, Brian Komei. *Making Home from War: Stories of Japanese American Exile and Resettlement*. Berkeley, CA: Heyday Books, 2011.

Dusselier, Jane E. *Artifacts of Loss: Crafting Survival in Japanese American Concentration Camps*. New Brunswick, NJ: Rutgers University Press, 2008.

Faderman, Lillian, and Barbara Bradshaw. *Speaking for Ourselves: American Ethnic Writing*. 2nd ed. Glenview, IL: Scott, Foresman, 1975.

Fiset, Louis. "Censored! U.S. Censors and Internment Camp Mail in World War II." In *Guilt by Association: Essays on Japanese Settlement, Internment, and Relocation in the Rocky Mountain West*, edited by Mike Mackey, 69–100. Powell, WY: Western History Publications, 2001.

Fiset, Louis. *Imprisoned Apart: The World War II Correspondence of an Issei Couple*. Seattle: University of Washington Press, 1997.

Fiset, Louis. "Public Health in World War II Assembly Centers for Japanese Americans." *Bulletin of the History of Medicine* 73, no. 4 (1999): 565–584.

Fryer, Heather. "Miné Okubo's War: *Citizen 13660's* Attack on Government Propaganda." In *Miné Okubo: Following Her Own Road*, edited by Greg Robinson and Elena Tajima Creef, 82–98. Seattle: University of Washington Press, 2008.

Fukuhara, Francis M. Interview by Tom Ikeda and Elmer Good. September 25, 1997. https://ddr.densho.org/interviews/ddr-densho-1000-9-16/. Densho, 1997.

Gesensway, Deborah, and Mindy Roseman. *Beyond Words: Images from America's Concentration Camps*. Ithaca, NY: Cornell University Press, 1987.

Hamill, Pete, and Diego Rivera. *Diego Rivera*. New York: Harry N. Abrams, 1999.

Harvey, Robert. *Amache: The Story of Japanese Internment in Colorado during World War II*. Dallas, TX: Taylor, 2003.

Hathaway, Heather. *Caribbean Waves: Relocating Claude McKay and Paule Marshall*. Bloomington: Indiana University Press, 1999.

Havey, Lily Yuriko Nakai. *Gasa Gasa Girl Goes to Camp: A Nisei Youth behind a World War II Fence*. Salt Lake City: Tanner Trust Fund, Marriott Library, University of Utah Press, 2014.

Hawley, Grace S. Interview by Megan Asaka. June 3, 2009. https://ddr.densho.org/interviews/ddr-densho-1000-246-11/. Densho, 2009.

Hayashi, Brian Masaru. *Democratizing the Enemy: The Japanese American Internment*. Princeton, NJ: Princeton University Press, 2004.

Helphand, Kenneth. *Defiant Gardens: Making Gardens in Wartime*. San Antonio, TX: Trinity University Press, 2006.

Hirabayashi, Gordon K., James A. Hirabayashi, and Lane Ryo Hirabayashi. *A Principled Stand: The Story of Hirabayashi v. United States*. Seattle: University of Washington Press, 2013.

Hirabayashi, Lane Ryo, Kenichiro Shimada, and Hikaru Iwasaki. *Japanese American Resettlement through the Lens: Hikaru Carl Iwasaki and the WRA's Photographic Section, 1943–1945*. Boulder: University Press of Colorado, 2009.

Hirahara, Naomi, and Gwenn M. Jensen. *Silent Scars of Healing Hands: Oral Histories of Japanese American Doctors in World War II Detention Camps*. Fullerton: Center for Oral and Public History, California State University, 2004.

Hirasuna, Delphine, and Kit Hinrichs. *The Art of Gaman: Arts and Crafts from the Japanese American Internment Camps, 1942–1946*. Berkeley, CA: Ten Speed Press, 2005.

Hong, Christine. "Illustrating the Postwar Peace: Miné Okubo, the 'Citizen-Subject' of Japan, and 'Fortune' Magazine." *American Quarterly* 67, no. 1 (2015): 105–140. http://www.jstor.org/stable/43823009.

Horikoshi, Peter. "Interview with Toshio Mori." In *Counterpoint: Perspectives on Asian America*, edited by Emma Gee, 472–479. Los Angeles: Asian American Studies Center, University of California, 1976.

Howard, John. *Concentration Camps on the Homefront: Japanese Americans in the House of Jim Crow*. Chicago: University of Chicago Press, 2008.

Ichihashi, Yamato, and Gordon H. Chang. *Morning Glory, Evening Shadow: Yamato Ichihashi and His Internment Writings, 1942–1945*. Stanford, CA: Stanford University Press, 1997.

Ichioka, Yuji, ed. *Views from Within: The Japanese American Evacuation and Resettlement Study*. Los Angeles: Asian American Studies Center, University of California–Los Angeles, 1989.

Ina, Satsuki, and PBS Online. *Children of the Camps*. Alexandria, VA: PBS Online, 2003. http://www.pbs.org/childofcamp/.

Inada, Lawson Fusao. *Drawing the Line: Poems*. Minneapolis: Coffee House Press, 1997.

Inada, Lawson Fusao. *Legends from Camp: Poems*. Minneapolis: Coffee House Press, 1993.

Inada, Lawson Fusao. "Standing on Seventh Street: An Introduction to the 1985 Edition." In *Yokohama, California* by Toshio Mori, v–xxvii. Seattle: University of Washington Press, 1985.

Inouye, Karen M. "Japanese American Wartime Experience: Tamotsu Shibutani and Methodological Innovation, 1935–1978." *Journal of the History of Behavioral Sciences* 48, no. 4 (2012): 318–338.

Inouye, Karen M. *The Long Afterlife of Nikkei Wartime Incarceration*. Stanford, CA: Stanford University Press, 2016.

Irons, Peter H. *Justice at War*. New York: Oxford University Press, 1983.

Ito, Leslie. "Japanese American Women and the Student Relocation Movement, 1942–1945." *Frontiers: A Journal of Women Studies* 21, no. 3 (2000): 1–24. doi:10.2307/3347107.

James, Thomas. *Exile Within: The Schooling of Japanese Americans, 1942–1945*. Cambridge, MA: Harvard University Press, 1987.

The Japanese Relocation. Directed by War Relocation Authority. Washington, DC: US Office of War Information, 1943.

Jensen, Gwenn M. "Dysentery, Dust, and Determination: Health Care in the World War II Japanese American Detention Camps." *Discover Nikkei*, June 28, 2008. Japanese American National Museum, 2008. http://www.discovernikkei.org/en/journal/2008/6/21/enduring-communities/.

Jensen, Gwenn M. "Health Care Deficiencies in the World War II Japanese American Detention Centers." *Bulletin of the History of Medicine* 73, no. 4 (1999): 602–628.

Jin, Michael. "Americans in the Pacific: Rethinking Race, Gender, Citizenship, and Diaspora at the Crossroads of Asian and Asian American Studies." *Critical Ethnic Studies* 2, no. 1 (2016): 128–147. doi:10.5749/jcritethnstud.2.1.0128. http://www.jstor.org/stable/10.5749/jcritethnstud.2.1.0128.

Jin, Michael. "A Transnational Generation: Japanese Americans in the Pacific before World War II." *Ritsumeikan Language and Culture Studies* 21, no. 4 (2010): 185.

Kadohata, Cynthia. *Weedflower*. New York: Atheneum Books for Young Readers, 2006.

Kashiwagi, Hiroshi. *Shoe Box Plays*. San Mateo, CA: Asian American Curriculum Project, 2008.

Kashiwagi, Hiroshi. *Swimming in the American: A Memoir and Selected Writings*. San Mateo, CA: Asian American Curriculum Project, 2005.

Kehoe, Karen. *City in the Sun*. New York: Dodd Mead, 1946.

Kessler, Lauren. "Fettered Freedoms: The Journalism of World War II Japanese Internment Camps." *Journalism History* 15, no. 2 (1988): 70–79.

Kim, Kristine, and Japanese American National Museum. *Henry Sugimoto: Painting an American Experience*. Berkeley, CA: Heyday Books, 2001.

Lange, Dorothea, Linda Gordon, and Gary Y. Okihiro. *Impounded: Dorothea Lange and the Censored Images of Japanese American Internment*. New York: W.W. Norton, 2006.

Lawrence, Keith, and Floyd Cheung. *Recovered Legacies: Authority and Identity in Early Asian American Literature*. Philadelphia, PA: Temple University Press, 2005.

Lee, Anthony W. *Painting on the Left: Diego Rivera, Radical Politics, and San Francisco's Public Murals*. Berkeley: University of California Press, 1999.

Leong, Russell. "An Interview with Toshio Mori." *Amerasia Journal* 7, no. 1 (1980): 89–108.

Lyon, Cherstin M. *Prisons and Patriots: Japanese American Wartime Citizenship, Civil Disobedience, and Historical Memory*. Philadelphia, PA: Temple University Press, 2012.

Magnet (Jerome). *Denson Magnet*. April 1943. Documents Section, Jerome Relocation Center, Denson, Arkansas, 1, Japanese American Evacuation and Resettlement Records, BANC MSS 67/14c, The Bancroft Library, University of California, Berkeley.

Manbo, Bill T., and Eric L. Muller. *Colors of Confinement: Rare Kodachrome Photographs of Japanese American Incarceration in World War II*. Chapel Hill, Durham: University of North Carolina Press. In association with the Center for Documentary Studies at Duke University, 2012.

Masaoka, Mike, and Bill Hosokawa. *They Call Me Moses Masaoka: An American Saga*. New York: Morrow, 1987.

Matsumoto, Valerie J. *Farming the Home Place: A Japanese American Community in California, 1919–1982*. Ithaca, NY: Cornell University Press, 1993.

Matsumoto, Valerie J. "Japanese American Women during World War II." *Frontiers: A Journal of Women Studies* 8, no. 1 (1984): 6–14.

McKay, Susan. *The Courage Our Stories Tell: The Daily Lives and Maternal Child Health Care of Japanese Americans at Heart Mountain*. Powell, WY: Western History Publications, 2002.

McNaughton, James C. "Japanese Americans and the U.S. Army." *Army History* 59 (Summer/Fall 2003): 4–15.

Mencken, H. L. *The American Language; an Inquiry into the Development of English in the United States*, 3rd revised and enlarged ed. New York: Knopf, 1923.

Mirikitani, Janice, and Japanese American Anthology Committee. *Ayumi: A Japanese American Anthology* [= *Ayumi : Nikkei Beijin Bungei Shū*]. San Francisco, CA: Japanese American Anthology Committee, 1980.

Miura, Kokichiro. "Walking on the Edge: Towards a Sociography of Discrimination against the Buraku: Lectures on Discrimination in Letter Format." *International Journal of Japanese Sociology* 23, no. 1 (2014): 46–62.

Mizuno, Takeya. "Censorship in a Different Name: Press 'Supervision' in Wartime Japanese American Camps 1942–1943." *Journalism and Mass Communication Quarterly* 88, no. 1 (2011): 121–141.

Mizuno, Takeya. "Government Suppression of the Japanese Language in World War II Assembly Camps." *Journalism and Mass Communication Quarterly* 80, no. 4 (2003): 849–865.

Mori, Steven Y., ed. *Unfinished Message: Selected Works of Toshio Mori*. Berkeley, CA: Heyday Books, 2000.

Mori, Toshio. "The Brothers Murata: A Novel." In *Unfinished Message: Selected Works of Toshio Mori*, edited by Steven Y. Mori, 137–205. Berkeley, CA: Heyday Books, 2000.

Mori, Toshio. *Yokohama, California*. Caldwell, ID: Caxton Printers, 1949.

Muller, Eric L. *American Inquisition: The Hunt for Japanese American Disloyalty in World War II*. Chapel Hill: University of North Carolina Press, 2007.

Myer, Dillon S. *Uprooted Americans: The Japanese Americans and the War Relocation Authority during World War II*. Tucson: University of Arizona Press, 1971.

Nagata, Donna K. *Legacy of Injustice: Exploring the Cross-Generational Impact of the Japanese American Internment*. New York: Plenum Press, 1993.

Nagata, Ted. Interviewed by Megan Asaka. June 3, 2008. https://ddr.densho.org/interviews/ddr-densho-1013-3-1/. Densho. Courtesy of the Topaz Museum Collection, 2008.

Nakagawa, Gordon. "'What Are We Doing Here with All These Japanese?': Subject-Constitution and Strategies of Discursive Closure Represented in Stories of Japanese American Internment." *Communication Quarterly* 38, no. 4 (1990): 388–402. doi:10.1080/01463379009369775.

Nakamura, Hiroshi. *Treadmill: A Documentary Novel*. Oakville, Ontario, Canada: Mosaic Press, 1996.

Nakamura, Mary Sato, and Isami Nakamura. "Hiroshi Nakamura, 1915–1973." In *Treadmill: A Documentary Novel*, i–iii. Oakville, Ontario, Canada: Mosaic Press, 1996.

Niiya, Brian. "Jerome." *Densho Encyclopedia*. Last modified August 2, 2021. https://encyclopedia.densho.org/Jerome.

Niiya, Brian. "Laughter and False Teeth (Play)." *Densho Encyclopedia*. Last modified October 5, 2020. https://encyclopedia.densho.org/Laughter%20and%20False%20Teeth%20(play).

Niiya, Brian. "Salt Lake City Governors' Meeting." *Densho Encyclopedia*. Last modified October 8, 2020. https://encyclopedia.densho.org/Salt%20Lake%20City%20governors%20meeting.

Nikkei for Civil Rights and Redress and Lane Ryo Hirabayashi. *NCRR: The Grassroots Struggle for Japanese American Redress and Reparations*. Los Angeles, CA: UCLA Asian American Studies Center Press, 2018.

Obata, Chiura. *Topaz Moon: Art of the Internment*. Edited by Kimi Kodani Hill. Berkeley, CA: Heyday Books, 2000.

Okihiro, Gary K. "Tule Lake under Martial Law: A Study in Japanese Resistance." *Journal of Ethnic Studies* 5, no. 3 (1977): 71. http://libus.csd.mu.edu/wamvalidate?url=https://www.proquest.com/scholarly-journals/tule-lake-under-martial-law-study-japanese/docview/1300556031/se-2?accountid=100.

Okubo, Miné. *Citizen 13660*. Rev. ed. Seattle: University of Washington Press, [1946] 2014.

Omori, Emiko, dir. *Rabbit in the Moon*. Norwood, MA: Furomoto Foundation, 2004.

Omura, James Matsumoto, and Arthur A. Hansen. *Nisei Naysayer: The Memoir of Militant Japanese American Journalist Jimmie Omura*. Stanford, CA: Stanford University Press, 2018.

Paik, A. Naomi. *Rightlessness: Testimony and Redress in U.S. Prison Camps since World War II*. Chapel Hill: University of North Carolina Press, 2016.

Parikh, Crystal, and Daniel Y. Kim. *The Cambridge Companion to Asian American Literature*. New York: Cambridge University Press, 2015.

Park, Robert E. "Racial Assimilation in Secondary Groups with Particular Reference to the Negro." *American Journal of Sociology* 19, no. 5 (1914): 606–623.

Patel, Reeya A., and Donna K. Nagata. "Historical Trauma and Descendants' Well-Being." *American Medical Association Journal of Ethics* 23, no. 6 (2021): 487–493. doi: 10.1001/amajethics.2021.487.

Pen (Rohwer). The Outpost. Rohwer Relocation Center. Relocation, Arkansas. Densho, 1943. denshopd-p167-00042.

Pennebaker, James W. "Writing about Emotional Experiences as a Therapeutic Process." *Psychological Science* 8, no. 3 (1997): 162–166.

Pulse (Amache/Granada). Amache/Granada Relocation Center. Amache/Granada, Colorado. Courtesy of the Library of Congress. Densho, 1943. https://ddr.densho.org/ddr-densho-147-337/

Rabbit in the Moon. Directed by Emiko Omori, Chizuko Omori, Frank Emi, et al. Hohokus, NJ: New Day Films, 1999.

Relocation, Arkansas: Aftermath of Incarceration. Directed by Vivienne Schiffer and Johanna Demetrakas. Houston, TX: Rescue Film Production, LLC, 2017.

Richardson, Susan. Introduction to *I Call to Remembrance: Toyo Suyemoto's Years of Internment*, edited by Susan Richardson, xvii–xlvi. Newark, NJ: Rutgers University Press, 2007.

Robinson, Greg. *After Camp: Portraits in Midcentury Japanese American Life and Politics*. Berkeley: University of California Press, 2012.

Robinson, Greg. "Birth of a Citizen: Miné Okubo and the Politics of Symbolism." In *Miné Okubo: Following Her Own Road*, edited by Greg Robinson and Elena Tajima Creef, 159–178. Seattle: University of Washington Press, 2008.

Robinson, Greg. *By Order of the President: FDR and the Internment of Japanese Americans*. Cambridge, MA: Harvard University Press, 2001.

Robinson, Greg. "The Great Unknown and the Unknown Great: Queer Non-Nikkei Figures in Japanese American History (Part V)." *Nichi Bei: A Mixed Plate of Japanese American News and Culture*. Last modified October 2, 2014. https://www.nichibei.org/2014/10/the-great-unknown-and-the-unknown-great-queer-non-nikkei-figures-in-japanese-american-history-part-v/.

Robinson, Greg. *A Tragedy of Democracy: Japanese Confinement in North America*. New York: Columbia University Press, 2009.

Robinson, Greg. "When Birthright Citizenship Was Last 'Reconsidered': Regan v. King and Asian Americans Part IV." *Faculty Lounge* (Blog), August 9, 2010. http://www.thefacultylounge.org/2010/08/page/3.

Robinson, Greg. "Writing the Internment." In *The Cambridge Companion to Asian American Literature*, edited by Crystal Parikh and Daniel Y. Kim, 45–58. Cambridge, UK: Cambridge University Press, 2015.

Robinson, Greg, and Elena Tajima Creef. *Miné Okub: Following Her Own Road*. Seattle: University of Washington Press, 2008.

Roxworthy, Emily. "Blackface behind Barbed Wire: Gender and Racial Triangulation in the Japanese American Internment Camps." *TDR: The Drama Review: A Journal of Performance Studies* 57, no. 2 (2013): 123–142.

Roxworthy, Emily. "Nisei Girls' Kabuki in Wartime Arkansas: Cultural Segregation and Cross-Dressing at Rohwer and Jerome." *Women and Performance* 20, no. 2 (2010): 185–203.

Saroyan, William. Introduction to *Yokohama, California*, edited by Toshio Mori, 1–4. Caldwell, ID: Caxton Printers, 1949.

Scheiber, Harry N., and Jane L. Scheiber. *Bayonets in Paradise: Martial Law in Hawai'i during World War II*. Honolulu: University of Hawai'i Press, 2016.

Schweik, Susan M. *A Gulf So Deeply Cut: American Women Poets and the Second World War*. Madison: University of Wisconsin Press, 1991.

Shimabukuro, Mira. *Relocating Authority: Japanese Americans Writing to Redress Mass Incarceration*. Boulder: University Press of Colorado, 2015.

Shimabukuro, Robert Sadamu. *Born in Seattle: The Campaign for Japanese American Redress*. Seattle: University of Washington Press, 2001.

Shimano, Eddie. "Blueprint for a Slum." *Common Ground* (Summer 1943): 78–85. https://www.unz.com/print/CommonGround-1943q2-0078/.

Simpson, Caroline Chung. *An Absent Presence: Japanese Americans in Postwar American Culture, 1945–1960*. Durham, NC: Duke University Press.

Smith, Susan Lynn. 1999. "Women Health Workers and the Color Line in the Japanese American 'Relocation Centers' of World War II." *Bulletin of the History of Medicine* 73, no. 4 (2001): 585–601.

Sollors, Werner. "From the Bottom Up: Foreword by Werner Sollors." In *The Life Stories of {Undistinguished} Americans, as Told by Themselves*, edited by Hamilton Holt, with a new introduction by Werner Sollors, xi–xxviii. New York: Routledge, 1990.

Streamas, John. "Toyo Suyemoto, Ansel Adams, and the Landscape of Justice." In *Recovered Legacies: Authority and Identity in Early Asian American Literature*, edited by Lawrence, Keith and Floyd Cheung, 141–157. Philadelphia, PA: Temple University Press, 2005.

Sunda, Mike. "Japan's Hidden Caste of Untouchables." *BBC News*. Last modified October 23, 2015. https://www.bbc.com/news/world-asia-34615972.

Suyemoto, Toyo, and Susan B. Richardson. *I Call to Remembrance: Toyo Suyemoto's Years of Internment*. New Brunswick, NJ: Rutgers University Press, 2007.

Suzuki, Peter. Introduction to *Treadmill: A Documentary Novel*, by Hiroshi Nakamura. Oakville, Ontario, CA: Mosaic Press, 1996.

Suzuki, Peter. "*Treadmill*: The Premier Novel of the Wartime Camps for Japanese Americans." *Asian Profile* 20, no. 2 (April 1992): 175–176.

Suzuki, Shoko. "In Search of the Lost *Oikos:* Japan after the Earthquake of 11 March 2011." In *Hazardous Future: Disaster, Representation and the Assessment of Risk*, edited by I. C. Gil and C. Wulf, 109–126. Boston, MA: DeGruyter, 2015.

Tajiri, Larry, Guyo Tajiri, and Greg Robinson. *Pacific Citizens: Larry and Guyo Tajiri and Japanese American Journalism in the World War II Era*. Urbana: University of Illinois Press, 2012.

Takei, Barbara. "Tule Lake." *Densho Encyclopedia*. Last modified October 16, 2020. https://encyclopedia.densho.org/Tule%20Lake.

Takemoto, Kenneth Kaname, Paul Howard Takemoto, and Alice Takemoto. *Nisei Memories: My Parents Talk about the War Years*. Seattle: University of Washington Press, 2006.

Tamura, Eileen. *In Defense of Justice: Joseph Kurihara and the Japanese American Struggle for Equality*. Urbana: University of Illinois Press, 2013.

Tang, Edward. *From Confinement to Containment: Japanese American Arts during the Early Cold War*. Philadelphia, PA: Temple University Press, 2019.

Tateishi, John. *And Justice for all: An Oral History of the Japanese American Detention Camps*. Seattle: University of Washington Press, 1984.

Tateishi, John. *Redress: The Inside Story of the Successful Campaign for Japanese American Reparations*. Berkeley, CA Heyday Books, 2020.

Taylor, Sandra C. *Jewel of the Desert: Japanese American Internment at Topaz*. Berkeley: University of California Press, 1993.

Tokiwa, Rudy. Interview by Tom Ikeda. July 2–3, 1998. https://ddr.densho.org/interviews/ddr-densho-1000-92-17/. Densho, 1998.

Toy, Eckard. "Whose Frontier? The Survey of Race Relations on the Pacific Coast in the 1920s." *Oregon Historical Quarterly* 107, no. 1 (2006): 36–63.

TREK (Topaz). Central Utah Relocation Center. Delta, UT. Courtesy of the Library of Congress. Densho (December) 1942. https://ddr.densho.org/ddr-densho-142-425/.

TREK (Topaz). Central Utah Relocation Center. Delta, UT. Courtesy of the Library of Congress. Densho (February) 1943. https://ddr.densho.org/ddr-densho-142-426/.

TREK (Topaz). Central Utah Relocation Center. Delta, UT. Courtesy of the Library of Congress. Densho (June) 1943. https://ddr.densho.org/ddr-densho-142-427/.

Tulean Dispatch Magazine (Tule Lake). Tule Lake Segregation Center. Tule Lake, CA. Courtesy of the Library of Congress. Tulean Dispatch Collection. Densho, 1942–1943. https://ddr.densho.org/search/?fulltext=tulean+dispatch+magazine.

United States Commission on Wartime Relocation and Internment of Civilians. *Personal Justice Denied*. Washington, DC; Seattle: Civil Liberties Public Education Fund; University of Washington Press, 1997.

Van der Kolk, Bessel A., Alexander C. McFarlane, and Lars Weisæth. *Traumatic Stress: The Effects of Overwhelming Experience on Mind, Body, and Society*. New York: Guilford Press, 2007.

Ward, Jason Morgan. "'No Jap Crow': Japanese Americans Encounter the World War II South." *Journal of Southern History* 73, no. 1 (2007): 75–104. https://www.proquest.com/scholarly-journals/no-jap-crow-japanese-americans-encounter-world/docview/215775271/se-2?accountid=100.

Wegars, Priscilla. *Imprisoned in Paradise: Japanese Internee Road Workers at the World War II Kooskia Internment Camp*. Asian American Comparative Collection. Moscow, ID: University of Idaho Press, 2010.

Weglyn, Michi. *Years of Infamy: The Untold Story of America's Concentration Camps*. Updated. Seattle: University of Washington Press, 1996.

Wirth-Nesher, Hana. "Between Mother Tongue and Native Language: Multilingualism in Henry Roth's *Call It Sleep*." *Prooftexts* 10, no. 2 (1990): 297–312.

Wright, Richard. *Black Boy: A Record of Childhood and Youth*. London: Gollancz. New York: Harper Collins, [1945] 1993.

Wu, Cynthia. "A Comparative Analysis of Indigenous Displacement and the World War II Japanese American Internment." *Amerasia Journal* 42, no. 1 (2016): 1–15.

Yamamoto, Hisaye. Introduction to *The Chauvinist and Other Stories*, by Toshio Mori, 1–14. Los Angeles: Asian American Studies Center, University of California, 1979.

Yamamoto, Hisaye. *Seventeen Syllables and Other Stories*. Revised and expanded ed. New Brunswick, NJ: Rutgers University Press, 2001.

Yamane, Kazuo. "Introduction to Yoshio Abe's *The Man of Dual Nationality*." *Journal of Ethnic Studies* 13, no. 4 (1985): 87–88.

Yasuda, Kenneth. *A Pepper-Pod*. New York: Alfred A. Knopf, 1947.

Yogi, Stan. "Japanese American Literature." In *An Interethnic Companion to Asian American Literature*, edited by King-Kok Cheung, 125–155. New York: Cambridge University Press, 1997.

Yoo, David. *Growing Up Nisei: Race, Generation, and Culture among Japanese Americans of California, 1924–49*. Urbana: University of Illinois Press, 2000.

Index

For the benefit of digital users, indexed terms that span two pages (e.g., 52–53) may, on occasion, appear on only one of those pages.